ACCOUNTING FOR BUSINESS

ICSA Certificate in Business Practice

Accounting for Business

MIKE EDWARDS

ICSA PUBLISHING

Published by ICSA Publishing Ltd
16 Park Crescent
London
W1B 1AH

© ICSA Publishing Ltd, 2005

Reprinted 2007

Typeset by Fakenham Photosetting Limited, Fakenham, Norfolk
Printed and bound in Great Britain by Marston Book Services Limited,
Oxford

British Library Cataloguing in Publication Data

A catalogue record for this book is available from the British Library.

ISBN 10: 1-86072-275-X

ISBN 13: 978-1-86072-275-2

Contents

How to Use this Study Text

All ICSA study texts developed to support the ICSA's Certificate and Diploma in Business Practice follow a standard format and include a range of navigational, self-testing and illustrative features to help you get the most out of the text.

Each study text is divided into three main sections:

- introductory material
- the text itself, divided into parts and chapters
- additional reference material

What follows shows you how to find your way around the text and make the most of its features.

Introductory material

The **Studying for the ICSA Certificate and Diploma in Business Practice** section gives an overview of the two programmes, how they fit into ICSA's suite of qualifications, recommended study routes and guidance on the examinations. We recommend that you read this before starting on the text itself, and

again as you approach revision and the examination itself.

It is followed by the detailed module syllabus and an extended syllabus overview, which gives a more detailed outline of the syllabus, highlights key topics and concepts and provides guidance on how best to approach the module and guarantee success in the examination.

Where relevant, the introductory section may also include other material such as a list of acronyms or list of legal cases.

The text itself

Each text **part** opens with a list of chapters, an overview of the topics covered and learning outcomes specific to that part. This should help you break the material down into manageable sections for study.

Part openings also include a **case study** which will be used as a business scenario throughout the part to test understanding and help apply theory into practice.

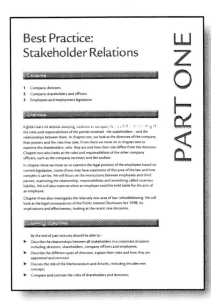

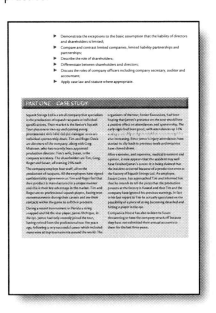

Every **chapter** opens with a list of topics covered and an introduction to what follows.

Features

The text is enhanced by a range of illustrative and self-testing features to assist understanding and to help you prepare for the examinations. Each feature is presented in a standard format so that you will become familiar with how you can use them in your study.

Each chapter ends with a summary, and each part with a series of practice questions based on the kind of questions you will face in the exams. Answers to the practice questions are given at the end of the text.

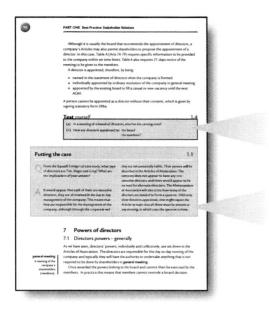

Test yourself

Short, revision-style questions to help you re-cap on core information and concepts.

Putting the case

Short questions, plus answers, based on the part opening case, designed to help you apply theory in practice.

Marginal definitions

Marginal definitions explain key terms and concepts.

Making it work

Making it work examples use real-life scenarios to illustrate and bring theory to life.

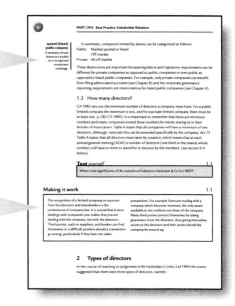

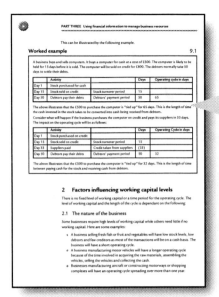

Worked examples

Worked examples are crucial to an understanding of accountancy-based modules. Questions and answers allow you to work through the calculation as part of your study.

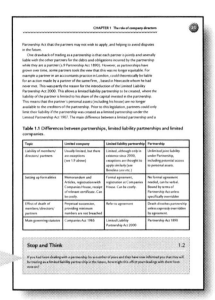

Stop and Think

Stop and Think boxes encourage you to think how your own experiences or common business scenarios relate to the topic under discussion.

Reference material

The text ends with a range of additional guidance and reference materials.

In addition to answers to practice questions, the text also includes a sample examination paper and suggested answers so that you can test your understanding of the subject against what will be expected of you in the examination.

Other reference material includes a glossary of key terms and a directory of further reading and web resources.

Studying for the ICSA Certificate and Diploma in Business Practice

The new ICSA Certificate and Diploma in Business Practice is designed to offer students a solid foundation in the principles and practice of contemporary business management.

The programmes provide well-rounded and practical professional business qualifications for students who may already be employed or seeking employment in a range of business organisations – large companies, small businesses, public sector bodies or voluntary organisations.

The ICSA Certificate and Diploma are each made up of four modules which can be studied full-time or part-time, by distance learning or self-study. The two levels provide the opportunity to earn an award from an internationally recognised professional body, which will enable you to continue your studies either through the ICSA, or by moving on to a further course of study, such as an honours degree.

In completing the eight modules which comprise the ICSA Certificate and Diploma you are completing programmes which are broadly the equivalent of the first two years of UK three-year undergraduate degree, or a Foundation degree without the work-based component. As these are professional examinations, candidates will be expected to demonstrate knowledge, understanding and the ability to apply at least some of the knowledge acquired.

Once you have successfully passed the four modules which make up the ICSA Certificate you will be entitled to use the designatory letters Cert ICSA (Business Practice) and after successfully completing the four modules which make up the ICSA Diploma, you will be entitled to use the designatory letters Dip ICSA (Business Practice).

Throughout your study of the Certificate or Diploma modules, you can rely on the integrity of the quality assurance process, predicated on more than 100 years' rigorous examinations offered with integrity by a senior international chartered body.

Themes and core concepts

You will be aware of a number of themes which are threaded through both the Certificate and the Diploma. These themes are based around:

- governance
- ethics and integrity
- best practice.

The Certificate and Diploma are designed to encourage reflective and effective business acumen delivered from an ethical standpoint. Both qualifications are structured to be of practical use in all types of business organisation, including small and medium-sized enterprises (SMEs), plcs, not-for-profit organisations, (NFPs), charities and local government.

Business Communications underpins all modules at Certificate and Diploma level.

The themes outlined in Business Environment (Cert) find their link in Business Law in Practice as well as in Marketing, Business Finance and Business Strategy and Planning.

Accounting for Business (Cert) is expanded in Business Finance but also in Business Law in Practice, Marketing and Business Strategy and Planning. Business Management links through to Business Strategy and Planning and Marketing. Business Environment underpins all other modules and links through to all of them.

Studying for the certificate and diploma

The ICSA study texts have been especially written to support candidates studying for the ICSA Certificate and Diploma in Business Practice. All material within each study text for a particular module can be examined. The style of the study text draws on case studies and real-life examples to give candidates a strong feel for the practical application of relevant knowledge to the workplace. Detailed syllabus overviews included in each of the texts give advice and guidance to students regarding approaching study of each module and the particular requirements of the examination.

Recommended study routes

You can work through the modules at your own pace and in different study combinations, however we strongly recommend the following pattern:

- Certificate
  Examination Session One: Business Communications with Business
                             Environment
  Examination Session Two: Business Management with Accounting for
                             Business

- Diploma
  Examination Session One: Business Law in Practice with Marketing
  Examination Session Two: Business Finance with Business Strategy and
                             Planning

Assessment

The examinations reflect the practical approach which underpins the modules. Both the Certificate and Diploma examinations contain a mix of short questions from any part of the syllabus and longer questions based on a case study which will have been issued prior to the exam.

Each examination paper is divided into two sections. Candidates can expect questions from any part of the syllabus. In section A, compulsory short-answer questions test your understanding and knowledge across the breadth of the syllabus, but not depth. You should aim to spend only a few minutes on each of these questions, and it is acceptable to give your answers in bullet points. It is not necessary in the short-answer questions to provide essay style answers.

Section B contains questions on a case study.

Certificate

The examination paper is two hours long, plus 15 minutes reading time. In Section A you are required to answer a set of compulsory questions which carry either 2 or 4 marks, making a total of 40 marks. In Section B you are required to answer two multi-part questions, each worth 30 marks, from a choice of five. Each part is worth 5, 10 or 15 marks.

Look carefully at the timing for the paper and take care that you allocate your time appropriately. You need only spend a few minutes on each of the Section A questions (2.5 minutes on a 2-mark questions and just over five minutes for 4-mark questions). In Section B we suggest you set aside approximately 35 minutes per 30-mark question as follows:

5 mark Section B question:	around 6 minutes
10 mark Section B question	around 11 minutes
15 mark Section B question	around 18 minutes

Diploma

The Diploma examinations are three hours long. Each examination comprises ten short-answer questions in Section A and three questions from a choice of five in Section B. Section A questions are worth 2 or 3 marks each. You should aim to spend around 3.5 minutes on a 2-mark question and no more than 5.5 minutes on a 3-mark question. For questions in Section B, you should allocate 45 minutes for the whole question, split as follows:

5 mark Section B questions	around 9 minutes
10 mark Section B questions	around 14 minutes
15 mark Section B questions	around 22 minutes

Tackling case studies

The case studies in Part B of the examination are based on real-life scenarios. This gives candidates the opportunity to demonstrate and apply their knowledge in business situations so that they can be assessed in as practical a manner as possible.

The case study will be available on the website six weeks before the date of the examinations to enable candidates and tuition providers to research the case study and prepare to answer on any aspect across the entire syllabus.

Additionally, the case study will be provided on the examination paper.

When accessing the case study, candidates should bear in mind that the Chief Examiner attempts to ensure that the questions based on the case study cover the whole syllabus. When faced by a case study, many students try to predict the questions which will arise. This is unwise and can add to the stress in the exam room when the questions you have prepared don't appear! A more reliable method is to consider the topics covered by the case study in relation to the study text and use this to try to identify the broad syllabus areas to which the Chief Examiner has referred. If you are familiar with and, most importantly, understand fully the study text, then you should be able to answer the questions in the case study.

It is worth remembering that the Chief Examiner has made considerable efforts in producing the case study and the questions based on it. In practice, this means that you must remember to refer to the case study in each answer to each question. The Chief Examiner is looking to see that you understand the practical implications of the material you have learned from the text and any candidate who can bring relevant experience to an answer will gain marks. The relevant experience to which you refer can have been obtained in employment or in your private life, or it could be something you have read about and can relate to this scenario. However, you must always remember to relate your experience to the scenario outlined in the case study.

In summary, examiners are looking for answers that are expressed in candidates' own words, that demonstrate understanding and apply the relevant knowledge to the question being asked. Candidates should read all questions carefully and answer all parts. Do not reproduce everything you know about a topic. Tailor your answer to the context and requirements of the question.

We hope you enjoy studying with the ICSA.

Good luck!

The Accounting for Business Syllabus

Position of the module in overall syllabus

- The Accounting for Business module at Certificate level is one of four areas of activity considered essential for those seeking ICSA entry-level qualifications in business practice.
- This module is expanded in the Diploma level module 'Business Finance'. 'Accounting for Business' and 'Business Finance' also provide a sound underpinning for the Professional Programme 1 modules 'Financial Accounting' and 'Management Accounting' and the Professional Programme 2 module 'Corporate Financial Management'.

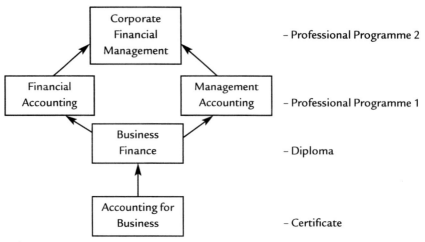

Aims

- The module is intended for aspiring managers with little or no formal financial training or experience, whose present and future positions will affect the acquisition and use of business resources.
- This module looks at the financial aspects of managing business resources.
- The module will help students to understand the basic terminology, concepts and techniques that underpin both financial and management accounting.
- This module is designed to improve students' understanding and use of financial information.

Learning outcomes

On successful completion of this module, candidates will be able to:

- Appreciate and understand the part that accounting and finance play within business.

- Understand the need for accounting information in business decision-making and the differing needs of various stakeholders.
- Understand the process underlying the preparation and presentation of financial information and the accounting conventions and principles used.
- Analyse basic financial information and draw appropriate conclusions.

Syllabus content

Introduction to accounting and finance   10%

- The role of accounting in business.
- Who needs to use accounting information.
- The distinction between financial accounting and management accounting.
- Basic concepts and terms underpinning accounting information.
- The regulatory framework.

Recording and reporting business activity   40%

- The accounting equation.
- Recording business transactions in ledger accounts.
- Function of profit and loss accounts and balance sheets.
- Why adjustments are made to figures in the accounts.
- Simple profit and loss accounts and balance sheets for a small business.
- Using computerised systems.
- How to deal with assets, stocks and bad debts when recording and reporting accounting information.

Using financial information to manage business resources – an introduction   30%

- Why cash management is important to an organisation.
- Cash flow budgets.
- The working capital cycle.
- How cost information can assist managers in planning and controlling the use of business resources.
- Costs including variable and fixed costs.
- Breakeven analysis in simple situations.

An introduction to the construction and use of budgets in managing business resources   20%

- Preparing budgets.
- Using budgets to control business resources.

The syllabus explained

Introduction to accounting and finance

As a starting point to the module it is useful to consider financial information as being made up of two aspects. These, for the purpose of this overview, are termed financial accounting and management accounting. The first two areas of the syllabus focus on financial accounting in that the module explains the nature and role of accounting within business and why non-accountants need to understand the fundamentals of accounting and finance. The intention is to examine the wide spectrum of users of financial information and explain their differing needs. The module will explain the basic concepts on which accounting information is based and refer to the regulatory framework within which accounting operates.

Recording and reporting business activity

It is important to realise that the module does not aim to turn students into bookkeepers or accountants. However, as business managers, it is important to know how business transactions impact on the finances of a business. Thus it is useful to be able to describe a simple system for recording business transactions from source documents such as invoices through to the accounting ledgers.

It is essential that managers can describe the format of the key financial statements – namely, profit and loss accounts and balance sheets. The focus here is on examining how these statements measure the financial performance and financial position of the organisation. Having focused on the description of business transactions and financial statements, candidates will also be asked to demonstrate an ability to prepare simple profit and loss accounts and balance sheets for a small business at the end of an accounting period. This will involve demonstrating a knowledge of how to make adjustments at the year-end.

As many businesses base their information systems on computers it is important that candidates can describe the operation and benefits of using a computerised system to record and report business activity.

Using financial information to manage business resources – an introduction

The final two parts of the syllabus focus on management accounting. In contrast with financial accounting, this information assists managers in making decisions about the future policy and operations of their business. This part of the syllabus focuses on the information business managers receive about the costs of the resources they use. This covers the planned and actual cost of resources, including staff, inventory and buildings. The information on costs will help managers in their decision-making. Candidates will need to explain how the use of cost information can assist managers in planning and controlling the use of business resources. In particular candidates should be able to describe and explain the key terms used in classifying and attributing costs to specific units or activities within organisations.

In order to assist decision-making, managers should be able to explain and apply the traditional methods of absorbing overhead to unit costs. Decision-making is assisted if managers can distinguish between variable and fixed costs and explain why the difference is important. This distinction can be applied by candidates using breakeven analysis in simple situations.

Finally, as cash as well as profit is the lifeblood of a business, the syllabus requires candidates to describe why cash management is important to a business and to prepare and interpret a simple cash flow budget. This will lead candidates to describe the working capital cycle and illustrate how it can be managed.

Introduction to the construction and use of budgets in managing business resources

This part of the syllabus helps managers and administrators use budgets to plan, monitor and control the use of their business resources. Thus candidates are expected to define a simple budget and explain their objectives within the context of an organisation.

Having set the scene, the syllabus moves on to consider the construction and operation of budgets. The syllabus considers different approaches to budget preparation and describes the process of preparing the various budgets within an organisation. There is a requirement to prepare simple budgets from relevant data.

The syllabus concludes by introducing managers to interpreting and acting on the information produced by budgetary control systems. This involves managers describing the use of budgets in exercising control over business resources.

Excluded topics

Questions are likely to be set in the examination in either section from any part of the syllabus. All aspects of the syllabus will be examined over time, though not all topics can be covered in any one examination. In addition, to ensure that we test students' understanding effectively, the case study will mean that individual questions will be set that require knowledge of material contained across a number of different syllabus areas. A narrow focus on selected areas of the syllabus is ill advised.

Questions calling for an understanding of new legislation will not be set for examinations held less than six months after the statute received Royal Assent, or statutory instrument takes effect.

Study hours

It is recommended that students undertake approximately 200 hours' study for each module. This includes face-to-face tuition, self-study, examination preparation and reflection on work experiences.

Key areas of the syllabus

As a starting point to the module it is useful to consider financial information as being made up of two aspects: financial accounting and management accounting.

The module is not aimed at turning supervisors and aspiring managers into bookkeepers or accountants. However, as aspiring business managers it is important that you know how business transactions impact on the finances of a business. The module concentrates on trying to make the subject more understandable and relevant to both your job and career needs.

It is essential that managers can describe the format of the key financial statements, namely the profit and loss account and the balance sheet.

Assessment approach

This module will be assessed by a closed book examination of 2 hours' duration. Section A comprises 15-short answer questions, which account for 40 marks, designed to test both breadth and depth of the syllabus. Section B requires candidates to answer two multi-part questions from a choice of five, which account for 60 marks (2 × 30). The questions are based on a pre-released case study, which is circulated six weeks before the examination to enable students to research the case study.

Relevant study materials

Students will be expected to use the ICSA Accounting for Business study text as their primary text. For those seeking to broaden their knowledge of the subject area, the following supplementary study materials are recommended:

- www.accaglobal.com – choose an article, a paper, professional articles and technical articles.
- Financial Reporting Council – www.frc.org.uk with links to www.asb.org.uk – the Accounting Standards Board and to www.frrp.org.uk – the Financial Reporting Review Panel.
- International Accounting Standards Board – www.iasb.org.
- *The Economist* – www.economist.com.
- The Financial Times – www.news.ft.com.uk.
- *Accountancy Magazine* – www.accountancymag.co.uk – articles on tax, audit and finance.
- www.accountingweb.co.uk – resources on auditing and financial reporting.

The professional bodies' websites:
- www.acca.co.uk.
- www.cipfa.org.uk (not for profit body).
- www.icaew.co.uk.
- www.cimaglobal.com – good for online resources with articles from Financial Management.
- www.aia.org.uk – The Association of International Accountants.

- www.companieshouse.gov.uk – company reports.
- www.bized.ac.uk – this is a very informative site. It is a collection of resources for business, economics and accounting maintained by The Institute for Learning and Research Technology at the University of Bristol. It contains company information and Internet resources. You can search by subject, including accounting, economics and business studies. There are sites for students and lecturers. It contains glossaries, interactive worksheets and accounting theories.

Syllabus Overview

The place of Accounting for Business in the ICSA Certificate in Business Practice

The Accounting for Business module at Certificate level is one of four areas of activity considered essential for those seeking entry-level qualifications in business practice. The ICSA views the study of the business environment, management, communications and accounting as applied to business organisations as complementary elements in shaping business practitioners.

The module does *not* attempt to teach students to be accountants, but concentrates on trying to make the subject more understandable and relevant to their job and career needs.

The module looks at the financial aspects of managing business resources. It is intended for aspiring managers with little or no formal financial training or experience, whose present and future positions will affect the acquisition and use of business resources. The module will help students understand the basic terminology, concepts and techniques that underpin both financial and management accounting. In summary, the module aims to improve students' understanding and use of financial information.

The focus is on taking away some of the mystery from a subject that, it can be argued, is full of jargon, terminology and number-crunching. To this end, there is a very extensive glossary of technical accountancy terms in the Study Text, which provides definitions of the key terms used. This should be referred to throughout your studies.

Similarly, while numbers are used in accounting, they should not overwhelm business managers. The module does, however, expect you to produce simple figures in a clear and understandable form.

The point is that business managers' work can be made easier if they understand how fellow professionals produce information to assist decision-making as well as the terminology used in that information.

Finally, to those students who are confident of their ability to calculate and produce numeric tables and statements, it is important to appreciate that this is not the end of the story. The numbers may be accurate, but the results have to be interpreted and communicated to others involved in business decision-making. This may involve business managers communicating financial information via written reports and/or verbal presentations. The module will develop and test these skills in the examination.

Why Accounting for Business is important to business organisations

Financial information plays a part in achieving the key elements of the successful management of a business namely:

1 Planning the future operations and direction of a business by assessing the financial implications of setting company objectives; for example, the benefits and drawbacks of borrowing money to finance company expansion.

2   Controlling the daily activities and operations of a business; for example, by comparing actual costs with budgeted costs so as to identify under- or over-spending.

3   Continually reviewing the direction, activities and operations of a business to allow the business to predict and react to changing environments; for example, by identifying why sales income has dropped below the planned level and deciding to increase advertising costs to boost sales.

Key elements of the syllabus

There are four main areas within the Accounting for Business syllabus. They are:

* Introduction to accounting and finance   10%
* Recording and reporting business activity   40%
* Using financial information to manage business
  resources – an introduction   30%
* An introduction to the construction and use of
  budgets in managing business resources   20%

The syllabus explained

Introduction to accounting and finance

As a starting point it is useful to consider financial information as being made up of two aspects. For the purpose of this overview, these are termed financial accounting and management accounting. The first two areas of the syllabus focus on financial accounting in that the module explains the nature and role of accounting in business and why non-accountants need to understand the fundamentals of accounting and finance. The intention is to examine the wide spectrum of users of financial information and explain their differing needs. The module explains the basic concepts on which accounting information is based and refers to the regulatory framework within which accounting operates.

Recording and reporting business activity

It is important that business managers know how business transactions impact on the finances of a business. Thus it useful to be able to describe a simple system in which to record business transactions from source documents (such as invoices) through to the accounting ledgers.

It is essential that managers can at least describe the format of the key financial statements – namely, profit and loss accounts and balance sheets. The focus here is on examining how these statements measure the financial performance and the financial position of the organisation. Having focused on the description of business transactions and financial statements, candidates will also be asked to demonstrate an ability to prepare simple profit and loss accounts and balance sheets for a small business at the end of an accounting period. This will involve demonstrating an ability to make adjustments at the year-end.

Many businesses base their information systems on computers, so it is important that candidates can describe the operation and benefits of using a computerised system to record and report business activity.

Using financial information to manage business resources – an introduction

Parts 3 and 4 of the syllabus focus on management accounting. In contrast to financial accounting, this information assists managers in making decisions about the future policy and operations of the business.

This half of the syllabus focuses on the information business managers receive about the cost of the resources they use. This covers the planned and actual costs of resources, including staff, inventory and buildings. The information on costs helps managers make decisions. Candidates will have to explain how the use of cost information can assist in planning and controlling the use of business resources. In particular, candidates should be able to describe and explain the key terms used in classifying and attributing costs to specific units or activities within organisations.

In order to assist decision-making, managers should be able to explain and apply the traditional methods of absorbing overhead to unit costs. Decision-making is assisted if managers can distinguish between variable and fixed costs and explain why the distinction is important. This difference between the two can be applied by candidates using breakeven analysis in simple situations.

Finally, as cash as well as profit are the lifeblood of a business, the syllabus requires candidates to describe why cash management is important to a business and to prepare and interpret a simple cash flow budget. This will lead candidates to describe the working capital cycle and illustrate how it can be managed.

Introduction to the construction and use of budgets in managing business resources

This part of the syllabus assists managers to use budgets to plan, monitor and control the use of their business resources. Thus candidates are expected to define a simple budget and explain their objectives within the context of an organisation.

Having set the scene, the syllabus moves on to consider the construction and operation of budgets. It considers different approaches to budget preparation and describes the process of preparing the various budgets within an organisation. There is a requirement to prepare simple budgets from relevant data.

The syllabus concludes by introducing managers to interpreting and acting on the information produced by budgetary control systems. This involves describing the use of budgets in exercising control over business resources.

How to approach the study of Accounting for Business

Because accounting and finance use numbers, many people believe that there is only one answer. This is not always the case. Accounting is not like a natural science such as physics or chemistry where statements of what occurs in nature are found by observation and experiment to be true.

Accounting information is often produced by a combination of mathematical techniques and judgement. For example, a business purchases a vehicle for £20,000 and makes a judgement that the vehicle will have an estimated life of four years. This means that the business estimates the cost of depreciation to be £5,000 per year. This contrasts with an annual depreciation estimate of £4,000 if the estimated life is five years. This is one simple illustration of how accounting information is not always verifiable by experiment. The module encourages students to question how financial information is produced and to understand the accounting concepts and principles that underpin such information. This does not mean that accountants can produce figures based exclusively on judgements. Their judgements need to take note of accounting standards and concepts as well as relevant legislation.

It is useful to approach accounting information in terms of the frameworks and concepts that underpin the information. In the above example the business has several methods of determining the estimated annual depreciation charge. This will have different impacts on the annual profit of the business. Thus once the business selects a particular method it is expected to be consistent in applying it from year to year. This does not prevent the business from changing its method, but there have to be good reasons to change. This example illustrates the application of the 'consistency' concept in preparing financial information. The study of many topics in the module can be better understood by reference to accounting frameworks and concepts, which assist in the preparation of financial information.

Using and developing your experience of accounting

Candidates may or may not be currently in a management role with a responsibility for finance. Whatever your situation, there are a number of options open to you to increase your practical knowledge which can be applied in studying this module. You could:

- Establish a contact from the finance department of your organisation and ask them to help you with finding practical examples to illustrate the module theory.
- Refer to the financial secretary of an organisation you are a member of, say a sports club or music society.
- Obtain a copy of the annual report and accounts of a company either directly, via the web, or from national newspapers and use these as the basis of examples.
- Make use of the contacts you have with the not-for-profit sector – local authorities, charities and health authorities all produce financial accounts. You may even contribute to them through taxation or donations and might want to know how your money is spent. The financial terminology of the profit and not-for-profit sectors is increasingly generic, i.e. has common characteristics.

How to succeed in the examination

Preparing for examination

Candidates need a clear idea of what is expected of them in terms of assessment – in this case a revealed or pre-released case study. The key is to prepare for the case study as your work progresses rather than cram everything in to the last couple of weeks. Candidates will find it useful to highlight and/or summarise the key points of the various accounting concepts and techniques as they come across them; this might be on the Study Text itself or on study cards so they can be reviewed at regular intervals. This approach allows you to consolidate and rationalise your study material prior to the examination.

Another key point is to get to know the examination paper and what is required. With this module a case study will be made available to candidates six weeks prior to the examination. The examination is of 2 hours' duration and is in two parts. Section A is made up of 15 short-answer questions, which account for 40 marks. Ten questions have 2 marks each and five questions have 4 marks each, which can relate to any part of the syllabus. In the main the 2-mark questions ask for short, factual answers such as 'Identify FOUR different groups who use the published annual accounts of a business'. Candidates could gain the 2 marks by listing (for example): The Inland Revenue, Shareholders, Creditors and Employees (0.5 mark each). The short 4-mark questions normally require more than a listing of points. They will ask you, for example, to outline the advantages and/or disadvantages of an accounting technique or they could require short numerical answers. For example, Capital International Travel Company has a financial year ending on 31 March. On 1 June the company purchased a company car. The annual insurance premium of £432 was paid on the same day. What is the correct amount that should be included for the cost of insurance in the profit and loss account for the year ended 31 December? What accounting concept is being applied in calculating your answer? The 4 marks available could be gained by:

£432
12 months = £36 per month × 10 months

£360 charged to profit and loss account. (2 marks)

The concept is called the accruals concept with £72 being prepaid. (2 marks)

Section B comprises a choice of questions based on the case study. Candidates are required to answer two questions from a choice of five, which account for 60 marks (2 × 30 marks). Each of the five Section B questions is in at least three parts. These questions will be a mix of numerical and discursive questions.

The case study

The case study is made available six weeks before the examination so time management is essential in the preparatory period as well as during the two-hour examination.

In the six-week preparatory period, candidates need to spend time reading and understanding the case study. Initially, it is probably better not to question spot, but rather to identify the main points and themes. The themes will always be clearly signposted. After you have read the case study a few times, consider making a list of the possible topics/areas for further research. This could provide a structure for any preparatory work and so avoid focusing on one key area to the exclusion of others. Remember, there will be five questions for candidates to choose from and they could be taken from any part of the syllabus. In addition, a single question may cover several parts of a syllabus.

The case study material presents you with a situation you as a business manager could find in your workplace. Thus it may relate to a business that has several factories located throughout the world and you may take the role of a business administrator located in the central accounting department. You may be given a specific job, e.g. communicating information and advice between the accounting department and factory managers. Having read the case study you might identify five key themes that appear in the case study e.g. 1) Budgeting, 2) Profit calculation and accounting concepts, 3) Fixed and current asset records, 4) Decision-making and 5) Accounting records and systems. The themes identified are clearly wide-ranging, e.g. budgeting can cover both budget preparation and budgetary control. Other themes also overlap, so questions on fixed assets could cover accounting records and accounting concepts. It would be risky or even foolish for a candidate to focus on two areas in their preparation for the examination to the exclusion of the others.

What are the questions looking for?

Some questions expect you to produce, say, a simple profit and loss account or to work out the cost of a product. On the other hand, the majority of questions will require you to explain and interpret the content of financial information.

The verb used in the question will give you a good indication of what the examiner expects. At this level, the questions may ask you to do one or more of the following:

- 'List', 'define' or 'state' asks you to display your knowledge of a subject in a concise and clear way, e.g. 'List FIVE potential benefits to a business of introducing a budgeting system'.
- 'Explain', 'describe', 'distinguish' or 'identify' asks you to make the meaning of something clear in order to display your comprehension of a topic, e.g. 'Explain the key differences between the terms revenue and capital expenditure'.
- 'Illustrate' asks you to explain something using examples – these could be examples you have experienced at work, selected from elsewhere or ones you have created yourself – e.g. 'Give THREE examples which illustrate the drawbacks of using manual accounting systems'.
- 'Calculate' or 'compute' asks you to ascertain a result mathematically or via an accounting technique, e.g. 'Calculate both the annual depreciation charge and the net book value of the equipment at the end of its first year of use'.
- 'Discuss' 'interpret' or 'analyse' asks you to analyse the detail of what you have learned, e.g. 'Discuss the opinion that depreciation should be calculated on replacement cost instead of the original capital cost'.

Common pitfalls to avoid

It is important to remember that the examination is a closed book examination so you cannot take any notes or the Study Text into the examination room. You will be given a fresh copy of the case study and the examination paper. Although it is a case study, candidates should still focus on avoiding the three most common errors seen at examinations:

- *Managing your time* – This is a big factor in passing examinations. A two-hour examination of 100 marks means that each mark is worth 1.2 minutes. Thus the 40 marks available in Part A merit only 48 minutes and the two 30 mark questions in Part B merit only 36 minutes each. This might seem very precise, but helps candidates remember the need to attempt all the required questions and not spend too much time on one question. Remember the first few marks are easier to score in the last question than the final few marks in a question a candidate has been working on. Do not get stuck on one question – you can return to it later.
- *Answer the questions asked* – and not the one you would have liked to have been asked. This is particularly important when you have focused in great detail on one area in your case study preparation and it does not appear in the form you expected in the examination paper. It is useful to keep referring back to the question as you write your answer to ensure you are not straying away from it.
- *Keep your answers simple* – in terms of writing straightforwardly and concisely. It is better to use simple English and make good use of full stops and paragraphs. In this module it is essential that you include clear and full workings to support your calculations. A wrong answer with no workings will gain no marks. Marks can be awarded if a wrong answer is supported by workings which reveal the correct methodology.

Summary

This syllabus overview is intended to give you guidance about how best to approach the Accounting for Business module and the ways in which you can score highly in the examination. The case study will be a challenge, but try to focus on the vocabulary used in the questions as they will give you a good indication as to the examiner's expectations. Plan your time during the six-week preparatory period in terms of reading and understanding the case study. Initially, it is probably better not to question spot, but rather to identify the main points and themes of the case study. These will always be clearly signposted.

Manage your time in the examination. This is a big factor in gaining a pass.

Keep your answers straightforward. Write simply and concisely. In this module it is essential that you include clear and full workings to support calculations.

Your answers should be clear, well written, make appropriate use of accounting concepts and techniques and reflect the professional approach expected of candidates of the ICSA Certificate.

Finally, remember that the examiner wants you to pass. There are no tricks.

Introduction to Accounting and Finance

Contents

Overview

As a starting point to this module it is useful to consider financial information as being made up of two aspects. These, for the purpose of this overview, are termed financial accounting and management accounting. The first two areas of the syllabus focus on financial accounting in so far as the module explains the nature and role of accounting within business and why non-accountants need to understand the fundamentals of accounting and finance. The intention is to examine the wide spectrum of users of financial information and explain their differing needs. The module describes the basic concepts on which accounting information is based and refers to the regulatory framework within which accounting operates. In particular, it focuses on the role of legislation, the European Union, the professional accountancy bodies and the Accounting Standards Board in determining the format, content and purpose of financial statements. The final section of chapter 2 illustrates the importance and impact of accounting concepts and accounting standards in providing a degree of standardisation to facilitate user comparability.

Learning objectives

At the end of this chapter students will be able to:

▶ Explain the nature and role of accounting and the uses of accounting information.
▶ Describe and distinguish between the terms financial accounting and management accounting.
▶ Explain the key accounting concepts and their effects.
▶ Describe the regulatory framework.
▶ Describe how the accounting standard process developed in the UK.

Accounting information and concepts

Chris Smith has recently joined a manufacturing company as a trainee general manager. The company's training programme involves him gaining experience in various departments throughout the factory. As an experienced business manager you have been appointed to be Chris's mentor. Your role includes meeting Chris to discuss issues and problems the company has faced during their moves throughout the business.

One of Chris's first jobs is to go to a meeting attended by the factory manager and factory department supervisors. The meeting is chaired by the factory accountant and the aim is to discuss the content of the monthly budget factory statements and also to start planning the factory budget for next year. Chris observes the meeting which lasts for two hours.

The main speaker is the factory accountant, who takes up most of the time explaining the content of the budget statements and the problems the company is facing because factory expenditure is well over budget. There are a very few comments from the factory manager and none at all from departmental supervisors. The meeting is continually interrupted as the operatives from the shop floor come in and raise difficulties being experienced on the production line which require the supervisors' immediate attention.

The factory accountant concludes the meeting by explaining the paperwork for next year's budget. This is to be completed by the factory manger and supervisors. One of the departmental supervisors suddenly stands up and, pushing their copy of the paperwork into the middle of the table, comments: 'I can see no reason for factory managers and supervisors to be involved with accounting and budgets. The time spent on meetings like today's plus involvement with monthly budget statements would be better spent on improving production methods.' No one comments until the factory manager suggests the meeting is closed and reconvened at a later date.

When seconded to the Information Technology department Chris is involved in putting the company's main financial accounting statements for the last financial year on the company website. This proves to be a difficult task but Chris is pleased to gain experience in website design.

A few days later Chris is involved in collecting the mail from the Finance Department. There is a mail sack full of letters which include copies of the main financial statements. These are being sent to all company shareholders.

Chris has noticed references to accounting standards in the financial statements. Chris again sees the need for accounting standards to be questionable. Chris suggests that accounting standards are not necessary because the accountancy profession is perfectly capable of deciding what accounting principles to use.

When reading the company's financial statements Chris came across the term accounting concepts and references to 'going concern' and 'prudence'. The notion of concepts or ideas in accounting seem a little strange to Chris who took it for granted that accounting was concerned with numbers and producing right or wrong answers.

Introduction to accounting information and concepts

1

Introduction

This chapter discusses how non-accountants can benefit from developing their knowledge and understanding of accounting and finance. It also considers the role of accounting as part of an information system in managing business resources. The chapter identifies the principal individuals and groups who make decisions using accounting information. Managers will find it useful to distinguish between the internal and external users of accounting information as this allows a discussion of the two fields of accounting information as management accounting and financial accounting. The chapter invites business managers to consider the basic characteristics or qualities financial statements should possess.

Accounting concepts and conventions is the term given to the broad underlying assumptions that underpin accounting practice. They provide the basis for the rules and guidelines which accountants follow when preparing accounting information. It is useful for non-accountants to understand these concepts and conventions before getting involved in the mechanics of accounting, which are introduced in Part 2. It should make it easier for non-accountants to understand the finished products of the accounting process and be in a better position to question their content.

Students are advised to seek out a couple of examples of accounting information produced for use in their organisation or department, and consider its content and purpose in light of comments made in chapter 1.

> **accounting concepts and conventions**
> The broad, underlying assumptions that underpin accounting practice.

1 Organisations and the management of resources

Organisations of all types need resources to function. It is the responsibility of managers to acquire, use and control these resources to achieve the organisation's objectives. The resources come in all forms but can be classified to include such things as employees, equipment and vehicles, and the space and money used by the organisation. In the main these resources are tangible in that they can be seen and touched and have a monetary or financial value placed upon them.

Managers are continually making decisions which centre on the use of business resources. For example, they will look at the current and planned use of business resources and ask questions such as:

1   Are we acquiring our raw materials at the best possible price?
2   Are we using our buildings for the best possible purposes?
3   Are we putting our cash into the most profitable investments?
4   Should we put more cash into one type of resource, say buildings as opposed to people?
5   What profit is the organisation expecting to get back from investing in a certain combination of resources?

The decisions that managers face are continually changing. In order to assist in reaching these decisions managers need information on the use of these resources in the activities and processes of the organisation.

Putting the case   1.1

 Chris asks you to provide FIVE reasons, illustrated by relevant examples, which explain why the factory manager and departmental supervisors need to be involved in the production and use of financial information produced by the factory accountant.

 Five reasons with examples include:

1   Factory supervisors and managers frequently make, or contribute to, production-line decisions that have financial consequences. For example, what are the financial consequences of, say, changing the supplier of the raw materials used in the production process?

2   Factory supervisors and managers often have to interpret a range of financial information to fulfil their roles. For example, monthly budget statements can be used as an aid in controlling the production-line activities such as identifying excessive waste of raw materials during the production process.

3   Factory supervisors and managers are often involved in communication with colleagues

which involves using financial terms and terminology. For example, a factory manager may ask the stores manager what the latest replacement price of a particular raw material is so that they can contribute to the preparation of a quotation to an existing customer.

4   Factory supervisors and managers are likely to ask for increased business resources, for example, bids for new factory machinery or more staff for the production line. The company will have limited financial resources so it is essential for supervisors and managers to be able to make a strong case, including the financial aspects, to support their bid.

5   Factory supervisors and managers play a key role in achieving the company's objectives. For example, the business may have as an objective increasing the profit of the company so it is useful to be aware of the costs involved in production so that cost savings can be achieved.

2 Definition of accounting

Accounting can play a key role in providing information to decision-makers. The CIMA Management Accounting official terminology defines accounting as:

- the classification and recording of monetary transactions;
- the presentation and interpretation of the results of those transactions in order to assess performance over a period and the financial position at a given date; and
- the monetary projection of future activities arising from alternative planned courses of action.

In its broadest form, **accounting** is concerned with identifying, collecting, measuring, recording, summarising and communicating the financial aspects of an organisation's activities. This can be illustrated by reference to Table 1.1, which provides accounting information relating to the use of human resources:

accounting
Identifying, collecting, measuring, recording, summarising and communicating the financial aspects of an organisation's activities.

Identifying	Collecting	Measuring	Recording	Summarising	Communicating
The payment of wages.	The raw data from timesheets.	The value of the employee hours in £, $, etc.	The manual or computer entry in an accounting book.	The totalling of all wages transactions during a period.	Preparing summarised reports to show the results of an organisation's activities involving the use of human resources.

Table 1.1 Accounting information for human resources

2.1 Accounting as an information system

Accounting gathers data from both inside and outside an organisation. The accounting system converts these data into a form which helps managers and other interested parties to make decisions. This revised form is called information and is communicated to the users of the information. An accounting information system is summarised in Figure 1.1.

Stop and Think   1.1

Some of your colleagues, who are all non-accountants, have expressed their dismay at having to become more involved in the financial aspects of your organisation as they are already very busy in delivering your organisation's products and services. Can you produce three reasons, supported by specific examples taken from your organisation, explaining why it would be useful to your colleagues to spend some time improving their knowledge and understanding of the accounting?

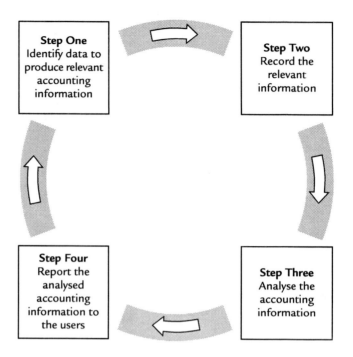

Figure 1.1 Accounting infomation system

3   Users of accounting information

Accounting information is used by any individuals or groups involved in decision-making. The principal individuals and groups who make decisions include the following:

- *Managers* – the people appointed to manage an organisation's day-to-day activities and operations. These individuals need information about the organisation's past, current and future financial position. This allows them to carry out the key elements of successful management – namely, planning and controlling their operations.
- *Shareholders* – the owners of the business who provide the money needed to start and keep the business operating. They may not be involved in the day-to-day operations of the business, but need to know if their business is making a profit, if that profit is satisfactory and how the profit is to be allocated.

- *Lenders of finance* want to know if their monies are safe. Lenders include banks which provide long-term loans and need to be assured that the business will be able not only to make interest payments but also repay the principal when required.
- *Financial analysts* include stockbrokers, financial advisers and financial journalists who want to be able to assess whether or not the business is a good investment. Financial analysts assess what potential profit investors can expect from their investment. This involves a review of accounting information provided from a number of sources such as the annual accounts and statements made to the media.
- *Suppliers* who provide goods and services to an organisation on credit want to know if they are going to be paid and how quickly. The financial information provides data on how long a company takes to pay its bills.
- *Government bodies*, such as the local and national taxation authorities, need some idea of how much taxation the organisation owes. This allows government bodies to plan how much they have to spend and to ensure that accounting records comply with the law. The government also uses accounting information for the regulation of industry and compilation of national statistics.
- *Customers* who are going to do business with an organisation want to know if it is financially able to continue in existence. It is essential that a customer who purchases goods or services from the organisation has confidence that they will have a regular supply of those goods and services. Customers may also be in a dependency relationship if they have product warranties/guarantees or need replacement of specialist parts.
- *Employees* rely on the organisation to provide their principal source of regular income. They use financial information to assess their job security and the organisation's ability to make pay awards. Similarly, past employees are interested in their pensions whilst potential employees may require accounting information to assist their decision to join an organisation.
- *The general public* are likely to be members of any of the groups mentioned above; for example, they may be employees and customers of the organisation. However, in their role as members of the general public they are likely to have a wider interest in the financial performance of an organisation. Thus they might be interested to know if the business is spending sufficient money to protect the environment from damage caused by its production processes.

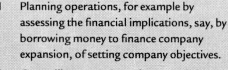

Putting the case   1.2

Chris has heard that there are several key elements of successful management. He asks you to list TWO elements and provide TWO examples of a way in which financial information can contribute to the three key elements of managing business operations.

Financial information plays a part in achieving the key elements of successful management namely:

1   Planning operations, for example by assessing the financial implications, say, by borrowing money to finance company expansion, of setting company objectives.

2   Controlling operations, for example by identifying why sales income has dropped below the planned level and deciding to increase advertising costs to boost sales.

3.1   External and internal users

The users listed above can be grouped into those who are within the organisation, such as the managers, while the rest can be classified as being outside the organisation. The distinction is somewhat arbitrary because in some small businesses the owners are both the key investors and the employees involved in the day-to-day operations. Notwithstanding this situation it is useful to distinguish between internal and external users of accounting information, namely management accounting and financial accounting.

3.2   Financial accounting

financial accounting

Reporting the financial performance of an organisation for external users via the organisation's financial statements.

This is the most traditional form of accounting and is aimed at satisfying the information needs of external users. **Financial accounting** involves:

- The contents and outlook of the three main accounting statements – namely the profit and loss account, the balance sheet and the cash flow statement – are principally historical in nature. These statements are explained in more detail later in this study text but at this stage it is useful to note that the respective statements reveal the profit (or loss) made during the last financial period, the impact of the profit (or loss) made on the overall wealth of a business and the impact of business transactions on its cash position.

- The content and format of financial accounting statements are largely shaped by the legal requirements of a particular country. For example, in the UK, companies need to comply with the financial reporting requirements contained in the Companies Acts. Similarly not-for-profit bodies such as charities and local authorities must conform to relevant legislation.

accounting standard

An authoritative statement of how particular types of transactions and other events should be reflected in financial statements.

- As organisations become increasingly global the content and format of financial accounting statements are subjected to a wider range of influences, including international law, stock exchange requirements and the **accounting standards**.

- Financial accounting statements for each financial year should give a 'true and fair view' of the organisation's performance and financial position at the end of the year. This term will be developed throughout the study text, but at this stage it can

be taken to mean that the statements comply with relevant legislation and accounting standards and that any judgements included in the accounts, say on the level of bad debts likely to incurred by the company, are reasonable and prudent.
- In financial accounting the unit of account is monetary and the emphasis is on accuracy.

3.3 Management accounting

Management accounting is aimed at satisfying the information needs of internal users. Key points about management accounting are as follows:

- The outlook of management accounting not only focuses on past results but also plans for the future. Thus the management accountant will not only review the financial performance of, say, the last financial year but will also assist in planning for the future by preparing a budget for the following financial year.
- The format and content of management accounting are not prescribed by legislation but are prepared to help managers plan, control and review their operations. In short, management accounting is concerned with assisting decision-making in day-to-day operations and long-term strategies.
- Management accounting information is prepared for all levels of management – senior managers, company accountants, supervisors and operational managers.
- The unit of account in management accounting is monetary but can also be physical, for example the number of units required to break even. The emphasis is also different in that management accounting often focuses on speed of producing the information rather than accuracy.

These distinctions are summarised in table 1.2.

management accounting
Management accounts are prepared by management accountants for internal users within an organisation.

Test *yourself*   1.2

(a) Explain the key difference between the content and format of financial accounts as compared with management accounting.
(b) How would you define the term 'accounting'?

	Financial Accounting	Management Accounting
Prepared for	External user groups	Internal user groups
Purpose	Satisfy information needs of external users	Assist managerial decision making, planning and control
Level of detail	Summarised or aggregated at organisational level	Detailed and specific information on parts of the organisations operations
Frequency of information	Usually annual accounts	As required by managers, e.g. monthly budget statements
Time horizon	The past, i.e. historical	The future, i.e. forecasts plus past information, e.g. budgets, used for control purposes
Constraints on content	Normally, legal requirements and accounting standards influence the content and format of financial statements	None – content can be tailor made to meet managerial requirements

Table 1.2 The distinctions between financial accounting and management accounting

Putting the case   1.3

Chris is mystified about why the company's main financial accounting statements for the last financial year are placed on the company's website as every shareholder receives a paper copy of the main financial statements. Chris asks you to list FIVE other groups who would be interested in having access to the financial statements, together with an example of the sort of information they would be looking for in the statements.

The shareholders are not the only group who may have an interest in the company's financial statements. The following are illustrations of interested groups together with an example of their interest:

1   Competitors will be interested in making financial comparisons in terms sales turnover, running costs and profits made.

2   Employees involved in share option schemes will be interested in the company's survival, its ability to pay dividends and the market price of the shares.

3   Lenders of money to the company such as banks will be interested in the company's ability to continue trading. This will make the lender more confident that they will receive interest and loan repayments as they fall due.

4   Government bodies such as taxation departments will be interested in the figures as a basis for working out taxes due and their collection. These could include company tax and value added tax.

5   The general public may be interested in the environmental impact of the manufacturing business, for example finding out how much the business is spending on limiting the emission of greenhouse gases or land pollution.

4 Characteristics of accounting information

If financial statements are to be of any use, they need certain basic characteristics or qualities. A comprehensive list of such characteristics would be very long; the main ones are summarised below:

- *Relevance*. The financial information provided should be relevant to the decision-making requirements of the users. In the case of financial statements, a wide range of information is needed to satisfy the interested parties identified above. Financial information should not be produced if it cannot influence decisions.
- *Reliability*. The financial information must be free from error and bias. The users must be able to rely on the information they receive, otherwise it is useless. The reliability of financial information is enhanced if information is independently verified. The law requires that the accounts published by limited companies should be examined by an **external auditor**, who must be independent of the company and hold an approved accountancy qualification. The auditor certifies that the financial accounting statements for each financial year give a 'true and fair view' of the organisation's results and its financial position.
- *Comparability*. Financial information should be produced in a consistent format so that valid comparisons can be made over several periods and between different organisations including the accounts of similar companies operating in the same business sector.
- *Understandability*. Financial information must be understood by the users it is intended for. This is not a one-way process in that the users of the information are expected to have a reasonable knowledge of business and accounting terminology and techniques.
- *Timeliness*. The usefulness of financial information is limited if there is too much delay in producing it. However, information produced too hastily may reduce its reliability. Timeliness is judged in terms of satisfying the decision-making needs of managers. For example, external users such as shareholders are normally satisfied to see accounts produced annually. Contrast this with internal users such as a factory manager who may require monthly factory accounts.

external auditor
A suitably qualified person who certifies that the financial accounting statements for give a 'true and fair view' of the organisation's performance and financial position.

4.1 Limitations of financial statements

Financial statements are a good way of communicating information about the financial performance of an organisation over a period of time and its financial position at a point in time. In particular, they allow users of the information to compare:

- changes to the organisation's financial position on a year-to-year basis;
- performance with similar businesses;
- performance against planned or budgeted figures.

However, at this early stage students will be aware that accounting information has certain limitations. These occur despite the application of accounting standards, accounting legislation and legislation. The limitations are as follows:

- Financial statements are prepared from historical or out-of-date information and may not reflect the current or future thinking about the business.
- The preparation of financial statements involves making subjective judgements and estimates, such as how long an asset will last for depreciation purposes.
- Accounting concepts and accounting standards will have an effect on figures used in the financial statements.
- The information presented in published financial statements is often a legal minimum as required by legislation and accounting standards.
- Financial statements are only one source of information about the performance of a business. Managers require information about all aspects of the performance of the business, e.g. delivering quality products and services which meet customer demands.
- Financial statements tend to include information which can be measured in monetary terms. This means that key elements of a business, e.g. skills of workforce are ignored.
- Financial statements tend to ignore the major external factors which can impact on a business, including a change of government policy, European or central government legislation, international or national shortages of raw materials or labour.

Test *yourself*   1.3

What do you understand by the term 'objective measurement' in relation to the production of accounting information?

5   Accounting concepts and conventions

Understanding accounting information would be relatively easy if every number in the information was verifiable by tangible evidence – for example, the economic value placed on every piece of equipment and building could be verified by reference to the historic cost of the equipment as revealed by the relevant invoice. In reality, many pieces of accounting information are based on personal judgements, in other words, they are subjective. The piece of equipment referred to above might be valued subjectively in accounting statements at replacement price. In order to provide a framework to these subjective judgements, the accounting profession has developed accounting concepts, conventions and accounting standards. These are the rules financial accountants and auditors are expected to comply with when preparing financial statements. These accounting standards are laid down by a body, in the UK called the Accounting Standards Board, which comprises representatives of the country's accounting bodies. These aim to increase the objectivity of the methods used to record the business activities in financial statements.

As a manager faced with reviewing accounting information it is important that you:

- Understand the accounting concepts, conventions and standards the accountant has adopted.

- Consider whether the concepts, conventions and standards adopted are appropriate to the particular situation.
- Consider questioning the accountant on the concepts, conventions and standards adopted.

5.1 Basic accounting concepts

A full list of accounting concepts would be quite extensive, so as a starting point it is useful to consider four basic concepts which are followed in preparing accounts. Not following them would result in the accounts not showing a 'true and fair view'. The four basic concepts or assumptions are:

1 Going concern.
2 Prudence.
3 Accruals or matching.
4 Consistency.

5.2 The going concern concept

The **going concern concept** is the assumption that the business will continue to operate in the foreseeable future – that there is no intention to close it and no intention to make significant cutbacks to the nature of the business. This approach means that the information provided by financial statements is most relevant.

The implication of this concept is that the **assets** of a business such as buildings and equipment will normally be valued at their historic cost, i.e. their original purchase cost. The issue here is that the assets of the business should *not* be valued at their break-up value, i.e. the amount they would sell for if they were to be sold one at a time. The break-up values tend not to be relevant to the users of accounts who are assuming that the business will continue to operate over the remaining useful life of the asset. As an example, if a business acquires machinery at a cost of £100,000 which is expected to last five years, it is usual to write off the cost of the asset over the five-year period against the profits to which the assets has contributed.

This practice of writing off the cost of a long-term asset over its useful life helps to ensure that as the asset deteriorates physically or operationally, its cost in the accounting records is reduced to reflect that loss. This is done over the life of the asset because it would be inappropriate to charge the full purchase cost to any single accounting period. The profit would be understated for that period, while in subsequent periods the profit would be overstated. Equally, to show the asset at nil value in the accounts would be misleading as it would imply either no asset or a valueless asset. The accountant must therefore have evidence that the asset will last beyond the end of the year. The yearly reduction in the cost of the asset is called depreciation and appears as one of the expenses in the profit and loss account. Depreciation is dealt with more fully in chapter 4.

Going concern applies to other assets such as stock and debtors (customers who owe the business money for goods or services provided) where a similar assumption regarding the sale of stock or the collection of the debt applies.

going concern concept
The assumption that the entity will continue in operational existence for the foreseeable future.

asset
Any tangible or intangible possession which has value.

The concept can also be observed being applied in relation to long-term loans or liabilities owed by the business. If the going concern concept were not applied it is likely that these would become payable immediately and classed as short-term debts or liabilities.

The assumption that the business is a going concern really justifies the use of the historic cost concept, which in turn emphasises the high importance given to the qualities of objectivity and verifiability in accounting data.

5.3   The prudence concept

prudence concept
The principle that income is included in the financial statements only when realised, while likely losses are included as soon as possible.

The **prudence concept** means that where a selection has to be made between different procedures or valuations, the one selected should be that which gives the most cautious presentation of the financial position or results of the business. It also follows that where a loss can be foreseen, it should be recognised and taken into account immediately.

The prudence concept reflects the traditional tendency for accountants to recognise likely losses as soon as possible but to defer recognition of potential income until it arises. The use of the prudence concept can be observed in the case of stock. Accepted accounting practice states that stock should be valued at the lower of historic cost and net realisable value. Thus if the stock is likely to be sold for less than was originally paid for it, a loss will be made. The accountant recognises this loss immediately by reducing the value of unsold stock to net realisable value. This concept is sometimes called 'conservatism'.

There are at least two reasons for following the prudence concept, namely:

- 'Understating' profit looks after the traditional interests of creditors and bankers.
- A conservative approach may counteract the natural optimism of some managers and owners.

5.4   The accruals concept

accruals concept
The principle that revenues and costs are matched with each other and dealt with in the profit and loss account of the period to which they relate, irrespective of the period of receipt or payment.

Profit is measured not by comparing cash received during the financial period with cash spent but by matching expenditure incurred with income earned. The **accruals concept** states that when computing profit the sales income (or sales revenue) earned should be matched only against the expenditure incurred when earning it.

This raises the question of when sales revenue (or income) should be recorded in the accounts. If goods are sold on credit, when should the revenue be shown? Traditionally, the question is answered by reference to the realisation or revenue recognition concept. The prudence concept stresses that sales revenue should be 'realised' and 'recognised' only when a critical event has occurred. This event would normally be when:

- A cash sale is made.
- The goods are delivered or the services provided and *not* when the sale proceeds are received. This will normally coincide with date on the invoice or the date of delivery if the issue of the invoice is delayed.

The accruals concept refers to this critical event as the point in time when the revenue is earned.

The accruals concept is extended to the area of expenditure or costs. Costs should be recognised as arising when they are incurred and not when the cash is paid. For example, where an annual insurance premium is paid in advance and spreads across two financial years, care has to be taken that each financial year takes the appropriate share of the premium. Where an amount paid in this financial year relates to the next financial year, there is a prepayment, or a payment in advance, which will be carried forward to be charged in the subsequent year's accounts. This avoids the accounting period when the insurance premium is paid incurring the cost of another accounting period.

Alternatively, some services, for example telephone, gas and electricity, are seen as being incurred or used on the date they are received. At the end of a financial year these services have been consumed or incurred but no invoice has been received by the company. The company will treat these as accrued expenses or expenses owing.

In practice the accruals concept shows profit/loss, as follows:

Revenue earned – Expenditure incurred = Profit (or loss) for an accounting period.

5.5 The consistency concept

It was stressed earlier that some accounting information is verifiable by tangible evidence and as such is objective. In contrast many pieces of accounting information are based on personal judgements, i.e. they are subjective.

In certain important areas, for example the valuation of stocks or the estimation of bad debts, a company has a choice of several equally valid methods. These have different effects on reported profits from year to year. Firms may be tempted to take advantage of these alternatives to show an apparent 'improvement' in their financial performance or strength. The use of the consistency concept provides a barrier to this being easily done.

Accordingly, once a company chooses a particular accounting treatment for an item it must be applied consistently within each accounting period and from one period to the next for similar items. For example, it is assumed that the method of valuing closing stock is the same as that used to value opening stock. This does not mean that the company is not allowed to change its accounting methods. It can, provided that there are good reasons for doing so. However, if it does, the effect on that year's profits should be highlighted in the financial statements to facilitate comparisons with previous years.

One aim of applying the consistency concept is to increase the usefulness of accounting information. The information can be compared with similar information about the company for some other period or point in time, and with similar information about other businesses.

consistency concept
The principle that there is uniformity of accounting treatment of like items within each accounting period and from one period to the next.

(a) What is the difference between break-up value and historic cost?

(b) What is the difference between a payment in advance and an accrued expense?

(c) What do you understand by consistency of accounting treatment in financial statements?

6   Further accounting concepts

The above four accounting concepts are widely viewed as being basic to the preparation and content of accounting information. However, there are other principles/concepts which the accountant uses in the preparation of financial statements.

6.1   The materiality concept

materiality concept
The principle that financial statements should separately disclose items which are significant enough to affect evaluation or decisions.

Materiality refers to the relative significance or importance of a particular matter in the context of the financial statements as a whole. A matter is material if its omission or misstatement would reasonably influence the decisions of a user of the accounts.

An item in the accounts which is too trivial to affect a user's understanding of the financial statements is referred to as immaterial. When preparing financial statements it is important to assess what is material and what is not so that resources are not wasted in the pursuit of excessive detail. Thus a low-value office clock or paper shredder may last for several years but is highly unlikely to be subject to an annual depreciation charge because it is not worth the effort of to keep such detailed records.

There is no absolute measure of materiality. Often a rule of thumb will be applied such as defining material items as those with, say, a value greater than 5% of the profit disclosed by the accounts, but it is really a question of judgement. In making the assessment of materiality both the amount and the context in which it appears must be considered. Five per cent of £5 million profits can hardly be regarded as trivial.

Stop and Think   1.2

The following statements have been extracted from the published accounts of a business:

● 'The financial statements are prepared on the going concern basis unless it is inappropriate to presume that the company will continue in existence.

● The accounts include judgements and estimates that are reasonable and prudent'.

Are you able to explain the above statements in terms that would be easily understood by a person who has little or no accounting knowledge?

6.2   The money measurement concept

The **money measurement concept** states that accounts will deal only with those items to which a monetary value can be attached. As we have seen, this is fairly straightforward in that the value can be taken from a source document such as an invoice. Thus if a company purchases a vehicle, an item of stock or uses electricity, the value can be taken from the relevant invoices. Such values may be easily attributed to assets such as machinery and equipment, but other assets such as managerial skills or workforce loyalty may be difficult to quantify. Because they cannot be evaluated in monetary terms they do not noramally appear in the accounts.

money measurement concept
The principle that financial accounting information relates only to those activities which can be expressed in money terms.

6.3   The business entity concept

The **business entity concept** means that accountants regard a business as a separate entity, distinct from its owners or managers. Company law recognises this by viewing the company as a separate legal entity independent of its directors and shareholders. Accountants also regard a sole proprietorship or partnership in the same way, but only for accounting purposes.

The distinction is important because the accountant is trying to measure the financial performance of the business and therefore needs to exclude the private assets and liabilities of the owner.

business entity concept
The principle that financial accounting information relates only to the activities of the business entity and not to the activities of its owner(s).

6.4   Historic cost concept

The **historic cost concept** is the basic principle of accounting that resources are normally stated in accounts at the amount which the business paid to acquire them. This ensures that the objectivity of accounts is improved as there is supporting independent evidence, such as an invoice, to verify the amount paid to purchase an asset or pay an expense. Objectivity is important as it prevents the accountant or management influencing the financial performance of the business by deciding on a value independently.

historic cost concept
The principle that resources are normally stated in accounts at the amount which was paid to acquire them.

The use of valuations is to be avoided where possible. Valuations may be regarded as subjective, so accountants prefer to deal with historic costs. Valuations also tend to vary according to what the valuation is to be used for and may include many assumptions.

On the other hand, whilst historic costs are objectively verifiable, they tend to be less useful in periods of inflation. Individual assets, such as land or property, tend to appreciate in value significantly whilst other assets such as vehicles tend to depreciate. For these reasons it is common to prepare modified historic cost accounts. This means that periodically companies include more up-to-date valuations for some of their assets. This is referred to as modified historic cost.

Test *yourself*   1.5

(a) Which accounting concept is being applied when accountants focus on measuring the financial performance of a company and exclude the personal assets and liabilities of the owner?

(b) In using historic cost what is the accountant attempting to be?

Summary

- Accounting information is not an end in itself but is produced to assist the users of the information in making decisions. It is therefore essential that non-accountants understand the fundamentals of accounting and finance.

- The chapter helps managers judge the effectiveness of accounting information by identifying both the characteristics which make accounting information useful and the limitations of such information.

- The chapter provides an introduction to the main accounting concepts which underlie financial accounts. The discussion and examples in the chapter explain how much of the information included in financial statements has been based on subjective judgements. This should make managers aware that, despite legislation and accounting standards, there can be no guarantees that financial statements produce the 'correct' or 'true' picture of the organisation.

- As you work through this book it is important when reviewing accounting information to consider which accounting concepts, conventions and standards the accountant has adopted in a particular situation. You should question whether the concepts, conventions and standards are appropriate to the particular situation. Adopting this approach will encourage you to think more about the ideas underpinning accounting rather than focusing on the mechanics of financial accounting.

The regulatory framework

2

Introduction

Chapter 1 introduced the key accounting concepts which underpin the production of financial statements. The concepts will have made students aware that much of the content of financial statements is based on estimates and subjective judgements. This does not mean that accountants can put any figure they choose into financial statements. In addition to the accounting concepts, businesses have to comply with a range of regulations and legislation.

This chapter also discusses the regulatory framework within which organisations and accounting operate. This includes descriptions of the role and impact of legislation, the professional accountancy bodies, the European Community, the Stock Exchange and the Accounting Standards Board on financial statements.

1   Types of business

In the United Kingdom there are three main types of business:

- The **sole trader** – where one person owns the business on their own.
- The **partnership** – where several people share the ownership of a business with others.
- The **limited liability company** – where the business is owned by shareholders and managed by directors; in many cases these can be the same people.

Each type of business is subject to different levels of regulation and legislation. For example, all types of business have to maintain records for taxation purposes which can be inspected by the Inland Revenue; they may also have to keep Value Added Tax (VAT) records which have to be sent to H.M. Revenue and Customs.

A sole trader is exempt from a good deal regulation. On the other hand, the activities and financial statements of limited companies are subject to a wide range of regulation and legislation.

1.1   Limited liability companies

These are businesses set up under the limited liability concept which treats a company as a separate legal entity. The capital of the company is divided into **shares** which have a fixed value per share. To become a member or shareholder of a limited company an

sole trader
A person carrying on business with sole legal responsibility for the business, not in partnership or as a company.

partnership
A business where ownership is shared among two or more people.

limited liability company
A legal entity which exists separately from its owners, directors and employees. The liability of the members is limited to the value of their shares.

share
A fixed identifiable unit of capital, e.g. a share of £1.

individual must purchase one or more shares. Once the shareholder has paid for their share(s), their liability for the company's debts is limited to those shares. Thus if a limited company loses all its assets, the maximum amount the shareholder can lose is the value of their shares.

It is beyond the scope of this module to go into great detail about the legislation and published accounts of limited companies; this is covered in other modules in the ICSA programmes. However, as the impact of the regulatory framework is so apparent in relation to limited companies this will be used as an illustration of the sources and impact of the regulation on financial statements.

Test *yourself*   2.1

(a) What are the three main types of business found in the UK?

(b) Explain what is meant by limited liability

2 Regulatory sources

The main regulatory bodies which are the sources of the legislation and regulations influencing accounting information are shown in Figure 2.1.

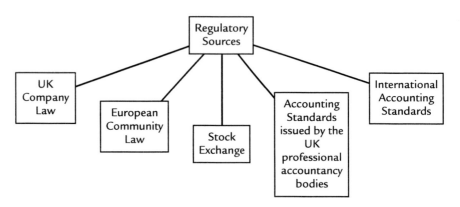

Figure 2.1 Regulatory sources

2.1 UK company law

Limited liability confers significant protection on the personal liability of shareholders. This in turn provides opportunities for limited companies and their shareholders to allow the company to develop. However, the limiting of liability has to be balanced with providing information which allows creditors, lenders, suppliers and employees to be confident in the financial position of the company. All existing company legislation was consolidated into the Companies Act 1985 as amended by the Companies Act 1989. Limited companies are required by the legislation to:

- send a copy of the annual accounts to shareholders;
- lodge a copy of the annual accounts with the Registrar of Companies, which will make it available for public inspection;
- comply with the legislation in terms of the formats, contents and rules for the preparation of the annual accounts.

We have seen that the primary requirement for financial statements in the Companies Acts is that they should show a 'true and fair view' of the company's position and performance. This concept is not specifically defined in the Act and the omission has posed problems over the years for accountants and non-accountants alike. As a starting point it is useful to say that true and fair does not guarantee that the information in the financial statements is correct in every detail as no accountant can be certain that every transaction in a limited company is correct. Consider the number of invoices paid or raised by a company; the number of pieces of equipment owned and used by company; the number of customers and countries dealt with by a company. It would be a brave, or perhaps foolish, statement to claim 100 per cent accuracy for the financial statements of such a company.

What UK company law does is require directors to prepare financial statements for each financial period which gives a true and fair view. In preparing the financial statements, the directors are required to:

- select suitable accounting policies and apply them consistently;
- make judgements and estimates that are reasonable and prudent;
- state whether applicable **accounting standards** have been followed, subject to any material departures being disclosed and explained in the financial statements; and
- prepare the financial statements on the going concern basis unless it is inappropriate to presume the business will continue in business.

Students will recall that the accounting concepts provide some explanation of what is meant by a true and fair view. The Companies Act 1985 enacted certain fundamental accounting concepts to be followed in arriving at the amounts to be included in company financial statements. The accounting concepts given by the Act include going concern, consistency, prudence and accruals.

UK company law also requires that the financial statements of a limited company *must* be audited, except in certain very specific circumstances. An **external audit** is an independent examination of the financial systems and controls of a business and an expression of an opinion on the financial statements. The business employs a firm of chartered or certified accountants to examine its accounting records and financial statements. This allows them to form an opinion of whether the financial statements give a true and fair view of the state of affairs of the business at a particular date. At the conclusion of the audit the auditors issue a report to the shareholders, which is published as part of the annual accounts.

A typical 'clean' audit report will end with the following statement:

accounting standards

Rules financial accountants and auditors must follow when preparing financial statements. In the UK the regulations are developed by the Accounting Standards Board.

external audit

An independent examination of the financial systems and controls of a business.

'In our opinion:

- The financial statements give a true and fair view of the state of affairs of the company as at 31 December 200X and of the profit for the year then ended: and
- The financial statements and the part of the directors' remuneration report to be audited have been prepared in accordance with the Companies Act 1985.'

However, some audit reports are qualified. An example of a qualified audit report was seen in relation to the interim accounts to June 2004 of Eurotunnel issued in September 2004. An extract from this qualified report is given below:

'Based on our review which was conducted in accordance with French accounting principles and regulations nothing has come to our attention that causes us to believe that the half year combined financial statements do not give a true and fair view of the financial position and the assets and liabilities of the Eurotunnel Group as at 30 June 2004 and of the results of the operations for the six month period then ended. Whilst giving this opinion, we draw attention to the disclosures made in note 2 to the half year combined financial statements concerning the two uncertainties the Group is facing:

- The first uncertainty relates to the going concern assumption after 2005 which is dependent upon the Group's ability to put in place a refinancing plan or, if not, to obtain an agreement with the Lenders under the existing credit Agreement within the next two years.
- The second uncertainty, in part related to the first one, relates to the carrying value at which the fixed assets are recorded in the financial statements. For the purposes of this valuation accounting regulations require the establishment of financial projections over the life of the Concession which have been prepared based on the assumption that the current contracts will be maintained and on the assumption of a level of debt lower than the current level ....

With the exception of the eventual outcome of the matters raised above, we have no further comments to make as to the fairness and consistency of the half year combined statements.'

2.2 EU law

The UK is a member of the European Union and as such is obliged to comply with the legal requirements issued by the EU. These are called Directives. The 4th, 7th and 8th Directives have been incorporated into UK Companies Acts and cover such matters as providing a set format for published accounts across the EU and auditors.

The harmonisation of accounting practices across Europe will not be achieved simply by issuing EU Directives. The European Community, and Europe as a whole, are not unified as far as accounting is concerned. European accounting is made up of national rules and practices influenced by EU laws. In addition, there are several reasons why it is difficult for Europe to achieve a standard approach to the content of financial statements. These include:

- The legal system of a country and its laws determine in part the format and content of financial statements. For example, in the UK, the legal system is specified in general principles only, whilst in countries heavily influenced by Roman law, including France and Germany, the legal system tends to include far more detail.
- The degree of difference between tax laws and accounting rules can be a significant obstacle to achieving standardisation. It is common, for example, in many northern European countries for certain tax allowances to be allowed only when the identical figure is included in the published financial statements. Contrast this with the UK, where financial statements tend to be prepared with little reference to tax regulation.
- The providers of finance to businesses determine the level of disclosure in financial statements. Thus in Germany, France and Italy, for example, where banks tend to supply the finance, the focus of the financial statements will be to protect the creditors. In other countries, including the UK and Ireland, much of business finance is supplied by shareholders. This results in the shareholders' and profit needs being satisfied by the contents of financial statements.

2.3 The Stock Exchange

Some companies have their share prices quoted on the Stock Exchange. These are known as 'quoted companies' or **listed companies**. In order to be listed the company has to comply with the Listing Rules issued by the UK Listing Authority (UKLA), which is part of the **Financial Services Authority**. The requirements are much more extensive than those included in the Companies Acts and relate to the disclosure of information to the market. The FSA is therefore another part of accounting's regulatory framework.

listed company
A company whose shares are traded on a recognised investment exchange.

Financial Services Authority (FSA)
The government authority that governs the regulatory framework of accounting in the UK.

Test *yourself*   2.2

> (a) List the FIVE main regulatory sources of accounting information.
> (b) Which is the key legislation which influences UK company accounts?

3 The development of accounting standards

Along with company law a significant part of the regulatory framework in the UK is the official statements or announcements issued by the professional accounting bodies. In the UK there are currently six accountancy bodies:

1 The Institute of Chartered Accountants in England and Wales (ICAEW).
2 The Institute of Chartered Accountants of Scotland (ICAS).
3 The Institute of Chartered Accountants in Ireland (ICAI).
4 The Chartered Association of Certified Accountants (ACCA).
5 The Chartered Institute of Management Accountants (CIMA).
6 The Chartered Institute of Public Finance and Accountancy (CIPFA).

These six bodies are represented by the Consultative Committee of Accountancy Bodies (CCAB).

During the 1970s the CCAB set up a joint committee of the governing bodies, the Accounting Standards Committee (ASC), with the aim of publishing accounting standards to answer the adverse criticism of the accounting profession. This criticism stemmed from a number of well-publicised cases where a variety of subjective accounting methods led to questionable profit and valuation figures appearing in published accounts. The work of the ASC was to develop Statements of Standard Accounting Practice (SSAPs). The ASC researched contentious accounting topics and consulted widely before issuing an SSAP which accountants and auditors were expected to comply with. The ASC issued its first standard in 1971 and 25 in total until it was disbanded in 1990.

The main criticisms of the ASC and SSAPs included the following:

- The ASC was too susceptible to political lobbying by the accountancy bodies and business organisations.
- The ASC did not have the power to issue standards in its own name but needed CCAB bodies' approval. This could mean compliance with a standard was patchy.
- The SSAPs often allowed more than one accounting treatment, so consistency was difficult to achieve.
- SSAPs were important documents but there was no reference to their existence in UK company law.

In 1990 a new process was established and the task of setting accounting standards was moved to the Accounting Standards Board (ASB).

Before outlining the new process it is important for managers to recognise that it was built on important views and changes prevalent at the time including the following:

- The government introduced provisions into company law in the 1989 Companies Act by formally recognising the existence of accounting standards. The Act laid down that companies should disclose and explain any departure from accounting standards in their accounts.
- The ASB can issue accounting standards on its own authority, without the approval of any other body.
- The new process took on board the view that the absence of regulation of financial statements is unlikely to provide the information that users need to make informed analysis of companies.
- The new process viewed accounting standards as assisting the promotion of comparability and consistency. This could mean that users have more confidence in companies' reports.
- The new process tried to involve non-accountants in the standard-setting process.
- The old system was slow and bureaucratic and run on a voluntary basis; only 25 standards were issued in 20 years.

The standard-setting structure is shown in Figure 2.2:

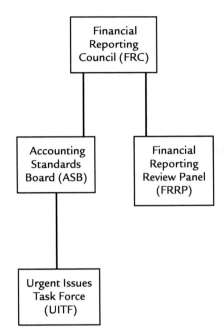

Figure 2.2 Accounting standard-setting structure

3.1   The Financial Reporting Council

The new structure comprises the **Financial Reporting Council (FRC)**, whose role is to promote good financial reporting and to act as the overarching and facilitating body for its two operational bodies, the ASB (Accounting Standards Board) and the FRRP (Financial Reporting Review Panel).

The role of the FRC includes 'responsibility for making, amending and withdrawing accounting standards'. It acts independently, and needs no external approval for its actions. The process through which standards are set includes pre-standard discussion papers and exposure drafts, i.e. full and open consultation.

Membership of the FRC is not restricted to accountants; rather, its membership comes from a wide number of accounts preparers and users. These include members of CCAB bodies, the Stock Exchange, institutional investors, industry and commerce. The key characteristic of the FRC is that it radically widens the field of those involved in the accounting standards process.

3.2   The Accounting Standards Board

The **ASB**, unlike its predecessor the ASC, can issue standards on its own authority. The FRC can give the ASB general policy guidance but has no say over the detail of any individual standard. However, the ASB cannot operate in isolation so it tries to work to a broad consent on the merit of the standards made. The ASB has full-time salaried officers so does not rely on voluntary help.

On its formation the ASB agreed to adopt the current SSAPs, thus ensuring continuity in accounting requirements. Any subsequent standards produced by the ASB

Financial Reporting Council (FRC)

Independent body responsible for making, amending and withdrawing accounting standards.

Accounting Standards Board (ASB)

The ASB is a subsidiary of the Financial Reporting Council. Its role is to produce, amend, issue and withdraw accounting standards on its own authority. Standards produced by the ASB are known as Financial Reporting Standards (FRSs).

Financial Reporting Standards (FRSs)
Accounting standards produced since 1990 by the Accounting Standards Board.

were to be known as **Financial Reporting Standards (FRSs)**. Prior to publication of an FRS the ASB circulates its proposals in the form of a **Financial Reporting Exposure Draft (FRED)** and invites comments.

In summary, the key points about accounting standards or FRSs as they are known are as follows:

Financial Reporting Exposure Draft (FRED)
Draft of an FRS circulated for consultation and comment.

- Standards have the force of law, namely, the Companies Acts, to back them up.
- Companies need to comply with standards to show a true and fair view.
- Departure from the standard is allowed only rarely.
- Departures from standards need to be fully disclosed and show the true economic effects.
- The Financial Reporting Review Panel, with the backing of the courts, have powers of investigation and restatement.

Stop and Think 2.1

Can you explain the benefits and drawbacks of issuing accounting standards?

3.3 The Financial Reporting Review Panel

Financial Reporting Review Panel (FRRP)
Part of the Financial Reporting Council responsible for ensuring that published company accounts comply with accounting requirements.

The FRC's other operating body, the **Financial Reporting Review Panel (FRRP)**, is charged with making 'enquiries into apparent departures from the accounting requirements of the Companies Acts in the annual published accounts of companies'. This focuses particularly on the requirement for accounts to show a true and fair view. The FRRP has legal backing in that if a company departs from an accounting standard the Panel may apply to the courts to seek remedial action. The courts may require the company to prepare revised accounts. In addition to the company law requirements that companies explain departures from standards, the Stock Exchange expects listed companies to comply with accounting standards.

3.4 The Urgent Issues Task Force

The Urgent Issues Task Force (UITF) is a sub-committee of the ASB. Its objectives are to assist the ASB in areas where an accounting standard or Companies Act provision exists, but where unsatisfactory or conflicting interpretations have developed or seem likely to develop. The UITF produces abstracts to tackle problem areas quickly (within one month) and these may be incorporated into subsequent standards.

Test *yourself*   2.3

(a) What is the role of the Financial Reporting Review Panel?

(b) What is the difference between an FRS and an FRED?

Stop and Think   2.2

List FIVE reasons why you would disagree with the suggestion that accounting standards are not necessary, because the accountancy profession can decide what accounting principles to use.

3.5 The International Accounting Standards Board

The International Accounting Standards Board (IASB) is an independent, privately funded accounting standard-setter, based in London. The Board has representatives from many countries, including the UK, Australia, Canada, New Zealand, Germany and the US. The IASB was preceded by the Board of the International Accounting Standards Committee (IASC), which operated from 1973 until 2001.

Standards issued by the IASB are designated International Financial Reporting Standards (IFRSs). Standards originally issued by the Board of the International Accounting Standards Committee (1973–2001) continue to be designated International Accounting Standards (IASs).

The IASB is committed to developing, in the public interest, a single set of high quality, understandable and enforceable global accounting standards that require transparent and comparable information in financial statements. In addition, the IASB co-operates with national accounting standard-setters to achieve convergence in accounting standards around the world.

The ASB also collaborates with accounting standard-setters from other countries and the IASB in order to influence the development of international standards and to ensure that its standards are developed with due regard to international developments. Full-time members of the IASB have formal liaison responsibilities with leading national accounting standard-setters. The IASB constitution envisages a partnership between the IASB and these national bodies as they work together to achieve the convergence of accounting standards worldwide.

This move towards convergence is illustrated by IFRS 1, First-time Adoption of International Financial Reporting Standards, which was issued by the International IASB in June 2003. It is particularly relevant to European listed companies (i.e. companies quoted on a stock exchange) because they are required to apply International Financial Reporting Standards (IFRS) to their consolidated financial statements for accounting periods beginning on or after 1 January 2005. IFRS 1 sets out the procedures that a company must follow when it adopts the IFRS for the first time. The objective of the IFRS is to ensure that financial statements contain high-quality information that is transparent and comparable.

International Accounting Standards Board (IASB)
The IASB is an independent, privately funded accounting standard-setter based in London. Standards issued by the International Accounting Standards Board are designated International Financial Reporting Standards (IFRSs).

Summary

- Organisations of all types have to comply with a range of regulations and legislation.
- In the UK, the regulators are the professional accountancy bodies, the European Community and the Financial Services Authority.
- Standards are set by The Financial Reporting Council, The Accounting Standards Board, The Financial Reporting Review Panel and The Urgent Issues Task Force.
- Since January 2005, the International Accounting Standards Board requires listed European companies to prepare financial statements according to new international financial reporting standards.

Part One Practice Questions

1.1 List THREE economic decisions which shareholders may make based on accounting information.

1.2 Provide a definition of accounting.

1.3 What are the two main branches of accounting?

1.4 Provide THREE limitations of using accounting information to make decisions.

1.5 A company has been asked by one of its suppliers to provide a credit reference. You are required to provide FIVE examples of type of information you will send to the suppliers.

1.6 What is a going concern?

1.7 What do accountants try to match when calculating profit?

1.8 What is the most common event used to determine when revenue is recognised?

1.9 Explain what you understand by the term modified historic cost. Illustrate your explanation with an example.

1.10 When are accountants allowed to value stock at a figure less than historic cost?

Recording and Reporting Business Activity

Contents

Overview

It is important that managers understand how business transactions impact on the finances of an organisation. While this module is not intended to turn managers into bookkeepers or accountants it is useful to be able to describe a simple system for recording business transactions from source documents such as invoice through to the accounting ledgers.

Managers should be able to describe the format of the key financial statements, namely the profit and loss account and the balance sheet. The focus here is on examining how these statements measure the financial performance and the financial position of the organisation. Having focused on the descriptions of business transactions and financial statements, candidates will also be asked to demonstrate an ability to prepare simple profit and loss accounts and balance sheets for a small business at the end of an accounting period. This will involve demonstrating an ability to make adjustments at the year-end.

As many businesses base their information systems around computers it is important that candidates can describe the operation and benefits of using a computerised system to record and report business activity.

Learning objectives

At the end of this part students will be able to:

► Define and explain the principal elements and operation of the accounting equation.

► Demonstrate the impact of business transactions on the balance sheet and the profit and loss account.

► Define and explain the nature and purpose of depreciation in the accounts of a business and apply the main methods of depreciating the cost of fixed assets.

- ▶ Describe and explain the purpose of the trading account for recording stock used during an accounting period.
- ▶ Describe and explain the purpose of recording debtors, the adjustments for bad debts and doubtful debts, and how they are recorded in financial statements.
- ▶ Understand what is meant by the double-entry bookkeeping system.
- ▶ Prepare a profit and loss account and balance sheet from a trial balance and incorporate year-end adjustments.
- ▶ Understand how computerised and manual accounting systems work.

PART TWO   CASE STUDY

Keeping track of financial information

Jane Smith owns and runs a business selling electronic equipment. Jane established her business about eighteen months ago and it has made a relatively successful start. There are ten members of staff, all of whom have great experience in retailing and electronic equipment. Smith is attempting to get to know more about the financial side of the business and has been gathering financial data over the past couple of months. She would like these data to be explained and represented so that she can make more sense of her business.

When she started her business her accountant used the term 'accounting equation' and said that when any business started, the equation represented the starting point of her business in financial terms. At the time Jane just agreed with her accountant and thanked him for making her aware of the equation. Having been faced with numerous financial statements since then she feels she may be missing a trick if she cannot understand the mysteries of the equation.

Jane's shop manager has asked her to consider investing in a computer information system at a cost of £80,000. The computer will enable the firm to maintain a management information system which will improve the marketing and sales capabilities of the company. The equipment will be purchased at the beginning of the next financial year. The shop manager has estimated that the equipment can be sold for £15,000 at the end of its five-year life. Jane has agreed in principle to this purchase but would like to include the financial consequences of the purchase into her long-term business plan.

Jane has extracted the following information from the books of her business at 31 January 200X as follows:

	£
Land and buildings	450,000
Owner's capital	300,000
Plant and equipment	42,200
Reserves	225,000
Vehicles	33,800
Trade creditors	30,000
Bank overdraft	18,000
Stocks	80,000
Loan from Western Bank	120,000
Cash	2,400
Trade debtors	84,600

Jane comments that the information in its present form means little or nothing. She finds difficulty with some of the accounting terms and in particular how they are used to confuse rather than help non-accountants. For example, accountants treat the capital she has invested in the company plus the reserves she has built up over the years as liabilities in just the same way as the loan from the bank as a liability. This seems bizarre to Jane as her investments in the business are surely assets.

A new member of staff has complained about the way the petty cash system operates as it seems to involve a lot of paperwork. She has said that in her previous job they operated an imprest petty cash system and that seemed to cause fewer problems. Jane says she will look into the matter.

Finally, Jane wants to increase the efficiency of her business and is considering investing in computerised accounting applications. She is particularly interested in how spreadsheets and databases might be used.

The accounting equation, the profit and loss account and balance sheet

3

Introduction

This chapter discusses how accountants attempt to record the financial position of an organisation. This is achieved by introducing the accounting equation, which summarises both the assets owned by an organisation and the sources from which those assets are obtained. The sources of the assets are explained in terms as those coming from the owner(s) and outsiders. These sources are seen as claims on the organisation's assets or liabilities to bodies outside the organisation. The accounting equation is explained as the basis for the balance sheet and students will be asked to demonstrate their ability to show the impact of business transactions on the balance sheet. This chapter will assist business managers in recognising how their actions and those of their colleagues impact on the balance sheet.

1 The accounting equation

In chapter 1, accounting was defined as being concerned with identifying, collecting, measuring, recording, summarising and communicating the financial aspects of an organisation's activities. In order to achieve this, accountants need to have a system that will methodically collect the financial aspects of such activities. The system they use is based on the accounting equation which is reflected in a **balance sheet**.

Throughout the chapter, the accounting equation will be introduced and developed with reference to a business owned and set up by one person. This type of business is referred to as a sole trader but the principles of the accounting equation demonstrated here can be applied to all types of business organisation.

balance sheet
A statement of the financial position of an entity at a given date, disclosing the assets, liabilities and accumulated funds.

The owner, Chris Black, started a business selling computers on 1 January 200X. Black opened a business bank account and paid in £100,000. This money is termed the **owner's capital** (see 2.1 below). This one action has brought into existence the financial position of the business. This can be depicted as follows in the form of an accounting equation:

owners' capital
The total of the original capital invested by the owner in the business, plus any retained profits or reserves from previous years, plus this year's profits less any drawings made by the owner during the year.

Claims on assets = Assets

Total liabilities = Total assets

Owner's capital £100,000 = Bank account £100,000

---

liabilities
The financial obligations of a business, e.g. creditors, bank and overdrafts.

To represent the owner's capital as a liability may be difficult to understand. A **liability** represents a sum owed by the business to another party. If this is the case, how can the owner's investments in the business be seen as a liability? You will recall that chapter 2 introduced the idea of the business entity concept which means that a business is seen as a separate entity, distinct from its owners or managers. Under this concept any monies put into a business by the owner can be regarded as a liability. In simple terms the monies put in by Chris Black have not been given to the business. From an accountant's viewpoint, the £100,000 has been loaned to the business. Chris Black may withdraw the £100,000 at any time provided there is sufficient cash at the bank. In effect, the business has a liability because, as a separate entity, it owes the owner £100,000.

The assets of the business represent the economic resources of the business. In this case the assets are represented in the form of cash at the bank.

The initial capital of the business records what the owner has contributed to the business from their private resources to start the business. In the above example this is represented by cash at the bank, but the capital could be in the form of a workshop or vehicle which the owner has 'given' to the business. The value of the workshop or vehicle represents the capital which the business owes the owner.

Test *yourself* 3.1

(a) Define the term 'accounting equation'.

(b) 'The capital of the owner is an asset of a business.' Is this TRUE or FALSE?

The accounting equation has the following important characteristics:

- The value of the assets is the same as the value of the liabilities.
- Both sides of the equation are of equal value, i.e. they balance.
- The assets of a business must come from somewhere; in fact, they are financed by the liabilities of the business in this case the owner's investment.
- The application of the business entity concept distinguishes the owner and the business and thus the business incurs a liability back to the owner of the invested capital.

The accounting equation as developed above expresses the business in terms of:

> Claims on assets = Assets
> Or
> Total capital + Total liabilities = Total assets

Chris Black may decide that his business requires more monies and so will borrow a further £150,000 from the bank. This bank loan is a liability of the business, but at the same time the asset has increased by £150,000. The financial position of the business can now be represented in the accounting equation as follows:

> Total capital + Total liabilities = Total assets
> £100,000 (owner) + £150,000 (debt) = £250,000 (bank)

You can see that there are two claims on the £250,000 of assets of the business. These are Chris Black's initial start-up capital of £100,000 and the bank's claim for the £150,000 loan.

The impact of any further business transactions on the financial position of the company can be reflected in the accounting equation. Chris Black carried out the following transactions during the first week of trading. He:

1   Purchased a motor vehicle for £15,000 paying by cheque.
2   Withdrew £1,000 from the bank for use as cash float.
3   Purchased shop premises for £60,000 paying by cheque.

The impact on the accounting equation of these two transactions will be as follows:

Total capital + Total liabilities = Total assets

Worked example   3.1

Transaction 1

£100,000 (owner) + £150,000 (debt) = £235,000 (bank) + £15,000 (vehicle)

£100,000 (owner) + £150,000 (liabilities) = £250,000 (assets)

Transaction 2

£100,000 (owner) + £150,000 (debt) = £234,000 (bank) + £15,000 (vehicle) + £1,000 (cash)

£100,000 (owner) + £150,000 (liabilities) = £250,000 (assets)

Transaction 3

£100,000 (owner) + £150,000 (debt) = £174,000 (bank) + £60,000 (premises) + £15,000 (vehicle) + £1,000 (cash)

£100,000 (owner) + £150,000 (liabilities) = £250,000 (assets)

Note that following all these transactions the accounting equation is still in balance.

Recording both aspects of a transaction keeps the accounting equation in balance and is the principle underlying bookkeeping systems. Although non-accountants need not concern themselves with the mechanics of double-entry bookkeeping, it is important to

profit and loss account
A statement which shows the income less the various expenses of an organisation to show the profit or loss for an accounting period.

appreciate that the accounting equation not only forms the basis of the balance sheet, but forms the foundation of the **profit and loss account**.

Test *yourself* 3.2

(a) Record the cumulative effect of the following on an accounting equation:
   - Started a business by putting £50,000 into a business bank account.
   - Purchased a building for £10,000.
   - Raised a bank loan of £20,000.

(b) When you have completed the accounting equation for (a), identify the two claims on the business's assets and their total value.

2   Classifying assets and liabilities

As a business grows it is likely to increase the number of transactions that will impact upon the value and structure of the capital, liabilities and assets, as represented in the accounting equation. Given that the equation forms the basis of the balance sheet it will be beneficial for the users if the capital, assets and liabilities are classified. Classification means putting them into groups because they have common characteristics.

The balance sheet takes the following accounting equation:

$$\text{Total capital} + \text{Total liabilities} = \text{Total assets}$$

and classifies the items as follows.

2.1 Capital

capital
The funds used by an entity for its operations.

The initial cash put in by the owner is called the **capital**. Capital is a liability of the business to the owner. The size and value of this initial capital may increase over the life of the business. The capital can increase in at least two ways:

retained profits
Non-distributed profits retained as revenue reserve. In a not-for-profit entity these are described as accumulated funds.

1 The owner can put in more of their own money into the business. The new funds increase the capital of the business.
2 The business itself can generate additional capital by selling goods or services at a profit. This profit is earned on behalf of the owner by the business. The profit belongs to the owner and, provided it is not taken out of the business by the owner, will increase the capital element of the accounting equation. These profits are called **retained profits**.

2.2 Liabilities

creditor
A person or business entity to whom money is owed.

Liabilities are the debts of the business. They represent what the business owes to external parties other than the owner. The external liabilities or obligations, called the **creditors** of a business, may be classified according to the time period within which they have to be settled. Thus there are:

- **Long-term liabilities**, which include bank loans which normally do *not* fall due for repayment within one year. These long-term liabilities are also called 'creditors: amounts falling due after one year'.
- **Current liabilities** or 'creditors: these are liabilities which will fall due for repayment within one year. An example will be monies owed to suppliers for goods bought on credit and are not paid for until some time after they have been delivered. These types of current liability are also called trade creditors. Other examples of current liabilities include bank overdrafts and taxes owed to the government, both of which have to be settled within twelve months.

2.3 Assets

An asset is something which has a value which a business owns or has the use of, e.g. factories, office buildings, warehouses, delivery vans, lorries, plant and machinery. They also include such things as computer equipment, office furniture and cash as well as stock or inventory held in store awaiting sale to customers. The term can also be used to cover raw materials and components held in store by a manufacturing business for use in production. They provide a benefit to the firm.

Assets can be divided into two broad categories:

1 **Fixed assets**: assets that are bought and expected to be used within the business for several years. Fixed assets are not bought with the intention of reselling/converting them. Fixed assets are permanent and give long-term benefits to the business, which is why they are termed fixed. Factories, office buildings and warehouses are clearly fixed and so are delivery vans, lorries and cars, even though they can move about.

2 **Current assets**: those assets which, within a short period of time, will change their form. These assets will be converted into cash within a year in the normal course of trading. The form of current assets is constantly changing. Examples of current assets include stock, **debtors**, bank and cash balances.

This classification allows us to amend the accounting equation from its original format:

> Total capital + Total liabilities = Total assets

to

> Total capital = Total assets − Total liabilities
>
> Or
>
> Capital = Fixed assets + Current assets − Current liabilities − Long-term liabilities
>
> £100,000 (owner) = £60,000 (premises) + £15,000 (vehicle) + £174,000 (bank) + £1,000 (cash) − £150,000 (debt)
>
> £100,000 = [£60,000 + £15,000] + [£174,000 + £1,000] − £150,000
>
> £100,000 = £75,000 + £175,000 − £150,000
>
> £100,000 = £250,000 − £150,000
>
> £100,000 = £100,000

long-term liabilities
Liabilities which fall due for payment after one year or more.

current liabilities
Liabilities which fall due for payment within one year, including that part of the long-tem loans due for repayment within one year.

fixed assets
Any asset, tangible or intangible, acquired to provide a service to the organisation, and not intended for resale in the normal course of trading.

current assets
Cash or other asset, e.g. stock, debtors and short-term investments, held for conversion into cash in the normal course of trading.

debtors
Money owed to a business by customers (trade debtors) or others.

Stop and Think   3.1

Assets	Liabilities	Capital
£	£	£
25,000	3,600	?
39,200	?	32,900
?	23,300	79,500

Intangible fixed assets

All the assets described above have a physical existence, but not all assets have a physical form. These assets are useful not because of their physical characteristics but because the rights they carry can be extremely valuable. The following are examples:

- *Patents* where the governments grants the patent owner the exclusive right for a period of years to produce and sell an invention such as a mini music system, personal disc assistant (PDA).
- *Trademarks* or *brand names* are the distinctive identifications by which customers recognise a product or service, for example the logos of Heinz, Coca Cola or AOL. These are intangible assets.

3   The balance sheet

The balance sheet is a development of the accounting equation. The balance sheet has the primary purpose of reporting the financial position of an organisation at a single point in time.

The financial position is shown as follows:

```
┌─────────────────────────────────────────┐
│              Fixed assets                 │
│                   +                       │
│             Current assets                │
│                   −                       │
│            Current liabilities            │
│                   −                       │
│           Long- term liabilities          │
│                   =                       │
│     Initial capital + Retained profits    │
└─────────────────────────────────────────┘
```

If we refer to the accounting equation created earlier we can create a very simple balance sheet as follows:

Worked example   3.2

Balance Sheet of Chris Black as at end of week 1		
Fixed Assets	£	£
Premises		60,000
Vehicles		15,000
		75,000
Current Assets		
Bank	174,000	
Cash	1,000	175,000
		250,000
Less **Current liabilities**	nil	
Less **Long-term liabilities**		
Bank loan		150,000
		100,000
Initial capital		100,000
Plus retained profits		nil
		100,000

3.1 Points to note

- The title of the balance sheet includes the business name, Chris Black, and is stated at a point in time: 'as at'. The balance sheet is a position statement or 'snapshot' of the business's assets and the claims on those assets at a point in time.
- The balance sheet format starts to group certain items together, for example the bank and cash as current assets.

- Certain figures are added to produce sub-totals and totals, for example the fixed assets, premises and vehicles, are added together to give a figure for total fixed assets.
- Grouping similar items and providing sub-totals are intended to assist the users of balance sheets. This point will be developed later in this chapter.
- The business, which is only just beginning, has not yet incurred any current liabilities such as creditors or overdrafts.
- Most importantly the business has not yet generated any profits so there are no retained profits.

Putting the case   3.1

Jane Smith has asked you to explain the term 'accounting equation' and its significance in accounting. She wants you to keep the explanation simple and so does not want you to use any figures in your explanation. She would, however, like you to provide definitions of the key elements in the equation.

The accounting equation is based on the fact that for any business the starting point in financial terms is as follows:

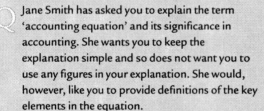

Resources used   Resources supplied
or owned   by the owner or others
Total assets =   Total liabilities

Assets are the general term for the resources in the business. An asset is something which has a value which a business owns or has the use of. Examples of assets include office buildings as well as such things as cash and stock or inventory held in store awaiting sale to customers. Assets may be divided into two broad categories: Fixed assets are those assets which are bought and expected to be used within the business for several years. Fixed assets are permanent and give long-term benefits to the business which is why they are termed fixed. Current assets are those assets which within a short period of time will change their form. These assets are converted into cash within a year in the normal course of trading. The form of current assets is constantly changing. Examples of current assets include stock, debtors, bank and cash balances.

Liabilities are the debts of the business. They represent what the business owes to external parties other than the owner. The external liabilities or obligations, called creditors (a person or business entity to whom money is owed of a business) can be classified according to the period within which they have to be settled. Long-term liabilities include bank loans which normally do *not* fall due for repayment within one year. Current liabilities, or 'creditors: amounts falling due within one year', are liabilities which will fall due for repayment within one year. An example is monies owed to suppliers for goods bought on credit.

The liabilities due to the owner are called the capital. Thus we can refine the accounting equation as follows:

Total assets = Owner's capital + Other liabilities

To identify the owner's capital more clearly it is possible to rearrange the equation as follows:

Total assets − Other liabilities = Owner's capital

Or

(Fixed assets + Current assets) − (Current liabilities − Long-term liabilities) = Owner's capital

The accounting equation is important because the equation will always balance, i.e. the value of items on each side of the equation will always be equal. This will be true no matter what transactions happen in the business.

This equality is reflected in the balance sheet and in the double-entry bookkeeping system of the business. Thus if a business borrows money from an outsider in the form of cash, then the equation will be kept in balance by two bookkeeping entries increasing both the asset – cash and the other liabilities – loans.

4 The impact of trading on the owner's investment in the business

So far the accounting equation recording the financial position of Chris Black has not involved buying or selling goods or incurring any expenses. These are essential activities if the business is to grow by selling its goods at profit.

Chris Black buys and sells computers. Computers are the goods the business buys with the intention of reselling. These are called **stocks**. In order to start, Chris Black decides in week 2 of trading to purchase £50,000 of computers on credit. This activity does not generate any profit as the transaction is only increasing the current asset stock and creating a creditor, or current liability, of £50,000. The revised balance sheet (with the impact of the purchase of the stock is shown in italic) appears as follows:

stocks
Stocks are made up of goods purchased for resale. The intention is to resell the stock so it will normally be kept in the business for a relatively short time.

Worked example 3.3

Balance Sheet of Chris Black as at end of week 2			
	£	£	£
Fixed Assets			
Premises			60,000
Vehicles			15,000
			75,000
Current Assets			
Stock	*50,000*		
Bank	174,000		
Cash	1,000	225,000	
Less **Current Liabilities**			
Trade Creditors		*50,000*	175,000
			250,000
Less **Long-term Liabilities**			
Bank Loan			150,000
			100,000
Initial Capital			100,000
Plus **Retained Profits**			nil
			100,000

Test *yourself* 3.4

(a) Define a balance sheet.
(b) Explain briefly the impact on a balance sheet of purchasing stock on credit.

During the third week of trading Chris Black's computers, which cost £10,000, were sold for £14,000. The customers all paid by cheque, which was banked on the same day. It is apparent that the sale of the computers has generated a profit of £4,000 – the difference between the cost price and the selling price. How will this impact on Chris Black's investment in the business, and in turn how will this affect the accounting equation and the balance sheet?

We saw in chapter 2 that accountants calculate profit (or loss) by applying the accruals concept. This concept states that when computing profit the sales income (or sales revenue) earned should be matched only against the expenditure incurred when earning it. In this case:

$$\text{Sales revenue} - \text{Expenses} = \text{Profit}$$
$$£14,000 - £10,000 = £4,000$$

The business has generated a profit on behalf of Chris Black and is owed to Chris Black by the business. Recording this liability of the business to Chris Black is shown on the liabilities side of the equation, specifically the capital and retained profits section. The profits earned in effect are additional capital reinvested by Chris Black and are called retained profits.

The sale of the computers that cost £10,000 has reduced the current asset stock by that amount. The proceeds of the sale have been banked, so the current asset at the bank has increased by £14,000. It is apparent that the accounting equation and balance sheet will not balance as the adjustments we made are not of equal value. In order to correct these imbalances we need to record the £4,000 on the liabilities side of the equation, specifically in the capital and retained profits section. In effect, the value of Chris Black's investment in the business has grown by £4,000. The impact of the sale of the computers and the profit it creates on both the accounting equation and the balance sheet is shown below:

$$\text{Total capital} = \text{Total assets} - \text{Total liabilities}$$

Or, allowing for the profit generated:

$$\text{Capital} + (\text{Revenues} - \text{Expenses}) = \text{Fixed assets} + (\text{Current assets} - \text{Currents liabilities})$$
$$- \text{Long-term liabilities}$$

$$£100,000 + (£14,000 - £10,000) = £75,000 + (£229,000 - £50,000) - £150,000$$

$$£104,000 = £104,000$$

Worked example

3.4

Balance Sheet of Chris Black as at end of week 3

Fixed Assets	£	£	£
Premises			60,000
Vehicles			15,000
			75,000
Current Assets			
Stock (−10,000)	40,000		
Bank (+14,000)	188,000		
Cash	1,000	229,000	
Less **Current Liabilities**			
Trade creditors		50,000	179,000
			254,000
Less Long-term Liabilities			
Bank loan			150,000
			104,000
Initial Capital			100,000
Plus Retained Profits (+4000)			4,000
			104,000

Points to note:

1 The sale of stock for cheque reduces the stock balance and increases the bank balance.

2 The sale of stock at a selling price greater than cost price will generate a profit.

3 The profit increases owner's investments in the business by increasing the retained profits.

4.1 Further examples

During the fourth week of trading the following activities take place:

1 Chris sells computers costing £6,000 for £11,000 but the customer was granted 30 days credit.

2 Paid wages by cheque of £500.

Obviously the value of the stock goes down by £6,000 and a profit of £5,000 is made on the sale of the computers. However, the customer owes the business £11,000 so the current asset, debtors, is increased by this amount.

Similarly, the payment of wages is an expense and will in reduce the profits for the period by £500. The current asset, bank balance, will be reduced by the £500 payment.

In summary:

1 Sales revenue − expenses = profit. In this example £11,000 (revenue) − £6,000 (stock) and £500 (wages) = £4,500 retained profits.

2 Stock and reduced by £6,000 and debtors increased by £11,000.
3 Bank balance reduced by £500.

Chris Black's investment in the business has grown in week 4 by a further £4,500. Total profits for the first month's trading amount to £8,500 (Week 3 £4,000 + Week 4 £4,500)

Worked example   3.5

	£	£	£
Balance Sheet of Chris Black as at the end of week 4			
Fixed Assets			
Premises			60,000
Vehicles			15,000
			75,000
Current Assets			
Debtors (+11,000)	11,000		
Stock (−6,000)	34,000		
Bank (−500)	187,500		
Cash	1,000	233,500	
Less Current Liabilities			
Trade creditors		50,000	183,500
			258,500
Less Long-term Liabilities			
Bank loan			150,000
			108,500
Initial Capital			100,000
Plus Retained Profits (+ 4,500)			8,500
			108,500

Points to note:

● The sale of stock reduces the current asset, stock and increases the expenses by the cost price of the stock that is sold. The selling price of the stock increases the revenue for the period.

● The sale is on credit so there is an increase in trade creditors by the selling price of the stock.

Test yourself   3.5

(a) Fill in the missing words in the following statements:

● The sale of stock paid for with a cheque reduces the —— balance and —— the bank balance.

● The profit increases owner's investment in the business by increasing the —— profits.

(b) Explain the impact of the following on the balance sheet of a business which sells some stock costing £5,500 for £9,000 but the customer will pay in one months time.

5 The profit and loss account

The transactions of Chris Black during January 2005 are summarised in the profit and loss account. This document shows how the business has generated profits/sustained losses, over a specified period. It is a period statement as described in its title 'Profit and Loss Account for year ended 200X'.

The calculation of profit involves identifying the sales revenue of a business and comparing this with the expenditure incurred in generating that income.

A typical profit and loss account for the first months trading, based on the information provided on Chris Black's business is shown in Worked example 3.6.

sales
Amounts derived from the provision of goods or services, after deducting returns, trade discounts, and value added tax. It is also called revenue.

Worked example   3.6

Chris Black

Profit and Loss Account for the month ended 31 January 200X

	£	£
Sales		25,000
Opening stock	Nil	
Add purchases	50,000	
	50,000	
Less Closing stock	34,000	
Cost of goods sold		16,000
Gross Profit		9,000
Less Expenses		
Wages		500
Net Profit		8,500

Points to note:

● **Sales**: this is the value of the goods sold, or services performed say in a hairdressing salon or an accounting practice. If a business sells goods on credit, it counts as sales the value of goods dispatched or services performed during the period *not* just the cash the business has received.

● It is usual to identify **gross profit**, that is sales revenue less the cost of goods sold. Gross profit results from matching the revenue earned and the expenditure incurred in providing the goods or services which is called the cost of goods sold.

● Cost of goods sold or **cost of sales** is calculated as follows:

	£
Opening stock	xxxx
Add purchases	xxxx
	xxxx
Less Closing stock	xxxx
Cost of goods sold	xxxx

gross profit

Sales less the cost of goods sold.

cost of sales

The sum of variable cost of sales plus factory overhead attributable to the turnover. It may also be referred to as production cost of sales or cost of goods sold.

purchases

Raw materials purchased for incorporation into products or finished goods purchased for resale.

expenses

The expenses of operating the business for the accounting period.

net profit

Gross profit less expenses.

This calculation is inset in the left-hand column between sales and cost of sales.

- The stock figure is the value of goods held for sale to customers at the beginning (opening stock) or end (closing period) of the accounting period.
- **Purchases** are the value of goods received in the accounting period. This does not equal the cash paid to creditors.
- **Expenses** are the expenses of operating the business for the accounting period. In the case of Chris Black the one expense is wages and the cost included is the same as the cash paid out. But there will be other bills such as telephone, rent, rates and insurance where the cost for the period is unlikely to be the same as those bills that have been paid. Refer back to the accruals concept as described in chapter 1.
- A profit and loss account matches the revenue earned in a period with the costs incurred in earning it.
- **Net profit** is gross profit minus expenses. Remember that a business can incur a net loss if its sales revenue is less than its expenses. Net profits will increase an owner's capital while a net loss will reduce the owner's capital.

Stop and Think   3.2

Explain why the profit and loss account will include all sales and expenses even though not all the cash has been received or paid out.

6   What goes where: profit and loss account or balance sheet?

Students need to be able to show the impact of business transactions on the balance sheet and profit and loss account. In order to assist business managers in recognising how their actions and the actions of their colleagues impact on the balance sheet and profit and loss account, Table 3.1 shows the transactions of Chris Black during January 200X. The table summarises the impact of the transactions in the accounting equation and identifies which of the financial statements each transaction is recorded in.

Transaction	Impact on Accounting Equation	Recorded in
Opened a business bank account and paid in £100,000.	Increases current asset, bank and increases owner's capital.	Balance sheet
Purchased a motor vehicle for £15,000 paying by cheque.	Increases fixed asset, vehicles and decreases current assets, bank.	Balance sheet
Withdrew £1,000 from the bank for use as cash float.	Decreases current asset, bank and increases current asset, cash.	Balance sheet
Purchased shop premises for £60,000 paying by cheque.	Increases fixed asset, premises and decreases current assets, bank.	Balance sheet
Purchased £50,000 of computers on credit.	Increases current asset, stock and increases current liability, trade creditors.	Balance sheet
Computers costing £10,000 are sold for £14,000. The customers all pay by cheque which is banked on the same day.	Decreases current asset, stock and increases current asset, bank. Increases revenue and increases expenses.	Balance sheet Profit and loss account
Computers costing £6,000 are sold for £11,000 but the customer is granted 30 days' credit.	Decreases current asset, stock and increases current asset, debtors. Increases revenue and increases expenses.	Balance Sheet Profit and loss account
Paid wages by cheque of £500.	Increases expenses and decreases current asset bank.	Profit and loss account Balance sheet

Table 3.1 What goes where: balance sheet or profit and loss account

It is important to understand the distinction between balance sheet items and profit and loss account items. A useful way of looking at it is to identify whether a payment has been for consumable items (expenses such as salaries, heating, lighting, bank interest, etc.) which are unlikely to be present at the year-end. These are all profit and loss items. Alternatively, payments may be for longer-term items (purchase of assets) which are all balance sheet items. These are likely to be there at the year-end.

Resources added to the business can come from the owner (capital), outside lenders (long-term loans) or traders granting credit (creditors). These are all balance sheet items. One point to note is that the purchase of stock involves payments which initially increase the asset stock and so are reflected in the balance sheet. However, when the stock is sold it turns into an expense and is shown in the profit and loss account through the cost of goods sold calculation.

Accounting systems will record the payment of invoices to suppliers of goods or services. A decision has to be made as to whether the bills received are recorded as an asset or an expense. This depends on whether the *benefit* of the goods or service being charged has been partly or fully received in the accounting period. For example, a business may purchase items of stock for resale. However, at the balance sheet date some of the stock items may remain unsold; the benefit from this unsold stock has not been received and so the closing stock is deducted from the expenditure related to the accounting period and is shown on the balance sheet as a current asset. The stock is charged, or 'expensed', in the period in which it is consumed.

Test *yourself*   3.6

(a) Explain the importance of gross profit?

(b) What is the equation for cost of sales?

Summary

- The accounting equation is fundamental to understanding a balance sheet. Total assets should always equal total liabilities. When recording a transaction it is important to remember to balance both sides of the equation. This is the principle behind double-entry bookkeeping.
- Asset is a general term for the resources in any organisation. Assets are classified into fixed assets, such as equipment, vans and buildings, which are bought for the medium to long term to bring benefit to the organisation, and current assets, which are items which will be converted into cash in the normal course of trading, such as stock, bank and cash balances.
- Liabilities, the external debts of the business, are classified into long-term liabilities – those obligations which do not fall due for repayment within one year – and current which are liabilities which are due for payment within a year. These include goods bought on credit.
- The balance sheet reports the financial position of the organisation at a point in time and shows total assets less total liabilities to provide retained profits and initial capital.
- The profit and loss account calculates profit by showing sales revenue less expenditure.

Depreciation, valuation and disposal of assets

4

Introduction

This chapter discusses the nature and distinction of capital and revenue expenditure in relation to fixed assets. Fixed assets were introduced in chapter 3 and this chapter explains how and why the costs of fixed assets are spread over the period the asset is owned by the business. Spreading the cost is achieved by annual depreciation charges. The main methods of depreciation are described and supported by practical illustrations of their application. These illustrations are used to discuss the impact of depreciation charges on the financial statements. The impact of purchasing and disposing of fixed assets is also illustrated. Throughout the chapter reference is made to the subjective nature of depreciation and the influence accounting concepts have on depreciation.

1   Capital and revenue expenditure

Accountants have to distinguish or classify expenditure (and income) into capital and revenue.

1.1   Capital expenditure

Capital expenditure is expenditure that is likely to provide a benefit to the organisation for more than one accounting period/financial year. The key points are as follows:

- The benefits and period of those benefits may be difficult to predict.
- Such expenditure can be defined as increasing the earning capacity of the business.
- Capital expenditure is incurred on the purchase of fixed assets such as land and buildings, plant and machinery, vehicles and fixtures and fittings and the cost of these fixed assets is, therefore, accounted for over their anticipated useful life.
- Capital expenditure usually involves an annual depreciation charge.
- Capital expenditure is concerned with purchasing high value, long-term and permanent fixed assets for use in the business. These assets are not bought to be resold.

capital expenditure
Expenditure that is likely to provide a benefit to the organisation for more than one accounting period/financial year.

capital income

The proceeds of
selling fixed assets.

- Central government capital grants are an example of **capital income**.
- The principle is that capital grants should be recognised in the profit and loss account so as to match with the expenditure to which they are intended to contribute.

1.2   Revenue expenditure and income

**revenue
expenditure**

Expenditure on the
supply and
manufacture of
goods and
provision of
services charged in
the accounting
period in which
they are consumed.

Revenue expenditure is expenditure which is necessary for the day-to-day operations of the business. The key points are as follows:

- It is expenditure that is likely to provide benefit to the organisation for only the current accounting/financial year and so is charged against profits in the period to which it relates.
- It is a cost used by the organisation in trading.
- Revenue expenditure include running costs such as electricity, business rates, wages and salaries of employees, interest charges, purchase of consumables such as stationery, goods purchased for resale etc.
- **Revenue income** includes income from the sale of goods to customers, rents received, dividends received, interest received, etc.

revenue income

Amounts derived
from the provision
of goods and
services falling
within the
company's
ordinary activities,
after deduction of
returns, trade
discounts and value
added tax; also
called
turnover/sales.

Importance of the distinction

The distinction between capital and revenue items is critical. If capital and revenue items are not classified accurately, the accounting profit will be incorrectly calculated. For example, if a capital expenditure item is included as revenue expenditure, then the annual profit will be understated. Similarly, if a capital grant were included in one year's accounts then the annual profits would be overstated.

Test *yourself*   4.1

> (a) List THREE features of capital expenditure which distinguish it from revenue expenditure.
>
> (b) If a revenue item of expenditure was incorrectly classified as capital expenditure what would be the impact on the annual profit?

2   The nature of depreciation

depreciation

The measure of
wearing out,
consumption or
other reduction in
the useful
economic life of a
fixed asset.

Depreciation is the measure of wearing out, consumption or other reduction in the useful economic life of a fixed asset, whether arising from use, passage of time or obsolescence through technological or market changes.

In referring to useful economic life the definition implies that the business will need to replace the fixed asset at some time in the future. The assumption is that the business is a 'going concern' and that the fixed assets will need to be replaced to maintain the operating capability of the business.

2.1   Depreciation and the accruals concept

Fixed assets are normally purchased for payment in cash. However, accountants do not charge the total cost of the acquisition to one accounting period. Rather, they spread the capital cost over several accounting periods. This is done by gradually writing off the asset's cost in the profit and loss account over several accounting periods corresponding to the asset's useful economic life. This is normally the period over which the present owner of the asset derives economic benefits from its use. The annual charge to the profit and loss account is called depreciation. The total amount to be depreciated is:

Cost – Residual value

The **residual value**, also known as the scrap value, is what the business expects to realise or receive at the end of its useful economic life. This represents the sale proceeds or trade-in value of the asset. This is in accordance with the accruals concept as it charges the annual depreciation in the profit and loss and matches it with the revenue sales generated during that same accounting period and avoids the cost of the acquisition being charged to one accounting period so producing a misleading profit figure. It also recognises that capital expenditure is different from revenue expenditure. The capital expenditure on a fixed asset, unlike expenditure on consumables and services, should not be written off in one year.

> **residual value**
> The actual or estimated value of a fixed asset, received on disposal.

Complying with the accruals concept by writing off of a fixed asset by an annual depreciation charge is subject to many subjective judgements. There are three key subjective judgements:

1 What is the estimated useful economic life of the fixed asset?
2 What will be the annual use of the fixed asset in each accounting period?
3 What is the estimated residual value?

2.2   Important points regarding depreciation

- As depreciation is an annual charge, it links capital expenditure to revenue expenditure in the profit and loss account and balance sheet.
- The aim of depreciation is to recoup the investment in fixed assets and to spread the cost of the fixed asset over the life of the asset.
- Depreciation is in accordance with the accruals concept, matching revenue earned with expenditure (including depreciation) incurred in generating the revenue.
- Depreciation recognises that fixed assets are used over several years by departments within the business and so the cost has to be charged against the departmental budgets.
- Capital expenditure, because of the financial size of a transaction, can have a significant impact on cash flow.
- The annual depreciation charge is a bookkeeping entry in both the profit and loss account and the fixed asset account which does *not* involve a cash payment.

● The accounts of a business are expected to show a 'true and fair view' of the financial position therefore reduced values cannot therefore be ignored.
● Like all other revenue expenses depreciation charges should be reflected in selling prices.

Stop and Think   4.1

If annual depreciation charges do not involve any cash payments, why do they appear as an expense in the annual profit and loss account?

Test *yourself*   4.2

Identify three estimates or judgements that have to be made in order to calculate a depreciation charge.

3   Methods of depreciation

The various methods give different arithmetical results in each accounting year, but are related to assumptions about the fixed asset concerning: the estimated useful economic life; the estimated residual value; and the estimated annual use of the fixed asset in each accounting period.

There are several different methods of calculating depreciation. These include:

● the straight-line method;
● the reducing balance method; and
● the machine hour method (sometimes called the units of output method).

The three methods are illustrated in the following example:

A firm acquires a piece of machinery on 1 January 200X at a cost of £60,000. Its estimated useful life is four years and it is anticipated that it can be sold for £14,400 at the end of this period. The asset will be used for 1,300 hours in year one, 1,400 hours in year two, 1,050 hours in year three and 810 hours in year four.

3.1   The straight-line method

As the name suggests, the total depreciable amount is charged in equal instalments in each accounting period over the expected useful life of the asset. This is the most commonly used method of all.

The formula for the annual depreciation charge is as follows:

$$\frac{\text{Cost of asset} - \text{residual value}}{\text{Expected useful life of the asset}}$$

The annual depreciation that is charged is often expressed at the rate of X per cent per annum on the net cost of the asset. For example, spreading the depreciable amount over four years uses a rate of 25% per annum.

Worked example

4.1

Using the information above:

$$\text{Annual charge} = \frac{\text{Asset cost} - \text{Residual value}}{\text{Life in years}}$$

$$= \frac{£60,000 - £14,400}{4}$$

$$= £11,400 \text{ per annum or } 25\% \text{ of the depreciable amount}$$

Across the life of the asset this is:

	£
Cost	60,000
Depreciation year 1	11,400
Net book value at end of year 1	48,600
Depreciation year	11,400
Net book value at end of year 2	37,200
Depreciation year 2	11,400
Net book value as at end of year 2	25,800
Depreciation year 3	11,400
Net book value as at end of year 3	14,400

3.2 The reducing balance method

This method of depreciation calculates the annual depreciation charge as a fixed percentage of the net book value of the asset, as at the end of the previous accounting period. The **net book value** is the historical cost of an asset less any accumulated depreciation from the date the asset was acquired. In order to arrive at the percentage, accountants use the following formula:

$$\text{Rate of depreciation} = 1 - \sqrt[n]{\frac{R}{C}}$$

Where: n = the estimated useful life of the asset
R = the estimated residual or scrap value of the asset
C = the historical cost of the asset

net book value
The historic cost of an asset less any accumulated depreciation or other provision for the diminution in value e.g. reduction to net realisable value.

The percentage rate to reduce the value from £60,000 to £14,400 over four years is 30%. Most managers do not need to calculate the percentage as it is provided by their accountants. It is more important to appreciate the mechanics of the calculation and the implications for the financial statements.

Worked example   4.2

Across the life of the asset this is as follows:

	£
Cost as at year 1	60,000
Depreciation year 1 (30% × cost)	18,000
Net book value as at end of year 1	42,000
Depreciation year 2 (30% × net book value)	12,600
Net book value as at end of year 2	29,400
Depreciation year 3 (30% × net book value)	8,820
Net book value as at end of year 3	20,580
Depreciation year 4 (30% × net book value)	6,180
Net book value as at end of year 4	14,400

Under the reducing balance method the annual charge for depreciation is higher in the earlier years of the asset's life and lower in the later years. The reducing balance method might therefore be used when it is considered fair to allocate a greater proportion of the total depreciable amount to the earlier years and a lower proportion to later years, on the assumption that the benefits obtained by the business from using the asset decline over time. It can be argued that, for some assets – motor vehicles, for example – the actual value of the assets declines quickly in the early years and more slowly in later years. At the same time the costs of repairs of a motor vehicle tend to increase as the asset gets older. Adopting the reducing balance method, in which the depreciation charge reduces as the asset gets older, tends to equalise the total cost of the asset over its life.

3.3   The machine hour and units of production methods

This method of depreciation is considered suitable for any asset where it is assumed that the loss in value is a direct function of the asset use rather than time. The depreciation charge is calculated according to the number of hours of asset use or units produced by the machine during the course of the period in relation to the total predicted use or production throughout the machine's life.

The life of the asset is estimated in hours (or other appropriate units) and each unit is given a money value for depreciation purposes. The rate of depreciation for each unit is calculated as:

$$\frac{\text{Cost of asset} - \text{estimated residual value}}{\text{Expected useful life of the asset in units}}$$

$$\text{Depreciation rate} = \frac{£60,000 - £14,400}{(1,300 + 1,400 + 1,050 + 810 = 4,560)\text{ hours}}$$

$$= £10.00 \text{ per hour}$$

Worked example 4.3

Across the life of the asset this looks like this:

	£
Cost as at 1 January year 1.	60,000
Depreciation year 1 (1,300 hours × £10)	13,000
Net book value as at 31 December year 1	47,000
Depreciation year 2 (1,400 hours × £10)	14,000
Net book value as at 31 December year 2	33,000
Depreciation year 3 (1,050 hours × £10)	10,500
Net book value as at 31 December year 3	22,500
Depreciation year 4 (810 hours × £10)	8,100
Net book value as at 31 December year 4	14,400

Test *yourself* 4.4

(a) If a fixed asset cost £36,000 in year 1 and is depreciated at 15% per annum using the straight line method what is the depreciation charge for year 2?

(b) If an asset is purchased in year 1 for £36,000 and is depreciated at 20% per annum using the reducing balance method what is the net book value of the asset at 31 December in year 3?

Putting the case 4.1

Jane asks you to provide the annual depreciation charge and the net book value of the computer equipment for the first two years after its purchase. She asks you to calculate these figures using both the straight-line method and the reducing balance method at a rate of 30%. She will include these figures in her business plan. Jane also asks you to provide THREE reasons why depreciation should be charged annually to the profit and loss account.

Depreciation – Straight-line method

$$\frac{\text{Cost} - \text{Scrap value}}{\text{Estimated life}} \quad \frac{80,000 - 15,000}{5 \text{ years}} = £13,000 \text{ per annum}$$

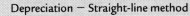

Straight-line method

Year	Annual Depreciation Charged to Profit and Loss Account	Cost of Fixed Asset	Accumulated Depreciation	Net Book Value Included on Balance Sheet
	£	£	£	£
1	13,000	80,000	13,000	67,000
2	13,000	80,000	26,000	54,000

Putting the case *(continued)* 4.1

Depreciation — Reducing balance method

30% of net book value per annum

Reducing balance method

Year	Annual Depreciation Charged to Profit and Loss Account	Cost of Fixed Asset	Accumulated Depreciation	Net Book Value Included on Balance Sheet
	£	£	£	£
1	24,000	80,000	24,000	56,000
2	16,800	80,000	40,800	39,200

There are three reasons for depreciation:

1 To reduce book value of fixed asset to more realistic levels in the balance sheet.

2 To comply with the accruals or matching concept. The annual depreciation charge represents the annual cost of using the fixed asset to generate sales for the business.

3 To reflect the loss in value of the equipment due to wear and tear, usage and the passage of time.

3.4 Impact of depreciation methods on financial statements

The three depreciation methods have different effects on the figures that appear in both the profit and loss account and the balance sheet. Over the four-year period the total depreciation charged to the profit and loss account is the same – £45,600 – using all three methods. Similarly, at the end of year 4 the net book value of the machine is the same, at £14,400. However, it is the different ways of apportioning the depreciation over the useful life of the asset which has an impact on the financial statements. In general terms the impact is revealed in two ways:

1 The annual depreciation expense charged to the profit and loss account differs for all three methods. This will have an impact on the annual profit figure.

2 The value of fixed asset in the accounts as revealed in the balance sheet by the net book value differs in all three methods. This will impact on the value of the total assets included in the balance sheet.

The following tables illustrate the impact.

Year	Annual Depreciation Charged to Profit and Loss Account	Cost of Fixed Asset	Accumulated Depreciation	Net Book Value Included in Balance Sheet
	£	£	£	£
1	11,400	60,000	11,400	48,600
2	11,400	60,000	22,800	37,200
3	11,400	60,000	34,200	25,800
4	11,400	60,000	45,600	14,400

Table 4.1 Straight-line method

- This method assumes that the business enjoys equal benefits from the use of the asset in every accounting period throughout its useful economic life. Thus it can be argued it produces a fair allocation of the total depreciable amount between the different accounting periods.
- The straight-line method has the merits of certainty, simplicity and equality of annual charge.
- It is the most widely used method of depreciation.
- It is particularly applicable to such assets as buildings, patents and leases where time is the important factor in the generating the benefits to be gained from the use of an asset.
- The method does not reflect the fact that, normally, the greatest loss in the market value of a fixed asset occurs in the first year of its use.
- The method does not reflect that there can be an unevenness of the loss in the market value of a fixed asset.
- The method does not provide an accurate measure of the cost to be charged in accounting periods.

Year	Annual Depreciation Charged to Profit and Loss Account	Cost of Fixed Asset	Accumulated Depreciation	Net Book Value Included in Balance Sheet
	£	£	£	£
1	18,000	60,000	18,000	42,000
2	12,600	60,000	30,600	29,400
3	8,820	60,000	39,420	20,580
4	6,180	60,000	45,600	14,400

Table 4.2 Reducing balance method

- The reducing balance method charges larger depreciation in the earlier years of the asset's life, and smaller amounts in later years.
- The method assumes that the benefits obtained by the business from using a fixed asset reduce over time.
- The method can be used when it is considered equitable to charge a greater proportion of the total depreciable amount to the earlier years and a lower proportion to later years.
- The reducing balance method approximates to reality in respect of certain fixed assets, e.g. motor vehicles where the depreciation calculated in the first year reflects the great loss in market value at the same time as when repairs are usually low.

Year	Annual Depreciation Charged to Profit and Loss Account	Cost of Fixed Asset	Accumulated Depreciation	Net Book Value Included on Balance Sheet
	£	£	£	£
1	13,000	60,000	13,000	47,000
2	14,000	60,000	27,000	33,000
3	10,500	60,000	37,500	22,500
4	8,100	60,000	45,600	14,400

Table 4.3 Machine hour and units of production methods

- This method is considered suitable for any asset where it is assumed that loss in value is a direct function of asset use rather than time and obsolescence.
- The machine hour method requires an estimate of usage well into the future at the time the asset is acquired.
- Depreciation is recorded only when the asset is used. The more units the asset produces or the hours used in a given year the greater the depreciation expense.
- This is used in some manufacturing companies.

3.5 Choosing a depreciation method

The business should choose the method most appropriate to the business. The method should be one that matches depreciation expense to the revenues that the fixed asset helped to generate. The accountancy bodies in their accounting standard on depreciation do not recommend one method over another. The standard says that the method should be the most appropriate to the fixed asset and to the assets use in the business.

The following is an extract from a typical set of notes to the published annual financial statements of company. It demonstrates clearly the importance of depreciation methods on both annual profits and fixed asset valuation:

'Tangible fixed assets

Depreciation is provided, normally on a straight line basis, to write off the cost or valuation of tangible fixed assets over their estimated useful economic lives to any estimated residual value, using the following rates:

Buildings	up to 50 years
Research equipment	8 years
Computing equipment and motor vehicles	3–5 years
Other equipment	10–15 years

No depreciation is provided on freehold land and assets in the course of construction'.

Test *yourself* 4.4

(a) Provide TWO examples which illustrate the impact on annual profit figures of using the straight line method of depreciation with the machine hour method.

(b) Give an example when it would be more appropriate to use the reducing balance method of depreciation.

4 Revaluation of fixed assets

Whatever method is chosen, depreciation is calculated using the historical cost of the fixed asset. The fact is, however, that the value of many fixed assets, particularly some land and buildings, rises over time, largely because of inflation. Some organisations periodically revalue their fixed assets to reflect the current market value, otherwise the total value of the assets might seem unrealistically low. The depreciation is then calculated on the revalued amount. The impact of the revaluation of fixed assets on the accounting equation is reflected in a corresponding increase in the owner's capital funds.

5 Disposal of fixed assets

In the normal course of trading, a business purchases and resells its fixed assets. This maintains the operating capability of the business as a going concern. The asset to be sold is recorded in the balance sheet at its net book value, i.e. its historic cost less depreciation to the date of sale. It is important to remember that the net book value does not represent an estimate of its market value. Net book value is its value to the business. The proceeds of the sale are thus likely to either exceed or be less than the net book value. This will result in either a paper profit or loss. A simple illustration of the profit or loss calculation is illustrated by using the example used earlier in the chapter.

Worked example   4.4

A firm acquires a piece of machinery on 1 January 200X at a cost of £60,000. Its estimated useful life is four years and it is anticipated that it can be sold for £14,400 at the end of this period. Suppose the machine was sold on 1 January in year 4 for £38,000. What was the profit or loss made on disposal of the machine?

	£	£
Cost of machinery		60,000
Less		
Cumulative depreciation to date		
of sale 3 years × £11,400	34,200	
Proceeds of sale	38,000	72,200
Profit on sale		12,200

The accounts have to be adjusted in the year of sale by:

● Removing the cost price and the cumulative depreciation of the asset sold from the balance sheet.
● Increasing the cash/bank balance by the sale proceeds.
● Transferring any profit on the sale to the profit and loss account as revenue income in the year of sale. Or
● Transferring any loss on sale to the profit and loss account as an expense in the year of sale

Obviously organisations purchase and sell assets at various times throughout the financial year. It is possible to calculate a proportionate amount of depreciation to reflect accurately when an asset was sold or purchased. This reflects the limited amount of use the business has had from the asset in that period. In practice, many organisations ignore the part-year depreciation, and charge a full year's depreciation on fixed assets in the year of their purchase (regardless of the point in time during the year at which they were acquired) and no depreciation in the year of sale/disposal of the asset. While a failure to apportion depreciation to the months of the year when an asset is only owned for a few months is actually contrary to the matching concept, it may be defended on the grounds of materiality.

5.1   Intangible fixed assets

There are a number of aspects of a business which may not have a monetary value placed on them. These include:

● A skilled, loyal and efficient work force.
● Excellent relations between management and the work force.
● The site of a business, say in a city centre or near a motorway, may give the business a competitive advantage.
● A range of well-known and trusted brand names.
● A range of products or services protected by patents or copyrights.
● A loyal customer base built up by the business's relations with customers.

These are all intangible assets and, as we saw in chapter 3, they are difficult to identify in monetary terms on a balance sheet, but they would nevertheless be valued by a prospective buyer. Intangible assets are frequently created or built up in the course of time by a business. The value of such intangible assets is not usually included in the balance sheet as accountants cannot place an objective value on them.

6   Accounting concepts and depreciation

Most managers do not need to be caught up in the technical aspects of depreciation but will need to understand the reasons why depreciation is included and its impact on financial statements. This approach is assisted by recognising that the recording of depreciation in financial statements is greatly influenced by the application of accounting concepts as follows:

- The *historic cost concept* directs that transactions, i.e. the purchase of fixed assets are recorded at the value at the time the transaction occurred.
- The *going concern concept* directs that assets are *not* recorded at their break-up value as it is assumed the business will continue in existence.
- The *matching/accruals concept* directs that the main objective of depreciation is to match the cost of the fixed asset against the revenue the asset is helping to generate.
- The *consistency concept* directs that the accounting treatment of depreciation should involve a method which is used consistently and gives comparability over accounting periods.

Test *yourself*   4.5

(a) Accountants can choose any method of depreciation. Provide TWO reasons why users of accounts can be confident that the depreciation is not used to manipulate profits.

(b) Define the terms 'net book value', 'residual value' and 'market value' in relation to fixed assets.

Summary

- If capital and revenue items are not classified accurately the accounting profit will be incorrectly calculated.
- Depreciation is a measure of wearing out, consumption or other reduction in the useful economic life of a fixed asset, whether arising from use, passage of time or obsolescence through technological or market changes. Depreciation charges are made in accordance with the accruals concept which charges the annual depreciation in the profit and loss and matches it with the sales revenue generated during the same accounting period. This avoids the cost of the acquisition being charged to one accounting period and so producing a misleading profit figure.
- Different depreciation methods produce different arithmetical results, but all methods are based on assumptions about the fixed assets' estimated useful economic life, its estimated residual value and the estimated annual use of the

fixed asset in each accounting period. A key point is that the business should choose a method which is a most appropriate to the business taking account of both the type of fixed asset and the asset's use in the business.

● Revaluation and disposal of fixed assets is significant and managers should be aware that there are ways of handling rising values. The impact of the revaluation of fixed assets on the accounting equation is reflected in a corresponding increase in the owner's capital funds. It is important to remember that at any time, including its disposal, a fixed asset will be recorded in the balance sheet at its net book value i.e. historic cost less depreciation to the date of sale. This net book value does not represent an estimate of its market value but its value to the organisation in the books of the business.

● Managers should focus on the reasons why depreciation is included and its impact on financial statements.

Adjustments for accruals, prepayments, stock and debtors

5

Introduction

This chapter discusses the need to make adjustments to accounting records prior to the preparation of period-end financial statements. Adjustments have to be made because it would be extremely unusual if the detail in the accounting records exactly mirrored the financial activity undertaken by a business in, say, the previous twelve months. There are several reasons for this, which this chapter develops, but one simple reason will be the time-lag between when a business activity occurs and the physical recording of the transaction in the accounting records.

A further issue raised in this chapter is that many of these adjustments involve the subjective judgements of accountants, which will ultimately influence such issues as the valuation of assets in the balance sheet and the profit or loss figure revealed by the profit and loss account.

The chapter illustrates and explains in simple terms how these adjustments are made, but without explaining the consequences of the adjustments in terms of double-entry bookkeeping. The important issue is that managers appreciate why these adjustments are carried out so that they can pinpoint the financial consequences of such adjustments and ask relevant and searching questions of financial accountants.

1   Adjustments for accruals and prepayments

We have seen that profit is measured not by comparing 'cash received' during the financial period with 'cash spent', but by matching expenditure incurred with income earned. The accruals concept states that when computing profit the sales revenue earned should be matched only against the expenditure incurred when earning it. They should be included in the profit and loss account of the period to which they relate, irrespective of when they are received or paid. This principle attempts to ensure that the profit and loss account for a period compares like with like.

prepayments
Expenditure on goods or services for future benefit, which is to be charged to future operations, e.g. rentals paid in advance.

accruals
Costs which have not so far been taken into account at the end of a period because they have not yet been invoiced - for example, gas or electricity, invoiced in arrears.

This concept is important as most businesses trade using credit terms. This means that a business is likely to sell its goods or services for cash or on credit or for a mixture of cash and credit. Similarly, businesses are likely to buy goods or services with a mix of cash and credit. Period-end adjustments are needed because goods or services sold or bought on credit have a cash time lag.

Costs should be recognised as arising when they are incurred and not when the cash is paid.

Some services – for example, telephone, gas and electricity – are seen as being incurred or used on the date they are received. At the end of a financial year these services have been consumed or incurred but no invoice has been received by the company. The company will treat these as **accruals**, or expenses owing.

Worked example   5.1

A business has a financial year ending on 31 December and during that year it had paid £12,000 for electricity to 30 September. The electricity bill of £4,950 for the final quarter (October–December) was not received and paid until 31 January in the next year. The business will need to make an adjustment for this outstanding electricity bill of £4,950 when preparing the accounts for the year ended 31 December. In the profit and loss account when listing the expenses for the year the business will include the total of the £12,000 paid + the accrued expense owing of £4,950, i.e. £16,950 is the expense of electricity consumed during the financial year. At the same time the £4,950 will be shown in the balance sheet under current liabilities as an accrual or expense owing.

Where an amount paid in this financial year relates to the next financial year, these are termed *prepayments or payments in advance*. For example, where an annual insurance premium is paid in advance the cash payment has been made before the benefit has been received from the insurance premium. When preparing the annual accounts these should be carried forward and charged in the subsequent year's accounts. The aim of the adjustment is to ensure that each financial year takes the appropriate share of the insurance premium.

Test *yourself*   5.1

(a) Provide ONE key reason why companies need to undertake year-end adjustments.

(b) Fill in the missing words in the following sentence: The —— concept states that when computing profit the sales revenue —— should be matched only against the —— incurred when earning it.

(c) Explain the term 'prepayment' or 'payment in advance'.

Worked example   5.2

> A business has a financial year ended 31 December 200X and it purchased a new car on 1 July 200X. On that date the business paid 12 months' vehicle taxation of £180. When preparing its profit and loss account for the year ending 31 December 200X the business needs to recognise that the cost of vehicle taxation is for the period 1 July-31 December 200X which would be 6 months or £90. The other £90 is a prepayment for following year and should be shown in the balance sheet current assets as a prepayment, or payment in advance.
>
> The adjustments required can be summarised as shown in Table 5.1.

Year-end Adjustment	Definition	Impact on Profit and Loss Account	Impact on the Balance Sheet
Accruals or expenses owing	The cash payment has been made AFTER the benefit has been received.	The relevant expense figure is increased by the amount of the accrual.	Show the amount of the accrual as a current liability on the balance sheet.
Prepayments or payments in advance	The cash payment has been made BEFORE the benefit has been received.	The relevant expense figure is decreased by the amount of the prepayment.	Show the amount of the prepayment as a current asset on the balance sheet.

Table 5.1 Year-end adjustments

2   Credit sales adjustments

If goods are sold on credit, when should the revenue be included in the profit and loss account? Traditionally, the question is answered by reference to **realisation** or revenue recognition **concept**. The prudence concept stresses that sales revenue should be 'realised' and 'recognised' only when a critical event has occurred. This event would normally be when:

realisation concept
The concept that profit is only accounted for when a good is sold and not when the cash is received.

- A cash sale is made.
- The goods are delivered or the services provided and *not* when the sale proceeds are received. This will normally coincide with date on the invoice or the date of delivery if the issue of the invoice is delayed.

For example, in a financial year a business may have made cash sales of £70,000 and credit sales of £320,000. If at the end of the year £25,000 of the credit sales revenue had not been received, the business has to decide what to include in the profit and loss account as total revenue for the financial year. Cash totalling £365,000 has been received but £390,000 sales have been 'realised'. This means that the £390,000 should be included in the profit and loss account for the financial year and the £25,000 credit sales revenue outstanding should be included in the balance sheet under current assets as trade debtors. Note that when the £25,000 is received in the business bank account in the following financial year it is has no impact on that year's sales – it merely increases the bank balance and reduces trade debtors.

Putting the case   5.1

Q
Jane is confused by the list of balances relating to her business and asks you to present the information to her in a more meaningful form. She wants the information to be in a form that tells her more about the financial state of her business at 31 January 200X.

A
The information should be presented as a balance sheet.

J. Smith Ltd
Balance Sheet as at 31 January 200X

	£	£	£
Fixed Assets			
Land and buildings			450,000
Plant and equipment			42,200
Vehicles			33,800
			526,000
Current Assets			
Stocks	80,000		
Trade debtors	84,600		
Cash	2,400		
		167,000	
Less **Current Liabilities**			
Trade creditors	30,000		
Bank overdraft	18,000	48,000	
Net current assets			119,000
			645,000
Less Long-term loan – Western Bank			120,000
Net assets			525,000
Financed By			
Owner's capital			300,000
Reserves			225,000
Owner's funds			525,000

Test *yourself*   5.2

What do you understand by the term 'total revenue' for an accounting period?

3   Debtor adjustment

The realisation concept allows a business to take the profit on credit sales before the cash is received from the debtor. Every time a business sells goods on credit it is taking a risk that payment may never be received from the debtor. In turn this means that the business is taking a risk in bringing the profit on credit sales into the profit and loss account of the period in which the sale is realised. If the debtor does not pay, the profit for that period will have been overestimated. In order to deal with this uncertainty accountants can make accounting adjustments which are explained below.

3.1 Bad debts

In general terms, debtors can initially be grouped in two categories: good debtors and bad debtors. Good debtors are those who settle their debt in full and normally within an agreed time frame of, say, 30 days. The cash received from the debtors is reflected in the accounting equation by increasing the cash balance and reducing the debtors balance.

There are some debtors, however, who cannot or will not pay their debts. Those who cannot pay are usually those who become insolvent and go out of business. Those debtors who will not pay are often in dispute with the business, for example about the quality of the goods or services they have received. These types of debts relate to specific debtors who have failed to pay the debt owed by them. The debt is still owed to the business but the business has to recognise the reality of the situation. It would be appropriate to follow the prudence concept and recognise these as **bad debts**. Consider how imprudent it would be if a debt is seen to be not receivable from the debtor and no adjustments were made; the total debtors' figure appearing under current assets in the balance sheet would be overstated. To provide a more realistic figure of both the financial performance and position of the business the bad debt should be written off.

> **bad debt**
> A debt which is, or is considered to be, uncollectible and is, therefore, written off as a charge to the profit and loss account.

Worked example 5.1

> A business has trade debtors of £280,000 at the end of the financial year to 31 December 200X. One of the trade debtors, A. Smith, has owed the business £18,000 for six years. The owner discovers that the debt is likely to be irrecoverable as Smith has not responded to any reminders and has even moved abroad. The owner decides to treat the £18,000 as a bad debt.
>
> This does not mean simply removing the £18,000 from the debtors balance as this would ignore the impact of the write-off on the profit earned. The adjustments required are:
>
> 1 The bad debt of £18,000 is shown as an expense in the profit and loss account for the year ended 31 December 200X.
>
> 2 The £18,000 bad debt is deducted from the total debtors figure in the balance sheet as at 31 December 200X. The trade debtors figure is now shown as £262,000 (£280,000 − £18,000).

It is common practice for business to conduct a regular review of debtors' balances throughout the financial year so that when information is received, for example concerning the bankruptcy of a debtor, the business will accumulate all bad debts to a bad debts expense account during the financial year and then transfer the total to the profit and loss account at the end of the period. The individual debtors' balances are reduced by the individual bad debt written off.

Finally, should the debtor subsequently pay the amount owing, the bad debt expense is reversed in the year the payment is received. This results in the business adding back the amount written off as bad debt to the profit in that year.

doubtful debts
An amount charged against profit and deducted from debtors which allows for the non-recovery of a proportion of the debts.

3.2 Provision for doubtful debts

At any time there is always a risk that debts will not be collected, which makes it difficult to put an exact value on debtors. A prudent business should make a reasonable estimate of how much of the debts may not be collected. This reasonable estimate is called a provision for doubtful debts and is charged as an expense in the profit and loss account and the debtors are shown in the balance sheet with the provision deducted.

Worked example   5.2

In Worked example 5.1, bad debts of £18,000 were written off as an expense in the profit and loss account for the year ended 31 December 200X. This resulted in a balance sheet figure for trade debtors of £262,000. Suppose the business, having looked at the history of the bad debts, estimates 10% of outstanding debtors are likely to be doubtful. The business would make a provision for doubtful debts in its accounts for the financial year to 31 December 200X of £26,200, i.e.10% of £262,000.

The adjustments required are as follows:

● The increase in provision for doubtful debt of £26,200 is shown as an expense in the profit and loss account for the year ended 31 December 200X.

● The trade debtors figure is now shown as £262,000 less £26,200.

Because the provision for doubtful debts is an estimate, the actual amount of bad debt is likely to be different from the estimate so it will be necessary to reassess the level of the provision every year.

Test *yourself*   5.3

(a) What is the purpose of a provision for doubtful debts? How is it recorded in the balance sheet?

(b) Provide TWO examples of why bad debts and provision for doubtful debts are different in nature and require different adjustments in the financial statements.

Debtor adjustments – key points

● Bad debts and provision for doubtful debts are different in nature and require different adjustments in the financial statements.

● Bad debts are *a fact* in that they comprise debtors who cannot or will not pay their debts.

● A provision for doubtful debts is a reasonable estimate of the value of debts which may not be collected.

● Bad debts relate to specific debtors who the business knows for a fact have failed to pay the debt owed by them.

● A provision for doubtful debts is different from bad debts in that it does not normally relate to specific debtors.

● The prudence concept (see chapter 1) requires that assets should not be valued in the balance sheet at a value more than they can reasonably be considered to be worth. At any time there is always a risk that debts will not be collected, which makes it difficult to value debtors exactly. Therefore a prudent business should make reasonable adjustments so that debtors reflect the value of debts that may not be collected.

4 Stock adjustments

During a financial year it is unlikely that all items purchased for resale will have been sold. The reality is that a business will be left with some items of stock in hand at the end of the financial year. At the end of the year a business has to calculate the gross profit for the financial year. This calculation is based on the principle that:

Gross profit = Sales − Cost of sales

This calculation is carried out in a section, called the trading account, at the beginning of the profit and loss account.

4.1 The trading account

In modern accounting, the **trading account** is normally incorporated within the profit and loss account rather than shown separately. A trading account is produced to:

trading account
An account which shows the gross profit or loss generated by an entity for a period.

- Establish the costs directly involved in buying in goods for resale.
- Measure the **gross profit** for the accounting period.

The calculation of cost of sales involves important adjustments for opening and closing stocks. These allow the calculation of the cost of goods sold during that period. This can be summarised as:

gross profit
This is sales less cost of sales.

Opening stock
+ Purchases
− _Closing stock_
= Cost of sales

The cost of sales can then be compared to the sales for the financial year and the gross profit can be calculated as follows.

Trading Account for month ending 30 November 200X		
	£	£
Sales		900,000
Opening stock	100,000	
Add Purchases	500,000	
	600,000	
Less Closing stock	340,000	
Cost of goods sold		260,000
Gross Profit		640,000

The gross profit represents the profit earned during the financial year through trading, but before the deduction of other expenses.

Test *yourself*   5.4

(a)   What do you understand by the terms gross profit and net profit?

(b)   The opening stock at the beginning of an accounting period was £36,000; during the period purchases totalled £1,400,000; at the end of the accounting period the closing stock was £76,000. What was the cost of sales for the period?

4.2   The valuation of stock

net realisable value (NRV)

The price at which the stock could be currently sold less any costs which would be incurred to complete the sale.

How stock is valued has an important bearing on the level of profit reported. Stocks are valued at the lower of cost price or **net realisable value** (**NRV**). This principle is based on the concept of prudence. By not overstating the value of stock the business is avoiding overstating profit.

The NRV is likely to be less than cost price if the stock is the subject of one or all of the following:

*   Obsolescence of stock due to technical developments.
*   Fall in market prices.
*   Physical deterioration of the stock.
*   Purchasing error.

first in first out

A method of pricing the issue of material using, first, the purchase price of the oldest unit in stock.

Most items of stock cannot be distinguished one from another, so it is difficult to keep track of each item throughout its life. If a firm has a delivery of raw materials over a period at different prices, how is it possible to identify the value of stock left? Was the oldest used first, was the latest used first, or was it a mix of the two? The answer has a significant bearing on how the remaining items (stock) are valued. Hence a few assumptions are permitted, including the following:

last in first out

A method of pricing the issue of material using, first, the purchase price of the latest unit in stock.

*   The goods are sold in chronological order and thus the closing stock is valued at latest cost price. The FIFO (**first in first out**) method.
*   The most recent purchases of stock were sold first and thus the closing stock is valued at the earliest cost price. The LIFO (**last in first out**) method.
*   A simple average where stock is not valued at actual cost price, but is based on average actual prices across all items in stock. The AVCO (**average cost**) method.

average cost

The total cost of an item of material in stock divided by the total quantity in stock; used for pricing issues from store.

Stock valuation calculations are not seen as a key task for most business managers. However it is important to understand the impact of the methods of stock valuation on:

*   Profit.
*   Closing stock valuation.

4.3 Impact of stock valuation methods on profit

Worked example

5.3

A new business has the following transactions during its first week of trading:

Day 1	Purchases one item of stock for £500
Day 2	Purchases a second piece of stock £700
Day 7	Sells one item of stock for £1,000

The impact of the three methods of stock valuation on profit is as follows:

	FIFO	LIFO	AVCO
	£	£	£
Sales revenue	1,000	1,000	1,000
Less cost of sales	500	700	600
Gross profit	500	300	400

The table identifies the following key issues which business managers should be aware of:

- LIFO will give a more realistic reflection of business operations.
- In times of rising prices LIFO by charging the latest prices will give a lower profit than FIFO.
- In times of falling prices LIFO will give a higher profit figure than FIFO.
- AVCO produces a profit figure half way between the two other methods.

The impact on closing stock valuation is as follows:

	FIFO	LIFO	AVCO
	£	£	£
Closing stock value	700	500	600

This table identifies the following key issues which business managers should be aware of:

- In times of rising prices LIFO stock values being based on earliest cost prices will tend to cause stock to be undervalued in relation to current replacement price levels.
- In times of rising prices FIFO will give a more realistic figure for stock as they are based on the latest cost price.
- AVCO produces a stock figure between the two other methods.

Test *yourself*

5.5

(a) Define the terms cost price and net realisable value as applied to stock.

(b) Explain the impact on profit of using LIFO as a stock valuation method in times of rising prices.

Summary

- Managers should appreciate why the adjustments are carried out, so that they can focus on the financial consequences and ask relevant and searching questions of financial accountants.
- Adjustments are made to ensure that the accounting records reflect the financial activity undertaken by a business in the previous financial period. The key reason for the adjustments is that there is a time lag between the financial transaction occurring and the physical recording of the transaction in the accounting records.
- Adjustments will be made for credit sales, for bad and doubtful debts and stock.
- Many adjustments involve the subjective judgements of accountants which ultimately influence such issues as the valuation of assets in the balance sheet and the profit or loss figure revealed by the profit and loss account.
- Stock needs to be valued carefully because incorrect valuation will result in the profit being incorrectly stated.

The accounting system and accounting records

6

Introduction

This chapter helps managers understand the role and function of source documents such as invoices and introduces the books of prime entry and the ledgers. We then look at the link between source documents and books of prime entry and the accounting ledgers. Examples of documents such as the cash book and petty cash records are illustrated. The chapter ends with the trial balance and how this is the basis of preparing the profit and loss account and the balance sheet.

1   Source documents

Business transactions are nearly always recorded on a document. These **source documents** contain information that is fed into an accounting system to form the basis of the information in the accounts. Such documents include the following:

- *Sales order* – a customer provides a written order detailing the goods or services they wish to buy.
- *Purchase order* – A business sends a written order to a supplier for the purchase of goods or materials.
- *Invoice from suppliers* – A business buys goods or services from a supplier and receives an invoice from the supplier. Note the goods or services received should correspond to the details on the purchase order.
- *Invoice sent to customers* – A business sells goods or services to a customer and sends an invoice to the customer. The details on the invoice should correspond to the details on the sales order. An example of the content of an invoice issued by the supplier A. B. Silver to the customer R. Blackburn Ltd is shown in Sample 6.1.

---

source documents
Source documents contain the information that is put into an accounting system.

sales order
An acknowledgement by a supplier of a purchase order. It may contain terms which override those of the purchaser.

purchase order
A written order for goods or services specifying quantities, price, delivery dates and contract terms.

invoice

A document prepared by a supplier showing the description, quantities, prices and values of goods delivered or services rendered. To the supplier this is a sales invoice; to the purchaser the same document is a purchase invoice.

Sample Invoice   6.1

A.B. Silver

6, Hudson Court,

Preston, PN7 6YG

Date: 31/01/0X

Your Order No. 15/Z/005

Invoice No: 230144

To: R. Blackburn Ltd.

10 Fishergate Hill

Manchester

M6 8JB

Date	Details	Unit Price	Total
23/12/0X	6 'BlueCool' Integrated Fridge Freezers Model Number BC756183 9.0 cu ft capacity	£399.00	£2,394.00
		Total Payable	£2,394.00
Terms 1% cash discount if paid within 1 month			

credit notes

Prepared by a seller notifying the purchaser that the account is being reduced, e.g. because of return of goods or cancellation.

goods received note

A record of the receipt and inspection of stock, used to verify the suppliers' invoice before it is passed for payment.

books of prime entry

A first record of transactions, such as sales or purchases, from which details or totals, as appropriate, are transferred to the ledgers.

Other source documents include:

- **Credit notes** from suppliers for purchases returned, or to customers for sales returned. Credit notes are sent out when goods or services are returned to the supplier by the customer. The credit note contains the same information as an invoice but is usually printed in red. In effect credit notes negative sales invoices.
- **Goods received note (GRN)** –These are sent with goods as they are shipped to the customer. The GRN is used to book the goods into the warehouse. A copy of the GRN is usually sent to the accounts department before an invoice can be paid.

2   Books of prime entry

In the early days of accounting the information on the source documents was copied each day by a clerk into a book. This book is the source of any accounting entry, and gives it authority; it is called a **book of prime entry**.

There is no such thing as a typical accounting system as many of these books have been computerised or replaced by files of invoices which carry out the same function. However, familiarity with the purpose, use and effects of these important accounting documents will help managers understand how basic accounting systems work.

Figure 6.1 lists the main books of prime entry:

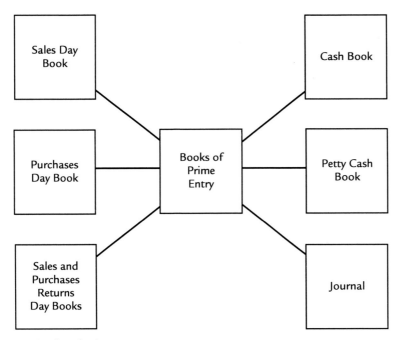

Figure 6.1 Books of prime entry

Test *yourself* 6.1

(a) Give THREE examples of and define the term accounting source documents.

(b) Give THREE examples of and define the term books of prime entry.

2.1 Sales day book

This book records all the sales invoices which a business has sent out to its customers. Every sale, both cash sales and on credit, should have an invoice raised. These invoices should be recorded in the sales day book. Each page of the sales day book is sequentially numbered to assist in the financial control of sales.

Sample Sales day book 6.2

Date	Invoice No.	Customer	Sales ledger page	Total invoiced
May 200X	1311	I. Back & Co.	SL 44	£15,000
	1312	L. Coe Ltd	SL 84	£ 3,400
				£18,400

At the end of each day, each invoice should be entered, or 'posted', to the individual customer's account in the sales ledger. This ledger contains an account for each customer and shows the business how much is owed by each of its customers i.e. its trade debtors. The customers' accounts can be found by reference to the sales ledger page.

Periodically, the total of the sales day book page is analysed between cash sales and credit sales and the totals posted or entered to the Sales account.

2.2   Sales returns day book

Goods sold to customers are often returned for some reason such as:

- The goods may be faulty; or
- The wrong goods may have been supplied.

This return may be for all the sold goods, in which case the entire original invoice has to be cancelled. Alternatively, only a few of the goods are returned, in which case only part of the invoice may be offset. To achieve this, credit notes are issued. The sales returns day book should be completed in exactly the same way as the sales day book in respect of goods returned from customers. When the individual entries are made to the sales ledger they will reduce the amount owed by the customer. The sales returns will also reduce the sales achieved by the business.

2.3   Purchases day book

This book contains information about the purchases made by a business and is a list of invoices from suppliers. It is completed in exactly the same way as the sales day book, with each page being sequentially numbered. The invoice is the source document and describes the goods and services provided and the price the buyer has to pay. It will also contain a cross-reference to the order number issued by the business to raise the purchase.

The individual invoices will be posted to the supplier's accounts in the purchases ledger which contains an account for each supplier. This account will record the individual invoices received from the supplier and ultimately the payments made to the supplier by the business. At any point in time the supplier's account shows the financial position between the business and the supplier.

Sample Purchases day book   6.3

Date	Purchases	Supplier ledger page	Total invoiced
May 200X			£
25th	ABC Ltd.	PL08	3,305
26th	XYZ Ltd	PL96	2,809
28th	RST & Co.	PL77	860

2.4   Purchases returns day book

Purchases returns are goods a business returns to a supplier. In effect they are negative purchases in that they reduce the amount owed to a supplier. This will be completed in exactly the same manner as the purchase day book. When the entries are made to the purchases ledger they will reduce the amounts owing to your suppliers and will reduce the purchases made by the business.

Test *yourself*   6.2

(a) Why would you make an entry in the sales returns book?

(b) Where will the entries in a purchases day book and a sales day book be 'posted' to?

3   Cash books

For accounting purposes 'cash' includes cash, cheques and bank transactions, unless specified as 'cash in hand' or 'petty cash' (see below). The **cash book** records all 'cash' transactions including coins, banknotes, cheques, direct debits, and credit transfers and banker's drafts. The cash book is split into columns for cash and bank transactions.

The cash book has one page for receipts from customers depending on whether it is in the form of cash or cheque. On the opposite side of the cash book will be a page for payments to creditors and for other expenses such as wages, electricity, etc.

3.1   Petty cash book

Sometimes an organisation regardless of its size finds itself in a situation where it has to make or reimburse small-value payments. Such payments may be for stamps, taxi fares, tea or coffee for the office or emergency purchases of stationery. Most businesses keep a small amount of cash on their premises for this purpose. This cash or float is called a **petty cash account**. As the cash used to finance the petty cash float is normally transferred from the bank account it is in effect a subsidiary of the main cash book. Petty cash payments and receipts are recorded in a **petty cash book**. The petty cash is usually the responsibility of the petty cashier.

A common way of maintaining petty cash is by using the **imprest system**. A fixed float is given to the petty cashier. When a purchase is made, a petty cash voucher is completed and filed, together with the proof of purchase such as a receipt. At any one time the balance of the petty cash plus the total of all the petty cash vouchers should equal the amount of the original cash float. This method acts as automatic internal check on the accuracy and honesty of the cashier. When the petty cashier needs to replenish the float he/she presents the vouchers to the main cashier who then reimburses the petty cashier with cash equal to the value of the vouchers. The petty cash vouchers are then entered in the expense accounts of the main accounting system.

cash book
A book which records the cash accounts of a business.

petty cash account
A record of relatively small cash receipts and payments, the balance representing the cash in the control of an individual, usually dealt with under an imprest system.

petty cash book
A book for recording receipts and payments made out of a petty cash account.

imprest system
A method of controlling cash or stock; when the cash or stock has been reduced by disbursements or issues it is restored to its original level.

Worked example   6.1

Running a petty cash book

Date		RECEIPTS Narrative	Total	Date	PAYMENTS Narrative	Total £	Taxis £	Stamps, £	etc. £
1.1.200X	Bank		100	3.1.0X	Meeting	22	22		
					Stamps	<u>35</u>	—	<u>35</u>	
			<u>100</u>			<u>57</u>	<u>22</u>	<u>35</u>	

An 'imprest' of £100 was received on the 1 January 200X. Up to the 3 January payments totalling £57 had been made out of petty cash. At that date the petty cash balance should be £43 which should be the amount held by the petty cashier and be the total of the petty cash vouchers. In other words:

	£
Cash still held in petty cash	43
Plus voucher payments	<u>57</u>
Must equal the agreed sum or float	<u>100</u>

4   The journal

journal
A record of financial transactions, such as transfers between accounts, not dealt with elsewhere.

The **journal** is used to make entries in the ledger that cannot be made through the other books of prime entry. Examples are the correction of posting errors in the ledger or the formal entry of accounting adjustments, such as depreciation and accruals, at the end of the year; correction of errors and large or unusual transactions.

Test *yourself*   6.3

(a) What do you understand by the term 'cash' as used in cash book?

(b) Why do organisations keep a petty cash book as well as a cash book?

Putting the case   6.1

 You are asked to prepare a note for Jane that will allow her to explain to her staff what a petty cash book is used for and how a petty cash imprest system operates.

 Petty cash is where a small amount of cash is kept on the premises for small-value payments such as stamps, local travel costs, provisions, etc. Petty cash books record the payments made supported by a petty cash voucher. The book also records cash received from the business bank account.

Petty cash is the responsibility of the petty cashier. An imprest system is where the petty cash is kept at an agreed sum or float, say £200, by topping up from the business bank account at regular intervals. Thus expense items are recorded in vouchers, say £130, as they occur, so that at any time the following illustration will apply:

	£
Petty cash vouchers	130
Plus cash still held in petty cash	<u>70</u>
Equals the agreed sum or float	<u>200</u>

The total of the petty cash vouchers is the amount reimbursed to the petty cashier at regular intervals.

5   The ledger accounts

The ledger is a book which consists of pages called accounts. There is an account in the ledger for each different type of item the business wishes to analyse. The accounts can be either:

- **Personal accounts** of the customers (debtors) which are kept in the **sales or debtors ledger**. Personal accounts of suppliers (creditors) which are kept in the **purchases or creditors ledger**.
- **Impersonal accounts**, which includes accounts such as sales, purchases, wages, depreciation, stocks, cash and bank, and fixed assets, capital and liabilities, etc. It will also include the total debtors and total creditors of the business. These accounts are kept in the **nominal ledger**.

5.1   Sales or debtors ledger

The sales ledger contains an account or record for each customer. Invoices raised will be posted to the account to increase the customer's indebtedness, while credit notes will be posted to reduce their indebtedness. Any cash received will be posted to the cash book and to the customer's account to reduce their indebtedness. The balance column on the account shows at any one time how much is owing to you by that customer.

5.2   Purchases or creditors ledger

This will be completed in a similar manner to the sales ledger. This ledger contains an account or record for each supplier. Invoices received will be posted to the account to increase the amount owed to the supplier, whilst the credit notes will be posted to reduce the business's indebtedness. Any cash paid will be posted to the cash book and to the suppliers account to reduce the business's indebtedness. The balance column on the account shows at any one time how much is owed by the business to that supplier.

5.3   Nominal (or general) ledger

This ledger is made up of all the non-personal accounts – in contrast to the personal ledgers which include the names of customers and suppliers.
    Examples of accounts in the nominal ledger include the following:

- Fixed assets at cost – a separate account for each type of fixed asset, e.g. motor vehicles, machinery, etc.
- Provision for depreciation of fixed assets – a separate account for each provision, e.g. provision for depreciation of motor vehicles, provision for depreciation of motor vehicles, etc.
- Capital account – of owner.
- Stocks of finished goods.
- Total debtors.
- Total creditors.

personal accounts
A record of amounts receivable from or payable to a person or an entity.

sales or debtors ledger
A collection of the accounts or records receivable from each customer.

purchases or creditors' ledger
A collection of the personal accounts payable to a person or an entity.

impersonal accounts
A record of the revenues and expenditures, liabilities and assets classified by their nature, e.g. sales, rent, wages, electricity. Sometimes called nominal accounts.

nominal ledger
A record of the revenues and expenditures, liabilities and assets classified by their nature, e.g. sales, rates, wages, electricity. Sometimes called impersonal accounts.

- Expense accounts – a separate account for each expense, e.g. salaries, heating, bank charges, petrol, etc.
- Sales income.
- Total cash.

These accounts form the basis for preparing the profit and loss account and balance sheet.

Test *yourself*   6.4

(a) Explain the difference between personal accounts and impersonal accounts?

(b) Explain the difference, if any, between the content of the sales ledger and the debtors ledger.

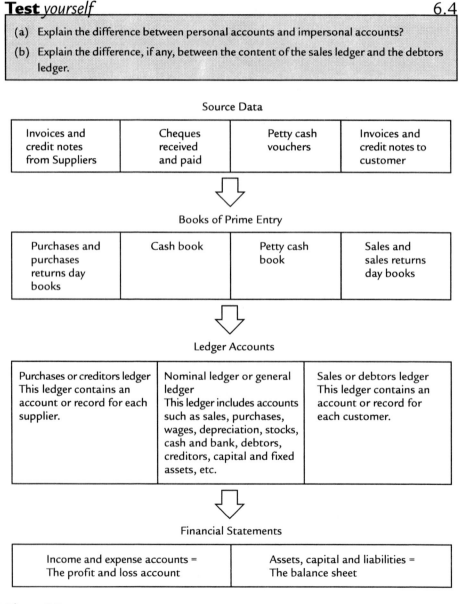

Source Data

Invoices and credit notes from Suppliers	Cheques received and paid	Petty cash vouchers	Invoices and credit notes to customer

Books of Prime Entry

Purchases and purchases returns day books	Cash book	Petty cash book	Sales and sales returns day books

Ledger Accounts

Purchases or creditors ledger This ledger contains an account or record for each supplier.	Nominal ledger or general ledger This ledger includes accounts such as sales, purchases, wages, depreciation, stocks, cash and bank, debtors, creditors, capital and fixed assets, etc.	Sales or debtors ledger This ledger contains an account or record for each customer.

Financial Statements

Income and expense accounts = The profit and loss account	Assets, capital and liabilities = The balance sheet

Figure 6.2

6 Putting it all together

We have described how accounting entries are recorded from the source documents to the books of prime entry to the individual accounts in the accounting books or ledger. This can be quite daunting to non-accountants as it is full of terminology complicated by the fact that many of the terms have alternative names. Figure 6.2 above helps to clarify the process.

Stop and Think	6.1

Try to find out a little about how accounting record-keeping works in the organisation where you work. Follow through a couple of transactions and investigate how they are recorded. For example, choose the payment of an invoice or the receipt of cash from a customer.

7 Double-entry bookkeeping

Most firms use a system which requires two entries to be recorded for each transaction undertaken by the business. This is known as **double-entry bookkeeping**. Before getting into the rules and operation of double-entry, students should remember that the entries will be recorded in the books of account as and when the transactions occur, not when money for these transactions is received or paid out. For example, if a sale is made on credit terms, it will be recorded in the bookkeeping system as a sale even though it may be several weeks before the customer pays for those goods or services.

double-entry bookkeeping
A method of recording transactions in ledger accounts so that the monetary value of the debits and credits always balance each other.

On the other hand, if goods are purchased on credit, the purchase will be recorded when it is made and not when the goods are actually paid for, i.e. when a valid invoice for the goods or services is received. This means that double-entry bookkeeping follows the accruals concept.

A double-entry system is a method in which each transaction is recorded in ledger accounts at least twice. The monetary value of the entries will exactly balance one another. Each entry has a left side – these are called debits – and a right side – these are called credits. The terms debits and credits are, at this stage best just accepted as the language of business and will become clearer as students begin to use them.

Figure 6.3 shows how debits and credits affect the different types of accounts.

Account Type	Debit	Credit
Assets	Increases	Decreases
Liabilities	Decreases	Increases
Owner's capital	Decreases	Increases
Revenues	Decreases	Increases
Expenses	Increases	Decreases

Figure 6.3 Debits and credits

You will have noted that the five account types identified in Figure 6.3 are the same as those which comprise the accounting equation:

$$\text{Capital} + (\text{Revenues} - \text{Expenses}) = \text{Total assets} - \text{Total liabilities}$$

You will recall that in order to keep the accounting equation in balance at least two items in the equation had to be adjusted. Similarly for each transaction a bookkeeping entry will have to show the impact of a transaction on each of the two items. This means that the bookkeeping system will have one entry showing an increase or decrease in one item and another entry showing the increase or decrease in the other item. Hence the term double-entry bookkeeping reflects the fact that each entry is made twice.

7.1 Recording business transactions

The following are examples of how the double entry system will record business transactions.

Paying expenses

The vast majority of transaction entries in expense accounts reflect an increase in expenses and are recorded on the debit side. A business enters an expense as a debit to increase the business record of what it has spent. For example, a business purchases cleaning materials at a cost of £200, paying by cheque. The business is decreasing its cash in the bank by £200 and is increasing its expenses by the same amount. These are the two bookkeeping entries – bank is an asset which is being decreased and gets a credit entry, and cleaning materials is an expense which is increased and gets a debit entry.

Instead of paying for the cleaning materials by cheque, suppose the business buys them on credit terms. The expense entry stays the same – the expense cleaning materials is increased, or debited. This time, however, the business is not using its bank instead the business has increased its liabilities or creditors. To increase a liability account, the business credits it. In short, the balancing entry is credit creditors.

Purchase of fixed assets

When a business purchases a fixed asset, such as a piece of equipment, the fixed asset account – equipment is debited as it is increased. For example, a business purchases a computer at a cost of £10,000, paying by cheque. The business is decreasing its cash at the bank by £10,000 and is increasing its fixed assets by the same amount. These are the two bookkeeping entries – bank is an asset which is being decreased and gets a credit entry, and fixed asset – computers are an asset which is increased and gets a debit entry.

Instead of paying for the computer by cheque, suppose the business agrees to pay 30 days after the computer is installed. The asset entry stays the same – the fixed asset (computers) is increased, or debited. This time, however, the business has increased its liabilities or creditors. To increase a liability account, the business credits it. In short the balancing entry is – debit fixed asset – computers, credit creditors.

The asset stock

Stock items are goods purchased for resale. The goods are usually sold at a selling price that is greater than cost price with the difference being profit. If this were not the case it would be possible for a business to have a stock account with debit entries recording increases (or purchases) in stock and credit entries recording decreases (or sales) in stock. The difference between the debit entries and the credit entries represents the cost of the unsold stock. However, because of the profit element in the sale of stock this situation does not apply.

Therefore, it is usual to record increases in stock in a purchases account. The purchases account should record only the purchase of goods which the business buys with the prime intention of selling. The purchases account will never record the purchase of items which are bought to be used in the business rather than resale.

Purchases are an expense and an increase in expenses is recorded as a debit entry in the purchases account. Another way of viewing this is to consider the simplest purchase, where the business purchases goods for cash. Making cash purchases decreases cash – credit cash. The balancing entry has got to be a debit entry – debiting purchases.

Similarly, decreases in stock are recorded in a separate sales account. The sales account should record only the sale of those goods which were bought with the prime intention of resale. It will never record the disposal of other items.

Sales are a source of revenue and an increase in revenue is recorded as a credit entry. This can be a difficult concept for students. A useful way of learning this is to think of the idea that 'making a sale is a credit to the business'. Another way to view the transaction is by thinking of the simplest sale, where the business sells goods for cash. Making a cash sale increases cash – debit cash. The balancing entry has got to be a credit entry – crediting sales.

Worked example   6.2

Double-entry bookkeeping

Work out the debit and the credit for each of the following transactions:

1 A sale for cash.

2 A purchase on credit terms (payment one month after delivery).

3 A new machine bought for cash.

4 Payment of wages for cash.

5   Owner invests more money in the business by paying money into the bank.

6 Firm borrows money from a lender.

1 Debit cash, credit sales. Cash is an asset (increases) and sales are a source of revenue.

2 Debit purchases, credit trade creditor (the supplier). Purchases are an expense and creditors are an increase in the liability of the firm.

3 Debit machinery, credit cash. Machinery is an asset which is increased by the acquisition. Cash is an asset which is decreased by the transaction amount.

4 Debit wages, credit cash. Wages is an expense and cash is an asset which is decreased by the amount of the transaction.

5 Debit cash at bank, credit owner's capital. The asset cash at bank is increased whilst the liability of the firm to the owner is increased.

6 Debit cash at bank, credit lender. The asset cash at bank is increased whilst the liability of the firm to the lender is recognised.

---

8   The trial balance

trial balance
A list of account balances in a double-entry accounting system.

Periodically, and certainly before the annual financial statements are prepared, a **trial balance** is drawn up from the nominal ledger. This is a list of all the nominal ledger balances. For example, if we look at the creditors account, the balance will be calculated by taking the total of invoices received from suppliers and deducting from this figure the total of the credit notes for purchases returns plus the total cash paid by suppliers. The balance represents the liability (money owed) of the organisation to the supplier.

If the balances comply with the rules of double-entry bookkeeping, the trial balance should balance because each transaction is recorded throughout the accounting period by at least two accounting entries of equal value. This is very similar to how the accounting equation was seen to balance in chapter 5.

The trial balance is not part of the double-entry system. It is only a summary sheet which checks the arithmetical accuracy of the ledger.

Worked example   6.3

T. Smith
Trial balance as at 31 December 200X

	£	£
Sales		70,000
Purchases	26,000	
Rent	8,000	
Sundry expenses	7,000	
Loan interest	2,000	
Debtors	2,000	
Cash	22,000	
Buildings	10,000	
Fixtures and Fittings	36,000	
Loan		20,000
Creditors		3,000
Capital		20,000
	113,000	113,000

The trial balance is used as a basis for the preparation of the financial accounts.

- The profit and loss account.
- The balance sheet.

Test *yourself*   6.5

(a) Identify FOUR period end adjustments that might be authorised in the journal.

(b) Explain, briefly, why a trial balance should balance?

Summary

- Business transactions are nearly always recorded on documents which are the source of the information in the accounts. The information is copied from source documents into books of prime entry. These books perform the key roles of not only being the being the source of all accounting entries but also give authority to those entries.

- The books of prime entry are linked to recording business transactions. The sales day book records all the sales invoices which a business has sent out to its customers. Goods returned by the customer are recorded in the sales returns day book. The purchases day book contains information about the purchases made by an organisation while the goods returned back to a supplier are recorded in the purchase returns day book. The cash book records cash movements in and out of the business.

- For accounting purposes cash includes cheques and bank transactions, coins, bank-notes, cheques, direct debits, and credit transfers and bankers drafts.

- The petty cash book is a book for recording small value payments. The Journal is the book used to make entries into the ledger that cannot be made through the other books of prime entry.

- The ledger records all the accounts of the business. There are the personal accounts of the customers and suppliers which are kept in sales or debtors ledger and the purchases or creditors ledger respectively. These ledgers contain an account or record for each customer and supplier.

- Impersonal accounts record sales, purchases, wages, depreciation, stocks, fixed assets, capital and liabilities, etc. These accounts are all kept in the nominal ledger. The accounts in the nominal ledger are used for preparing the profit and loss account and balance sheet.

- The trial balance is a list of balances on the accounts included in the ledger. The balances show the period end position on each account. For example, it will show how much customers owe a business or how much the business owes its supplier or how much cash we have at the bank, etc. The trial balance totals should be equal as each transaction is recorded throughout the accounting period by at least two accounting entries of equal value.

7 Preparing profit and loss accounts and balance sheets

Introduction

This chapter consolidates much of the coverage of Part 2, bringing together the content and purpose of financial statements. The chapter explains how financial statements are constructed from a trial balance and demonstrates how the trial balance will have to allow for year-end adjustments, including cost of goods sold, accruals, prepayments, depreciation, bad debts and provision for doubtful debts. It is useful to classify the items in the trial balance in terms of those that can be identified as profit and loss account items (revenues and expenses) and balance sheet items (assets, liabilities and capital). The chapter explains how to construct a profit and loss account and identify the gross profit and the net profit. Balance sheets are also constructed and list fixed assets, current assets, current liabilities and long term liabilities. The remainder of the balance sheet focuses on the capital of the owner.

1 The trial balance

nominal ledger
A record of the revenues and expenditures, liabilities and assets classified by their nature, e.g. sales, rates, wages, electricity. Sometimes called impersonal accounts.

Before the annual financial statements are prepared, a trial balance is drawn up from the **nominal ledger**. This is simply a list of all the nominal ledger balances. For example, if we look at the creditors account for a business, the balance will be calculated by taking the total of invoices received from suppliers and deducting from this figure the total of the credit notes for purchases returns plus the total cash paid by suppliers. The balance represents the liability (money owed) of the business to the supplier.

As we saw in chapter 6, if the balances comply with the rules of double-entry bookkeeping, the trial balance totals should be equal because each transaction has been recorded throughout the accounting period by at least two accounting entries of equal value.

Worked example   7.1

J. Brown Trial Balance as at 30 June 200X	£	£
Sales		70,000
Purchases	26,000	
Rent	8,000	
Sundry expenses	7,000	
Loan interest	2,000	
Debtors	2,000	
Cash	12,000	
Buildings	12,000	
Fixtures and fittings	36,000	
Loan		12,000
Profits brought forward from previous years		8,000
Creditors		3,000
Drawings	8,000	
Capital		20,000
	113,000	113,000

Students should be familiar by now with all the items in the above trial balance except for drawings and profit brought forward from previous years. **Drawings** represent monies or goods taken out of the business by the owner. These monies are for the owner's private use and are not expenses of the business so they are never recorded in the profit and loss account. Drawings represent a reduction in the funds the owner has invested in the business and are a reduction of the owner's capital and so are recorded in the balance sheet. Profit brought forward (b/f) from previous years represents the profits retained in the business; they are also called retained profits or reserves.

The trial balance is used as a basis for the preparation of the financial accounts.

drawings
Monies or goods taken out of the business by the owner for private use.

Test yourself   7.1

(a) What do you understand by the term trial balance?

(b) What does the term 'drawings' refer to?

2   Preparing a profit and loss account

The starting point in producing the profit and loss account is the trial balance. Assuming there are no year-end adjustments, the first step is to decide whether items in the trial balance should be included in the profit and loss account or the balance sheet. You will recall from chapter 4 that revenues and expenses are profit and loss items,

Worked example   7.2

J. Brown Trial Balance as at 30 June 200X			Profit and Loss	Balance Sheet
	£	£	£	£
Sales		70,000	70,000	
Purchases	26,000		26,000	
Rent	8,000		8,000	
Sundry expenses	7,000		7,000	
Loan interest	2,000		2,000	
Debtors	2,000			2,000
Cash	12,000			12,000
Buildings	12,000			12,000
Fixtures	36,000			36,000
Loan		12,000		12,000
Profits b/f		8,000		8,000
Creditors		3,000		3,000
Drawings	8,000	20,000		8,000
Capital				20,000
	113,000	113,000		

whilst assets, capital and liabilities are balance sheet items. Thus we can classify the trial balance items as shown in worked example 7.2. This trial balance lists all the items very neatly in terms of grouping profit and loss and balance sheet together. In reality, the trial balance items are likely to be mixed up so you must be confident that you can classify each item as to which financial statement it is entered in.

Worked example   7.3

J Brown Profit and Loss Account for the year ended 30 June 200X		
	£	£
Sales		70,000
Less Cost of sales		26,000
Gross profit		44,000
Expenses		
Rent	8,000	
Sundry expenses	7,000	
Loan interest	2,000	
		17,000
Net Profit		27,000

Worked example (continued)   7.3

- Sales represent the revenue from sales during the year.
- Gross profit represents sales revenue less cost of sales (Chapter 5).
- Net profit is gross profit minus the expenses of running the business.

3   Preparing the balance sheet

Worked example   7.4

J Brown
Balance Sheet as at 30 June 200X

	£	£	£
Fixed assets			
Buildings			12,000
Fixtures and fittings			36,000
			48,000
Current assets			
Debtors	2,000		
Cash	12,000	14,000	
Less **Current liabilities**			
Creditors		3,000	
Net current assets (working capital)			11,000
			59,000
Less **Long-term liabilities**			
Loan			12,000
Total Net Assets			47,000
Capital			
Owner's capital			20,000
Profits brought forward			8,000
Profit for year			27,000
			55,000
Less Drawings			8,000
Owner's Funds			47,000

The term 'net' is used in the balance sheet. This is the figure obtained if the total of one set of items is deducted from another set of items in the balance sheet. For example, net current assets (£11,000) is obtained by taking the total current assets (£14,000) and deducting the total current liabilities (£3,000)

There is no one way to lay out a balance sheet but the following are the key headings in the order they are found on a balance sheet:

- Fixed assets.
- Current assets.
- Current liabilities.
- Long-term liabilities.
- Capital.

The balance sheet should identify a sub-total for each of the above key items.

The term net current assets is a key figure on a balance sheet as it represents the **working capital** of the business. This is usually defined as current assets (stocks, debtors and cash) less current liabilities (creditors). Thus working capital represents the net investment in short-term assets. Such assets are continually flowing into and out of the business, and are essential to the day-to-day operations of the business. The importance of working capital is discussed further in chapter 9. For the present it is important to remember how it is calculated and shown on the balance sheet.

Total **net assets** (£47,000) is the figure obtained when a total is obtained by adding together the total fixed assets (£48,000) and the net current assets (£11,000) and deducting the long term liabilities (£12,000). In effect this figure represents the excess of the book value of all the assets of the business over the total external liabilities of the business.

The **owner's funds** is the total of the original capital invested by the owner in the business, plus any retained profits or reserves from previous years, plus this year's profits less any drawings made by the owner during the year.

The two totals – the owner's funds and total net assets – are equal; the balance sheet 'balances' for the same reasons explained in chapter 4 on the accounting equation.

working capital
The capital available for conducting the day to day operations of an organisation; normally the excess of current assets over current liabilities.

net assets
The excess of book value of assets over liabilities, including loan capital.

owners' funds
The total of the original capital invested by the owner in the business, plus any retained profits or reserves from previous years, plus this year's profits less any drawings made by the owner during the year.

Test *yourself*   7.2

(a) List THREE items in a trial balance which go into the balance sheet.

(b) What is the difference between net current assets and net assets?

4   Year-end adjustments

Earlier chapters have explained the need to make adjustments to accounting records prior to the preparation of period-end financial statements. This is because it is extremely unusual for the detail in the accounting records to mirror exactly the financial activity undertaken by an organisation in a financial period. A simple reason will be the time-lag between when a business activity occurs and the physical recording of the transaction in the accounting records.

Thus when a trial balance is produced it is simply a list of all the nominal ledger balances. These balances are before the year-end adjustments are made. Thus the balances need to be adjusted, where appropriate, so that the correct figures can be included in the profit and loss account and balance sheet.

A summary of the impact of the adjustments is provided in Table 7.1.

Year-end Adjustment	Definition	Impact on Profit and Loss Account	Impact on the Balance Sheet
Stocks	Finished goods bought or manufactured for resale.	Cost of sales as calculated below is included. Opening Stock + Purchases − *Closing stock* = Cost of sales	The closing stock is shown in the as a current asset.
Accruals or expenses owing	The cash payment has been made after the benefit has been received.	The relevant expense figure is increased by the amount of the accrual.	Show the amount of the accrual as a current liability on the balance sheet.
Prepayments or payments in advance	The cash payment has been made before the benefit has been received.	The relevant expense figure is decreased by the amount of the prepayment.	Show the amount of the prepayment as a current asset on the balance sheet.
Bad debts	An actual debt which is considered not to be collectable.	The business will accumulate all bad debts to a bad debts expense account during the financial year. This is the figure shown in the trial balance and is charged to the profit and loss account.	The individual debtors' balances will have been reduced throughout the year. There is no need to adjust the Debtors figure as shown in the trial balance.
Provision for doubtful debts	This is an estimate of the proportion of the year-end debtors which will not be paid.	The difference between last year's provision as shown in the trial balance and the provision for this year is included.	Last year's provision is removed and replaced by the provision for this year as calculated at the year end. This is shown as a deduction from the debtors in the balance sheet.
Provision for depreciation	The internal charge a business makes for the use and deterioration of fixed assets.	This year's annual depreciation is charged as an expense.	The fixed assets are shown as follows: (Cost of fixed asset − Cumulative depreciation) = Net book value

Table 7.1 Adjustments

Test *yourself*   7.3

(a) Describe how fixed assets are shown in a balance sheet.

(b) Describe how an accrual is recorded in a balance sheet.

5   Preparing annual financial statements

Worked example   7.5

Trial balance of P. Bronze as at 31 December 200X	£	£
Capital at 1 January		120,000
Premises at cost	100,000	
Provision for depreciation		30,000
Opening stock at 1 January	110,500	
Purchases	140,000	
Sales		315,600
Salaries	79,000	
Loan interest	2,000	
Office expenses	11,100	
Debtors	30,600	
Creditors		50,800
Long-term loan – 10%		15,000
Bank	40,200	
Cash	5,000	
Bad debts	2,000	
Drawings	11,000	
	£531,400	£531,400

The year-end adjustments which have to be allowed for in the profit and loss account and the balance sheet are as follows:

- Closing stock as at 31 December is valued at £120,500.
- Expenses accrued at 31 December were: salaries £700; office expenses £300.
- Prepaid expenses at the 31 December were: loan interest £500.
- Depreciation is to be charged on premises at 5% of cost.
- A provision for doubtful debts is to be created equal to 5% of debtors.

Worked example *(continued)*   7.5

Step 1   Classify the trial balance items

P. Bronze Trial Balance as at 31 December			Profit and Loss Item	Balance Sheet Item
	£	£	£	£
Capital at 1 January		120,000		120,000
Premises at cost	100,000			100,000
Provision for depreciation		30,000		30,000
Opening stock	110,500		110,500	110,500
Purchases	140,000		140,000	140,000
Sales		315,600	315,600	
Salaries	79,000		79,000	
Loan interest	2,000		2,000	
Office expenses	11,100		11,100	
Debtors	30,600			30,600
Creditors		50,800		50,800
Long-term loan – 10%		15,000	15,000	15,000
Bank	40,200			40,200
Cash	5,000			5,000
Bad debts	2,000		2,000	
Drawings	11,000			11,000
	531,400	531,400		

Step 2   Prepare the profit and loss account

Profit and loss account
for the year ended 31 December 20XX

	£	£	£
Sales			315,600
Opening stock		110,500	
Add Purchases		140,000	
		250,500	
Less Closing stock		120,500	
Cost of sales			130,000
Gross Profit			185,600
Less: Other expenses			
Salaries	79,000		
+ Accrual	+700	79,700	

Worked example (continued)   7.5

Office expenses	11,100	
+ Accrual	+300	11,400
Loan interest	2,000	
− Prepayment	−500	1,500
Depreciation (5% × £100,000)		5,000
Bad debts		2,000
Provision for doubtful debts (5% × £30,600)		1,530
Total expenses		101,130
Net Profit		84,470

Notes:

- The accruals increase the expenditure for the year.
- The prepayments reduce the expenditure for the year.
- The depreciation expense is the charge for the year.
- The bad debts expense is the actual bad debts written off during the year.
- The provision for bad debts is an estimate of the year end debtors who are unlikely to pay.
- The net profit is the link to the balance sheet as it increases the owner's funds.

Step 3   Prepare the balance sheet

Balance Sheet as at 31 December 200X			
	£	£	£
Fixed assets	Historic Cost	Cumulative Depreciation	Net Book Value
Premises	100,000	35,000	65,000
Current assets			
Closing stock		120,500	
Prepayment – Loan interest		500	
Debtors	30,600		
Less Provision for bad debts	1,530	29,070	
Bank		40,200	
Cash		5,000	
		195,270	
Less Current liabilities			
Creditors	50,800		
Accruals (£700 + £300)	1,000	51,800	
Net current assets			143,470
Less **Long-term Liabilities**			
Long-term loan			15,000
Total net assets			193,470
Capital			
Opening balance			120,000
Net profit for year			84,470
			204,470
Less Drawings			11,000
			193,470

Worked example *(continued)*   7.5

Notes:

● The fixed assets are shown at their net book value.

● The prepaid loan interest is shown as a current asset.

● The debtors are shown at the figure in the trial balance less the provision for bad debts.

● The accruals for salaries and office expenses are shown as a current liability.

● The net profit for the year increases the owner's funds.

● The drawings reduce the owner's funds.

Test *yourself*   7.3

(a) Where does the net profit appear in the balance sheet?

(b) Describe how a prepayment is recorded in both the profit and loss account and balance sheet.

(c) Describe the impact of a provision for doubtful debts on the financial statements.

(d) Explain why a prepayment is shown as a current asset in the balance sheet?

Putting the case   7.1

 Jane cannot understand why her capital and reserves are not recorded in the balance sheet as her assets. You are required to provide an answer.

The first point to make is that a business's accountant is interested in recording in the accounting records of a business, including the balance sheet, only the effect of various transactions on the business. The business's accountant is *not* interested in recording the impact of the transactions on the owners' private wealth. This division between private accounting records of owners and the accounting records of a business is based upon the entity concept. Thus no matter whether the business is a sole trader, a partnership or a limited company the business is considered to be a completely separate entity from the owner(s). Thus accounting records record the financial performance and position of a business.

This begins to explain why Jane's initial capital investment and subsequent retained profits or reserves are not shown as assets of the business. Capital and reserves represent a source of business finance provided by the owners to purchase assets for use in the business. In effect the business 'owes' the owner(s), in this case Jane, their original capital investment plus any accumulated reserves and as such are not listed as assets of the business on the balance sheet. The sum of capital plus reserves is called the owners interest or shareholders funds and represents the amount that should be left (in theory) when all the business assets are sold and any external liabilities such as long-term loans are repaid.

6   The accounts of not-for-profit organisations

Many organisations do not receive their income from sales income and are not created to generate a profit. These not-for-profit organisations are established with an objective of being non-profit-making. The heading covers a multitude of bodies including:

- Central government departments, including the Treasury, The Home Office, etc.
- Public corporations such as the British Broadcasting Corporation (BBC).
- Local authorities, including county, borough, district and parish councils.
- Health Authorities under the control of the Department of Health.
- Charities and voluntary bodies such as Oxfam, Age Concern.
- Clubs and societies, for example, a local swimming club or an amateur dramatic group.

These bodies are set up to provide services without making a profit. This is not to say that such organisations are not involved in some trading activities, but making a profit is not the driving force of their activity. Depending on their nature, size and sources of funding the accounting records of such bodies will vary. Many bodies maintain full accounting records, in which case the preparation of their accounts follow the normal process from trial balance to final accounts, making the necessary adjustments for accruals, prepayments and the like.

Some, like local authorities, universities and other government-funded bodies, follow accounting procedures which, although similar to those used in the private sector, also reflect the specialist nature of such bodies.

The accounting requirements of many of these bodies are determined by their legal form. For example a charity has to comply with the Charities Act and produces accruals-based accounts. Contrast this with smaller not-for-profit organisations such as clubs and societies which are run so that their members can undertake activities such as swimming, rambling, chess, amateur dramatics, etc. They are unlikely to draw up trading and profit and loss accounts and balance sheets.

The nature and accounting arrangements of not-for-profit bodies are so diverse and specialist that they are beyond the scope of this Study Text. However, we will focus on the accounts of clubs and societies which will allow managers to be introduced to receipts and payments accounts and income and expenditure accounts.

6.1   The income of clubs and societies

The sources of income for club and societies include the following:

- *Entrance fees or joining fees*. Entrance fees are charges made to new applicants on their admission as members.
- *Subscriptions*. These are the annual amounts receivable from members
- *Life membership fees*. A member pays a lump sum in return for membership for the rest of his or her life.
- Charges made to members for the use of club facilities.
- *Surpluses from trading activities* such as a licensed bar or car boot sale.

The accounts used to record the financial transactions of a clubs and societies are known as receipts and payments accounts or income and expenditure accounts.

6.2 The receipts and payments account

The receipts and payments account is a report of the cash transactions during a single financial period. It is used when it is not considered appropriate to distinguish between capital and revenue transactions or to include accruals. This means that there are no adjustments, including depreciation, doubtful debts, expenses owing, prepayments, etc.

In effect, the receipts and payments account is a summary of the cash transactions. The receipts and payments account records cash coming in, the receipts, and cash going out, the payments. The difference between the two sides represents the cash balance at the end of the accounting period.

Worked example 7.6 shows a receipts and payments account.

Worked example   7.6

The Merry Players Amateur Dramatics Club		
Receipts and Payments Account for the year ended 31 December 200X		
Receipts	£	£
Bank Balance at 1 January 200X		5,236
Subscriptions received		4,740
Rent received		114
Total receipts		10,090
Payments		
Caretaker's wages	2,728	
Costume expenses	296	
Purchase of lighting	3,000	
Committee expenses	750	
Printing and stationery	436	
Total payments		7,210
Bank balance at 31 December 200X		2,880

6.3 Review of receipts and payment account

Although relatively easy to produce, the receipts and payments account does not provide a comprehensive picture of the financial position of the club or society, because:

1 There is no distinction between capital and revenue. In the example above, the cash paid includes both the purchase price of a fixed asset and the wages paid to the caretaker.
2 Depreciation of fixed assets is not provided for; in the above example the full cost of the lighting is recorded in one year's accounts.
3 Accruals and prepayments are not included so members cannot determine whether the club has made a surplus or a deficit. For example, the members'

subscriptions included as receipts do not make adjustments for any subscriptions which are outstanding or paid in advance.

4 The assets and liabilities of the club are not disclosed. In the above the asset cash is recorded at the beginning and end of year but no allowance is made for assets purchased in earlier years or creditors and debtors at the end of the year.

5 No balance sheet is produced.

These weaknesses can be illustrated by reference to the above example.

In short, the receipts and payments account is simply to be regarded as the cash summary.

6.4   An income and expenditure account

This is a financial statement for not-for-profit entities such as clubs, associations and societies. It shows the surplus/deficit, i.e. the surplus of income over expenditure or vice versa, for a period, and is drawn up on the same accruals basis as a profit and loss account.

Rather than using the term profit and loss account the financial statement is normally called the income and expenditure account to emphasise that the main object of a club is to provide a service to its members rather than to make a profit. For the same reason, the balance at the end of the income and expenditure account is the surplus of income over expenditure, or excess of expenditure over income, for the period rather than profit or loss. The income and expenditure account is prepared following the same accounting rules as for trading and profit and loss accounts.

The club will also produce a balance sheet in which the capital account may be called the accumulated fund. Any surplus for the year is added to the club fund account exactly as a profit would be added to capital account in the balance sheet of a sole trader or small business.

The differences in the terminology used are as follows:

Profit-making business	Not-for-profit organisation
Trading and profit and loss account	Income and expenditure account
Net profit	Surplus of income over expenditure
Net loss	Excess of expenditure over income
Capital	Accumulated fund

Producing an income and expenditure account

The receipts and payments (or cash) account provides the basic information for producing the income and expenditure account. The receipts and payments account reveals when money was received or paid out. However, this does not give the organisation real information on its financial position because payments may be received or made in advance or in arrears.

When an organisation owns assets and has liabilities, the receipts and payments account is not an informative way of presenting the annual accounts. Other than the cash received and paid out, it shows only cash balances and omits other assets and liabilities. The income and expenditure account records all the transactions during the period whether or not money changed hands during the period, i.e. the accruals concept is applied. This will allow the organisation to see whether its capital has increased during the period. It also allows the organisation to produce a balance sheet.

For examination purposes it is useful to know about receipts and payments accounts because a question will often contain such a statement, along with other information, and ask for it to be converted into an income and expenditure account and balance sheet.

6.5 Subscription income

One of the major sources of income for clubs and societies are members' subscriptions. The process of working out the actual subscription income to be included in the income and expenditure account is complicated by the fact that subscriptions can be paid in advance or in arrears at both the beginning of the period and the end. It is important that students have their wits about them when they are working out the figure for subscriptions.

Students should remember that subscriptions owing at the beginning and end of the year are current assets of the organisation. In effect the members whose subscriptions are outstanding are debtors of the club or society. On the other hand, subscriptions paid in advance at the beginning and end of the period are current liabilities of the club. In effect, the members who pay there subscriptions before they are due are creditors of the club or society.

Another point is that subscriptions in arrears may never be received. In accordance with the prudence concept subscriptions in arrears should be reviewed regularly and those that have been outstanding for a long time should be written off as irrecoverable. If this is not done the organisations assets will be overvalued. In practice many clubs and societies follow the prudence concept fully and ignore subscriptions in arrears for final accounts purposes. The examination question should make clear exactly what the club's policy is in regard to such subscriptions. If in doubt, make an assumption and state it – for example, that all of the subscriptions in arrears will be collected and so included in the final accounts.

6.6 Calculating the subscription income for a period

To calculate the subscription income to be included in the income and expenditure account students will have to allow for the fact that subscriptions can be in advance or in arrears at both the beginning of the period and the end. This can be allowed for by adjusting the actual cash received for subscriptions. This is done as follows:
Cash received from members
Less (Subscriptions in arrears at beginning of year)
Plus Subscriptions in arrears at end of year
Plus Subscriptions in advance at beginning of year
Less (Subscriptions in advance at end of year)
Subscriptions to be included in income and expenditure account

These adjustments are illustrated in the Worked example 7.7.

Worked example   7.7

The South Bridge golf and country club charges its members an annual subscription of £1000, payable annually in advance. At 1 January 200X the club had received subscriptions in advance for the year for 13 members. Two members had failed to pay their subscription for the previous year at this date, but both did so early in 200X. The total amount received from members during 200X was £396,000 31 December 200X. At subscriptions received in advance for the next year amounted to £18,000 and three members failed to pay their 200X subscriptions. All three had promised to pay, and the committee had decided to prepare the club's accounts on the basis that they would in fact be received.

How much can be credited to the club's income and expenditure for subscriptions for the year 200X?

		£
Cash received from members		396,000
Less Subscriptions in arrears at beginning of year i.e. relate to previous year	2 members @ £1000	(2000)
Plus Subscriptions in arrears at end of year, i.e. due for 200X but not paid.	3 members @ £1000	3000
Plus Subscriptions in advance at beginning of year i.e. relate to 200X	13 members @ £1000	13,000
Less Subscriptions in advance at end of year, i.e. relate to following year.	18 members @ £1000	(18,000)
Subscriptions to be included in income and expenditure account for 200X		392,000

6.7 Other income

If the club operates a bar or similar activity, it may be necessary to prepare a trading account to calculate the profit or loss arising on that activity.

For other one-off activities such as a Christmas dance or concert where the club has income, perhaps from sales of tickets and related expenditure it is better to show the net result. This will clarify whether or not the activity covered its costs, rather than to include the receipts along with the income and the costs among the other items of expenditure.

6.8 Summary

Clubs' and societies' accounts normally consist of an income and expenditure account, which corresponds to the profit and loss account of a trading concern, and a balance sheet. A possible examination question is the preparation of the accounts from a receipts and payments account, which is a statement in the form of a summary of cash transactions.

The Worked example 7.8 illustrates the preparation and format of an income and expenditure account.

Worked example   7.8

The Hazlemere Sports and Social Club prepare its accounts to 31 December. The clubs assets and liabilities as 1 January 200X were as follows:

	£	£
Fixtures and fittings		68,000
Bar stocks		1,200
Rent prepaid		2,300
Balance at bank		2,200
		73,700
Less creditors		
Bar supplies	1,100	
Light and heat	500	1,600
Accumulated fund as at 1 January 200X		72,100

The club secretary has prepared a summary of the club's receipts and payments for the year to 31 December 200X:

Receipts	£	Payments	£
Bank balance at 1 January 200X	2,200	Bar purchases	27,500
Members' subscriptions	32,000	Heat and light	2,600
Loan	20,000	Rent	10,000
Bar sales	44,000	Manager's wages	12,000
Christmas dance receipts	7,500	General expenses	8,500
Total receipts	105,700	New pool tables	7,500
		Christmas dance expenses	5,100
		Loan interest	2,000
		Bar person's wages	8,000
		Bar expenses	5,000
		Total payments	88,200
		Bank balance	
		at 31 December 200X	17,500
	105,700		105,700

Worked example (continued)   7.8

The following information is also available:

1 At 31 December 200X rent prepaid was £3000 and electricity outstanding was £600.

2 The bar stocks at 31 December 200X were valued at £1400.

3 The club has decided to depreciate all fixed assets held at the year end by 10%.

4 Subscriptions owing by members on 31 December 200X amounted to £4550.

You are required to prepare the Club's income and expenditure account for the year to 31 December 200X and a balance sheet at that date. The club has asked that you prepare a separate account to show the profit or loss made by the bar.

Answer

A separate trading account to arrive at the profit from the bar is shown below. The profit is shown in the club's income and expenditure account. The separate trading account allows club members to see the financial results of operating the bar.

The Hazlemere Sports and Social Club
Bar Trading Account for year ended 31 December 200X

	£	£
Bar sales		44,000
Bar stock at 1 January 200X	1,200	
Add purchases (27,500 − 1100)*	26,400	
	27,600	
Less stock at 31 December 200X	1,400	
Less cost of sales		26,200
Gross profit		17,800
Less bar person's wages	8,000	
Bar expenses	5,000	13,000
Net profit to income and expenditure account		4,800

*Note the purchases are reduced by the creditor for bar purchases unpaid at 1 January 200X.

The Hazlemere Sports and Social Club
Income and Expenditure Account for year ended 31 December 200X

	£	£
Income		
Subscriptions for 200X (32,000 + 4550)		36,550
Profit from the bar		4,800
Christmas dance		
Receipts	7,500	
Less Expenses	5,100	2,400
Total income		43,750

Worked example *(continued)* 7.8

Expenditure

Heat and light (2600 − 500 + 600)	2,700	
Rent (10000 + 2300 − 3000)	9,300	
Loan interest	2,000	
General expenses	8,500	
Depreciation (68,000 + 7500) × 10%	7,550	
Manager's wages	<u>12,000</u>	<u>42,050</u>
Surplus of income over expenditure		<u>1,700</u>

Working notes to the income and expenditure account

1   The subscriptions of some members are arrears at the end of the year. The £4550 has to be added to the subscriptions received to determine the subscription income for the year.

2   For one-off activities such as the Christmas dance where the club has income, perhaps from sales of tickets, and related expenditure it is better to show the net result. This will clarify whether or not the activity covered its costs, rather than include the receipts along with the income and the costs among the other items of expenditure.

3   The heat and light figure of £2600 represents the cash paid, but £500 was a creditor for the previous year whilst £600 is owing for electricity at the end of 200X.

4   The rent figure of £10,000 has to be increased by the prepayment of £2300 at the beginning of the year and reduced by the prepayment of £3000 at the end of the year.

5   The depreciation is calculated at 10% on the fixed assets at the beginning of the year plus the fixed assets purchased during 200X.

Worked example (continued)   7.8

The Hazlemere Sports and Social Club
Balance Sheet as at 31 December 200X

Fixed Assets	Cost	Accumulated Depreciation	Net Book Value
	£	£	£
Fixtures and fittings	75,500	7,550	67,950
Current assets			
Bar stocks	1,400		
Rent, prepaid	3,000		
Subscriptions owing	4,550		
Bank	17,500	26,450	
Less Current liabilities			
Creditors — electricity		600	
Working capital			25,850
			93,800
Accumulated fund			
Balance at 1 January 200X			72,100
Add surplus for year			1,700
			73,800
Loan			20,000
			93,800

Working notes to balance sheet

1 The prepaid rent is shown as a current asset.
2 The subscriptions owing by the members at the end of 200X are a current asset.
3 The electricity owing is a current liability.
4 The surplus for the year is added to the accumulated fund.

Summary

- It is important to remember the link between the accounting equation and the financial statements.
- The financial statements are constructed from a trial balance which must allow for year-end adjustments for cost of goods sold, accruals, prepayments, depreciation, bad debts and provision for doubtful debts.
- A starting point is to classify the items in the trial balance in terms of those that can be identified as profit and loss account items (revenues and expenses) and balance sheet items (assets, liabilities and capital).
- The profit and loss account identifies the gross profit and the net profit.
- The first half of a balance sheet lists the fixed assets, current assets, current liabilities and long-term liabilities.
- The second half of the balance sheet lists the capital of the owner.

Computerised accounting systems

8

Introduction

Computerised accounting systems can offer significant benefits over manual systems because they can process inputs faster and can generate more reports for managers. The only difference between manual accounting records and the software packages is that the various bits of information, for example the ledgers, are held in computer files.

The chapter introduces some applications software; and the use of spreadsheets and databases is discussed in detail. The chapter concludes by introducing the topic of security in computerised accounting systems.

1 Computer applications in accounting

An accountant's main role is to provide information to meet user needs as well as regulatory requirements. Once the format and content are agreed, accounting reports and the financial statements can be prepared automatically using appropriate computer packages.

Here are some reasons why computers are used to produce accounting information:

- Business transactions and the accounting information produced from the transactions are recurring and repetitive in nature and are thus well suited to computerisation.
- Progressively standardised financial statements, including profit and loss accounts and balance sheets, lend themselves to being produced on a computer-based system.
- Legislation and accounting standards have increased the amount of financial information that has to be produced. Accountants have to produce more information which can be more efficiently produced using a computer and accounting software.
- The computer can produce cost savings for the business: for example, using accounting software allows accounting work previously carried out by qualified staff to be produced by less costly technicians.
- The timeliness of information is one of the essential characteristics of accounting information. Computers can produce this information promptly and at a relatively low cost.

● The accounting reports produced on a computer can have their content and presentation tailored to user needs.

1.1 Accounting software packages

accounting software packages
Collections of software or computer programs designed for computer hardware, the physical equipment that makes up the computer, to undertake specific accounting tasks.

It is important to remember that the same principles of manual accounting systems apply to computerised accounting systems. The terminology and concepts used are the same as in manual accounting records.

Accounting packages are merely collections of software or computer programs designed to undertake specific accounting tasks. The accounting software includes packages for:

● Maintaining ledger accounts including nominal ledger, purchase ledger, sales ledger, invoicing, VAT calculations and returns.
● Accounts production including nominal ledger, trial balance, final accounts and bank reconciliations.
● Stock control including purchases, sales, stock movements, stock pricing, etc.
● Financial planning and budgeting including the preparation and control of sales, production and cash budgets.
● Tax packages for personal and business tax calculations.

The only difference between manual accounting records and software packages is that the information (for example, the ledgers) is held electronically. The information held by the computer is expressed in the form of codes. Thus, the nominal ledger accounts are coded individually. For example, every account in the sales ledger and purchase ledger is given a unique code number for each debtor and creditor.

The code numbers allow the individual accounting entries, which keep the accounting equation in balance, to be made in the relevant accounts. Thus a purchase of stock for cash can be recorded in the purchases account and the cash account by using the correct code numbers. However, the accounting packages offer one great benefit over the manual system in that the data entered in the ledgers can be analysed in different ways to meet the needs of management. Thus managers might want further information on stock such as stock movements over defined periods, outstanding orders from suppliers, etc. This flexibility in accounting software allows the financial accounting and management information to be generated simultaneously.

1.2 Advantages of accounting packages

The advantages are as follows:

● The packages are frequently menu-driven and very user-friendly. This means that the packages can be used by non-specialists.
● The packages can process large amounts of data quickly.
● Although the packages cannot eliminate human error, there is less scope for error than in manual systems.

- One entry can update several accounting records so avoiding duplication of effort.
- The packages can rapidly analyse data to produce control information for managers.
- Many of the packages have a context-sensitive on-screen help facility.
- The packages include security systems which restrict use of the packages to nominated users. This helps to prevent fraud in accounting systems.
- The packages can produce a series of exception reports to highlight key areas, for example, credit limits listings and aged outstanding debtors.

1.3 Disadvantages of accounting packages

The disadvantages are:

- Training staff to use the packages can be costly.
- The accounting packages frequently require the use of a coding system which has to be created and installed.
- Employees may resist the introduction of the system because it involves change and could threaten their job security.

Test *yourself* 8.1

(a) Identify THREE reasons why accounting lends itself to the use of computers.

(b) List THREE advantages of using accounting software.

2 Ledger accounts software

This is software used to record daily financial transactions and prepare financial statements. An accounting package will comprise several modules, or programs, dealing with a particular part of the accounting system in the business. It is possible to purchase a standalone module which is a useful option for small businesses which can make do with one or two modules. Usually the package will contain several modules which together form a suite. It will also usually contain a report generator which allows information from the system to be output in a format designed by users to meet their specific needs. The software suite will usually have the following modules:

- Sales ledger.
- Invoicing.
- Nominal ledger.
- Stock control.
- Purchase ledger.
- Cash book.
- Payroll.
- Fixed asset register.
- Report generator.

2.1   Integrated accounting software

integrated accounting software

A set of accounting packages where each separate module is linked with others in the suite.

Integrated accounting software comprises a suite of accounting packages where each separate module is linked with others in the suite. This means that data input needs only one entry into one of the modules for its effect to be recorded automatically in other relevant modules throughout the suite. This is illustrated by the following example and Figure 8.1.

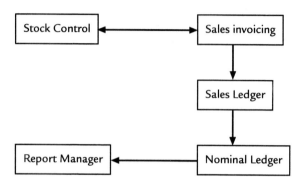

Figure 8.1 Integrated accounting software

- An input into the invoicing module authorises the raising of an invoice to a customer and may be automatically linked to –
- The sales ledger which is automatically updated by posting the invoice to the customer's account.
- The stock module automatically updates the stock file.
- The nominal ledger is automatically updated by posting the sale to the sales account.
- The report manager automatically updates the management reports, for example sales analysis by stock item customer.

Linking modules in this way means that data input into one module are transferred automatically to all other relevant modules. This facility increases the efficiency of the accounting system, assists in the reduction of errors and reduces workloads. On the other hand, integrated software requires more computer memory than separate (standalone) systems so there is less space in which to store actual data. Since one program has to do everything, the integrated package will frequently have fewer facilities than a set of specialised standalone modules.

Test *yourself*   8.2

(a) What do you understand by the term integrated packages?

(b) What is a report manger?

2.2 Sales ledger

A computerised sales ledger keeps the sales ledger up to date and produces certain outputs, such as statements of account to be sent to customers at the end of each month, and sales analysis reports. The content of the module can be divided into:

- Standing data.
- Transaction data.
- Output data.

2.3 Standing data

The data held on a sales ledger file consist of records for each customer account. It is known as a master file and is made up of standing data. The data tend to remain the same and change only occasionally. The customer's records will include:

- Customer name.
- Account number.
- Address.
- Telephone and e-mail.
- Ledger account number.
- Customer credit limit.
- Customer account sales analysis code.
- Settlement discount.

standing data
The master file of the records for individual accounts held on a ledger. The data tend to remain the same and change only occasionally.

2.4 Transaction data

Transactions are the inputs that are posted to the sales ledger. A typical list of transactions includes:

- Invoices.
- Credit notes.
- Cash received.
- Discounts.
- Journal entries, for example writing off bad debts.
- The program adjusts brought-forward balances, representing money owed, by adding or deducting the value of transactions inputted.
- The carried-forward balance becomes the new balance recorded on the customers account.

2.5 Output data

The outputs of a sales ledger could include the following:

- Customer record file.
- Customer statements.
- Reminder letters.
- VAT analysis.

output data
The outputs of a computerised ledger system.

- Aged debtors.
- Day book listing.
- Sales analysis reports by product type or customer.
- Sales and marketing information.

2.6 Purchase ledger

A computerised purchase ledger keeps the purchase ledger up to date, and produces various reports.

2.7 Standing data

- Supplier name.
- Account number.
- Address.
- Telephone and e-mail.
- Ledger account number.
- Supplier credit limit.
- Supplier account sales analysis code.
- Settlement discount.

2.8 Transaction data

- Purchases recorded on invoices.
- Returns to suppliers for which credit notes are received.
- Payments to suppliers.
- Invoices.
- Credit notes.
- Cash received.
- Discounts.
- The program adjusts brought-forward balances, representing money owed, by adding or deducting the value of transactions inputted.
- The carried-forward balance becomes the new balance recorded on the suppliers account.

2.9 Output data

The outputs of a purchases ledger include the following:

- Supplier record file.
- VAT analysis.
- Day book listing.
- Aged creditors reports.
- Suppliers account balances.
- Transaction histories.
- Purchases analysis reports by product type or customer.
- Purchasing information for example lead-time.

Test yourself 8.3

(a) What is the difference between standing data, transaction data and output data?

(b) Identify SIX items of output data from a sales ledger.

3 Computerised nominal ledger

The nominal ledger contains the accounts of assets, liabilities, capital, expenses and revenues. The accounts are fairly standard for most businesses and there is normally a standard list supplied with the software.

Sample 8.1 is an extract from a typical list.

Sample Nominal ledger codes 8.1

Fixed Assets	Code	Sales	
Property	00010	Product A	04000
Plant and Machinery	00020	Product B	04001
Office Equipment	00030	Rent income	04901
Furniture and Fittings	00040	Purchases	
Current Assets		Materials purchased	05000
Stock	01001	Discounts taken	05009
Debtors	01101	Opening stock	05200
Prepayments	01103	Closing stock	05201
Bank	01200	Overheads	
Current Liabilities		Wages	07000
Creditors	02100	Staff salaries	07003
Accruals	02109	Electricity	07200
Capital and Reserves		Printing	07500
Owner's Capital	03000	Cleaning	07802
Reserves	03100	Loan interest	07902
		Vehicle depreciation	08000
		Furniture depreciation	08004

This list of nominal ledger accounts is each given a unique computer code. These codes allow associated accounts to be grouped together. These groups can be categorised as follows:

Sales
Purchases   } Profit and loss account categories
Overheads

Fixed assets
Current assets
Current liabilities   } Balance sheet categories
Capital and reserves

Each business will select its own codes reflecting the type of business for its nominal ledger accounts. If the system is integrated, as soon as data are entered into the sales ledger module the relevant nominal ledger accounts will be updated. If the system is not integrated the output from the sales ledger module must be input into the nominal ledger by using journal entries.

3.1 Transaction data

The details required include the following:

- Date.
- Description.
- Amount.
- Account codes.

3.2 Output data

The outputs of a purchases ledger include the following:

- The trial balance.
- Financial statements.
- Listings of individual nominal ledger accounts.

Test *yourself*   8.4

(a) What is the role of a unique computer code in a nominal ledger package?

(b) The nominal ledger contains which types of accounts?

applications software
Computer programs which undertake specific tasks such as payroll or word processing.

4   Applications software

Applications software is a package of computer programs which undertake specific tasks such as payroll and word processing. They are a set of specific programs designed to process a specific application and are usually referred to as a computer package. A selection of the major applications software used by accountants is discussed below.

4.1 Spreadsheets

A spreadsheet helps the user to record, manipulate and analyse data in the form of a matrix. It appears on the computer monitor as a sheet of paper divided into columns and rows like a sheet of accountant's analysis paper. The spreadsheet stores the data on the computer as a large table of 'cells' organised in rows and columns. Each cell can hold text, a number or, most importantly, a formula that calculates a value for the cell from values held in cells elsewhere in the sheet. A key point is that if the numbers in those other cells change, the result displayed in the formula cell also change.

For example, you might want to produce a report containing a table of figures from different regions showing the sales for the last three months. You are preparing to present your report to your senior managers and would like information on, say, the percentage of total monthly sales for each region and figures for the increase, or decrease, of sales over the quarter with an average increase to compare them against.

You could use a spreadsheet application to label a number of rows with the names of the various regions and a set of columns with the months. Data for each month for the region would then be entered in the cell at the intersection of the row and the column. Total sales for each region could be calculated by adding along the rows and displayed in a further column; monthly sales would be column totals displayed in a lower row. Percentage figures and averages could be included in more rows and columns. The spreadsheet could be printed out for the meeting and the whole sheet saved on disk to update later.

Suppose you were at the meeting and someone asked what would happen to the sales figures if we introduced a new discounting structure. With the data held in a spreadsheet it can be a simple matter to change the entries in one or two cells, a row or column. The computer rapidly recalculates all the other values that are derived from them through the formulae that have been entered.

Spreadsheets can be used to create financial models, for example in setting budgets or in decision-making.

4.2 Databases

A database is used for data storage and retrieval. It consists of records which hold the data, for example about product, department, person, in a structured manner. Powerful data manipulation commands enable the records to be searched according to particular criteria. The software that runs the database is called the **database management system (DBMS)**. The data are input, and the DBMS software organises them into the database.

There is no need for different departments to keep different files with duplicated information as the database maintains a unique amount of data.

Databases allow individuals to cross-reference data between files. For example, a sales manager could find out which products are sold in each region to a particular customer. The database system would link all files of the customer across to the regions and then on to the product files to obtain the results. As the data are selected, the

---

spreadsheet
Software which allows data to be entered and stored in a 'grid' format. It provides a means of performing numerical and statistical calculations.

database
Data records held in a structured way which can be searched according to specific criteria.

database management system (DBMS)
The software that runs the database. The data is input, and the DBMS software organises it into the database.

reports can be displayed or printed showing just those parts of the record that are of interest to the manager.

Databases avoid the need to keep and maintain duplicate files across a business and the use of common data avoids conflicts between departments using inconsistent data. A database ensures that a central file is updated with all the latest changes so that everyone who is allowed access to the file sees the same, accurate data. However, the integrity of the database must be preserved. People using a database should not be allowed to alter the data on file as this spoils the database records for other users. Valid alterations will be allowed by authorised individuals to allow the legitimate updating of data on file.

Test *yourself*   8.5

(a) Explain the use of a 'what if' facility in a spreadsheet.

(b) What are TWO benefits of using a computer database?

5   Security and control

Security in computerised accounting systems is concerned with ensuring that access to data is restricted to people who need it to perform their jobs. For example, access to payroll records should be restricted to payroll staff and senior management. This approach is to maintain the privacy of the information. Security can be enhanced by controlling the use of accounting information by requiring users to give passwords or by restricting access to records to an agreed time-slot after which there is automatic logoff.

Another objective of computer security is to prevent fraud. This can be done not only by restricting access to records but also by restricting the ability to change accounting records to nominated employees.

Control can be enhanced if there is a sound system of internal check. This means that there is a division of duties relating to a single accounting transaction among several people. No single person should be responsible for a computing transaction from start to finish. For example, the computerised accounting system in relation to the purchase of goods needs to ensure that different people are responsible for recording different aspects of the transaction. Ordering the goods, recording the receipt of the goods and paying the bill are best recorded by separate individuals. This means not only that errors should be spotted as a matter of course but also that fraud is possible only by collusion.

Finally, losing accounting information can pose a real threat to control in a computerised system. For example, losing a list of trade debtors can be very costly. It might be possible to retrieve the information but this in itself would cost time and money. Thought has to be given to the availability of hard copies of key information and the regular creation of back-up files.

Putting the case 8.1

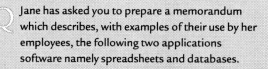

Jane has asked you to prepare a memorandum which describes, with examples of their use by her employees, the following two applications software namely spreadsheets and databases.

A spreadsheet consists of an on-screen worksheet ruled in a two-dimensional grid of columns and rows. It enables the user to perform, easily and quickly, routine calculations on-screen, which would otherwise be done manually or with a calculator.

The worksheet consists of a large number of cells, each cell being the intersection of a column and row. The user can enter text, numbers or formulas in the cells. The formulas will carry out calculations and will recalculate results should the initial data be changed. For example, in a sales budget calculation the selling price and number of units to be sold could be altered and the spreadsheet will produce the new budget.

The spreadsheet can be used by the business manager to prepare budgets, sales forecasts, cash forecasts, to create pro-forma balance sheets and profit and loss accounts, etc. The spreadsheet gives the user the ability to alter a key figure in any of these uses. For example, the cash forecast can be reproduced on the basis of a different debt collection period and/or a creditor payment policy.

A database package, sometimes referred to as a database management system (DBMS), is a computer program which enables a set of records or files to be set up and to be updated at regular intervals.

The files are created by inputting data from which information is obtained. The database is thus a pool of information which may be accessed and used in a variety of ways. The business manager may have a database of customer information which they might search to get results on sales by product type, by geographical area, by type of customer or by a combination of the above.

Summary

- Computerised accounting is the same as manual accounting, but has advantages, in particular, improved speed and efficiency. Computerised systems also enable the user to analyse the data in many different ways, quickly and easily.
- An accounting package consists of a number of 'modules' which perform all the tasks needed to maintain a normal accounting function. These modules may or may not be integrated with each other.
- Coding numbers play a key role in the operation of a computerised system because computers classify accounts by code numbers.
- Applications are packages of computer programs which undertake specific tasks. Examples include spreadsheets which are used to manipulate data, while databases are used for data storage and retrieval.
- With appropriate procedures in place, computerised accounting systems can bring improved confidentiality (for example in the case of sensitive information such as payroll) and can enhance security against error and fraud.

Part Two Practice Questions

2.1 Explain, providing TWO examples, what you understand by claims against a business.

2.2 How would you calculate the cost of sales for an accounting period?

2.3 Identify which of the following are shown under the wrong classification for J. Smith's business:

Assets	Liabilities
Cash in hand	Debtors
Creditors	Bank loan
Loan from A. Jones	Stock of raw materials
Buildings	
Office furniture	
Bank overdraft	

2.4 Fill in the gaps in the following table:

Assets	Liabilities	Capital
£	£	£
56,000	9,800	?
33,600	?	25,000
?	12,600	38,400

2.5 The accounts of the business of T. Judge on 31 January 200X revealed the following: Cash at bank £6,300; Stock £10,800; Debtor A. Cowan £876; Debtor A. Phillips £3,048; Creditor S. Richards £648; Office Furniture £4,320; Creditor P. Fiddler £828 Motor Vehicle £9,360.
Calculate T. Judge's capital as at 31 January 200X.

2.6 During the financial year just ended a business made payments in respect of expenses as follows:

	£
Rent	6,640
Insurance	2,160
Power	3,140

The following year-end adjustments need to be made in respect of the above expenses.

	£
Rent owing	1,603
Insurance prepaid	524
Power owing	820

Show the amount of the expenses to be included in the profit and loss account for the period.

2.7 The following adjustments to expenses have been identified as being required at the end of a financial year: insurance prepaid £2000; petrol owing £2550; rent and rates prepaid £2035; salaries owing £3,050.
Explain how the adjustments would be recorded in the balance sheet as at the end of the financial year.

2.8 The following information in respect of equipment has been extracted from the accounts of a business:

Cost	£125,000
Expected life	5 years
Expected scrap value	£12,500

Using the straight-line method of depreciation produce a table which shows the values of the equipment on the balance sheets over the life of the asset.

2.9 A manufacturing company purchased an assembly machine for £125,000. The machine has an estimated working life of 30,000 hours and an expected scrap value of £5,000. In its first year of use it worked 4,500 hours and in its second year 12,000 hours.
Calculate the depreciation charges for the first and second years of use, and the balance sheet value of the assembly machine at the end of the second year.

Using Financial Information to Manage Business Resources

Contents

Overview

Parts 3 and 4 of the syllabus concentrate on management accounting.

Part 3 focuses on the information managers need about the costs of making their products or providing their services to help them in planning and controlling the use of resources. This includes the planned and actual cost of staff, inventory and buildings as well as raw materials.

This part also helps managers to explain and apply the traditional methods of absorbing overhead to unit costs, distinguish between variable and fixed costs and explain why the difference is important.

Cash, like profit, is the lifeblood of a business and the syllabus requires candidates to describe why cash management is important to a business, and to be able to prepare and interpret a simple cash flow budget.

Learning objectives

After working through this part, you should be able to:

▶ Identify the main elements of the working capital cycle and describe the key factors to be considered when managing each part.

▶ Prepare a cash budget and understand its uses in managing cash flow.

▶ Identify the main ways in which costs may be classified.

▶ Define and explain the importance of the distinctions between direct and indirect costs and fixed and variable costs.

▶ Understand and apply the methods of absorbing overheads into products or departments.

▶ Understand how marginal costing can aid decision-making.

▶ Understand how to calculate and chart the breakeven point.

Financial information for decision-making

Blackstock Ltd is a manufacturing company with several factories located throughout the UK. The information listed below has been produced by the company's management accountants.

The first piece of information, which relates to the previous financial year, has been collected in respect of the working capital of the company.

	Previous Financial Year
Trade debtors collection period	44 days
Trade creditors payment period	53 days
Raw materials turnover period	90 days
Production period	29 days
Finished stock turnover period	68 days

Working Capital	£
Current assets	122,000
Less Current liabilities	20,000
Working Capital	102,000

The company has many factories manufacturing different types of products. One of the factories manufactures bread and pastry products. The factory is controlled by several cost centres (or departments) including the following: bakery, hygiene function, human resources, despatch, sales, engineering function, information technology, vehicle maintenance and administration. The factory manager has received a report of costs which he finds very difficult to understand. He is particularly confused about the difference between a direct and indirect cost and would be helped by some specific examples from the materials and labour costs incurred by the factory.

The manager of a factory in Birmingham has been to a presentation at the local Chamber of Commerce in which different types of costing methods were discussed. Reference was made to process costing and job costing. The manager is confused as to what these terms mean and has asked for some clarification of these costing methods. Attached to this request is the following information in relation to Job No. Ed 5555.

Direct material issues

Labour costs	£1,800
Machining section	30 hours @ £14.00 per hour basic and 6 hours at double-time
Assembly Section	14 hours @ £12.00 per hour
Finishing Section	8 hours a@ £12.50 per hour

Extract from the overhead analysis

	Machining	Department Assembly	Finishing
Budgeted overheads this year	£270,000	£170,000	£85,000
Budgeted labour hours this year	4,100	4,500	1,950
Budgeted machine hours this year	6,600	180	210

This information is to be used to calculate the factory cost of Job No. Ed 5555.

Another factory, located in Newcastle, produces a single product which sells at £15. The firm has analysed its costs and found that its fixed costs amount to £50,000 per annum and its variable costs are £10 per unit produced. The firm produces 15,000 units every year. The factory manager has asked you for two profit statements using the above information. One of the statements should be presented using traditional absorption costing methods whilst the second should identify the total and unit contribution made by the product.

Working capital and cash budgets

9

Introduction

This chapter discusses the importance of cash to all organisations and is based on the premise that profit is a necessary though not sufficient condition for the longer-term survival of a business. Cash is required to pay for the resources the organisation consumes. For example, there has to be sufficient cash to pay wages or other bills or purchase stock. Organisations have to manage their liquidity – the speed at which a business manages its **cash flow** – so an understanding of managing the main elements of working capital is vital. We also introduce the idea of the working capital cycle, emphasising that a business has to make profit in the long term, but this cannot be achieved unless the business continues to trade. There is no fixed level of working capital or a time period for the operating cycle. These will depend on the nature of the business, the impact of seasonal trade and the creditworthiness of the business.

We also look at the management of stocks – raw materials, work in progress and finished goods – and then examine the management of debtors, creditors and cash. Students will be given the opportunity to produce, interpret and use a cash budget, an essential tool of the financial manager.

1 The main elements of working capital

The **working capital** of a business is the difference between the short-term assets (**current assets**) and the short-term debt (**creditors**), amounts falling due within one year. In short it is current assets less **current liabilities**.

The main components of working capital are:

Current assets (stock, debtors and cash)	LESS	Current liabilities (trade creditors and bank overdrafts)

We discussed current assets and liabilities in chapter 3. To recap, current assets are cash or near-cash items in that they are either already cash or will soon be converted into cash. A business sells its stock on credit which creates debtors. The debtors pay cash to

cash flow
The difference between cash generated and cash spent in a period.

working capital
The capital available for conducting the day to day operations of an organisation; normally the excess of current assets over current liabilities.

current assets
Cash or other asset, e.g. stock, debtors and short-term investments, held for conversion into cash in the normal course of trading.

creditor
A person or business entity to whom money is owed.

current liabilities
Liabilities which fall due for payment within one year, including that part of the long-tem loans due for repayment within one year.

settle their debts. Note the term 'current' refers to conversion into cash within the normal course of trading.

Current liabilities are items that will soon have to be paid for with cash. A business may purchase its stock on credit which will have to be paid in the near future. Sometimes a business will have a bank overdraft which will have to be repaid at very short notice. Note the term 'current' refers to liabilities which will fall due for payment within one year.

Current assets and current liabilities are linked together and in the short term form a continuing and ever changing cycle. This is called the working capital cycle.

1.1　The working capital cycle

The working capital cycle is illustrated in Figure 9.1.

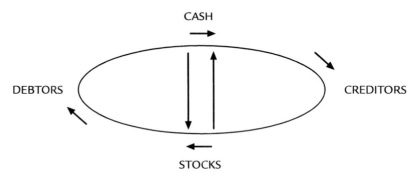

Figure 9.1　The working capital cycle

Figure 9.1 illustrates that a business can buy and sell its stock of finished goods for cash. However the majority of businesses buy and sell their stocks on credit terms and this creates the working capital cycle. Cash is used to pay suppliers for stock items or to pay trade creditors for stock bought on credit terms. The stock is sold either for cash or for credit. In the case of credit customers, there will be a delay before the cash is received from the sales. The receipt of this cash completes the cycle. It is vital that this cycle is actively managed to minimise the cost to the business while ensuring profitability and liquidity.

liquidity
The ability a business has to convert its assets into cash so as to meet its liabilities.

A business has to make profit in the long term, but this cannot be achieved unless the business continues to trade. **Liquidity** is the ability a business has to convert its assets into cash to meet its liabilities. A business must have access to sufficient working capital to ensure its short-term survival. At the same time it must decide what its net investment in short-term assets will be. Therefore working capital and cash flow management are extremely important factors in determining the success of a business.

1.2 The operating cycle or cash conversion cycle

A starting point to determine the level of working capital is to measure the length of time:

- between the purchase of stocks and the receipt of cash from debtors for the sale of the stock; and
- the interval between when the cash is paid out for stocks and the cash is received in from debtors.

This is illustrated in Worked example 9.1.

> **operating cycle or cash conversion cycle**
> The length of time between the purchase of stocks and the receipt of cash from debtors for the sale of the stock; and between when the cash is paid out for stocks and the cash is received in from debtors.

Worked example   9.1

A business buys and sells computers. It buys a computer for cash at a cost of £500. The computer is likely to be held for 15 days before it is sold. The computer will be sold on credit for £800. The debtors normally take 50 days to settle their debts.

	Activity		Days	Operating Cycle – days
Day 1	Stock purchased for cash			
Day 15	Stock sold on credit	Stock turnover period	15	
Day 50	Debtors pay their debts	Debtors' payment period	50	65

This illustrates that the £500 to purchase the computer is tied up for 65 days. This is the length of time the cash invested in the stock takes to be converted into cash being received from debtors.

Consider what will happen if the business purchases the computer on credit and pays its suppliers in 33 days. The impact on the operating cycle will be as follows:

	Activity		Days	Operating Cycle – days
Day 1	Stock purchased on credit			
Day 15	Stock sold on credit	Stock turnover period	15	
Day 33	Suppliers paid	Credit taken from suppliers	(33)	
Day 50	Debtors pay their debts	Debtors' payment period	50	32

This illustrates that the £500 to purchase the computer is tied up for 32 days. This is the length of time between paying cash for the stock and receiving cash from debtors.

2   Factors influencing working capital levels

There is no fixed level of working capital or a time period for the operating cycle. The level of working capital and the length of the cycle is dependent on the following:

2.1   The nature of the business

Some businesses require high levels of working capital while others need little if no working capital. Here are some examples:

- A business selling fresh fish or fruit and vegetables will have low stock levels, low debtors and few creditors as most of the transactions will be on a cash basis. The business will have a short operating cycle.
- A business manufacturing motor vehicles will have a longer operating cycle because of the time involved in acquiring the **raw materials**, assembling the vehicles, selling the vehicles and collecting the cash.
- Businesses manufacturing aircraft or constructing motorways or shopping complexes will have an operating cycle spreading over more than one year.

raw materials

Goods purchased for incorporation into products for sale.

2.2   The seasonality of the business

In some businesses, sales are seasonal. For example, a manufacturer of computer games should experience an increased demand at Christmas while a business selling ice cream and cold drinks should see sales rising in the summer. Businesses will have to determine working capital policies to cope with these situations. This may involve increasing working capital levels to cope with increased stocks and the extra labour costs to meet these seasonal changes.

2.3   The creditworthiness of the business

This is measured in terms of the willingness of suppliers to give credit to the business. The credit period granted will depend on the length of time the business has been in existence, the track record of the business in paying its debts and the terms of trade expected in the industry. The level of credit granted will influence the level of working capital required to keep a business ticking over on a day-to-day basis.

Stop and Think   9.1

Can you explain why you, as an individual, should plan and control your personal cash flow? How might an individual manage a cash shortfall?

3 Working capital management

Managers need to manage all the elements of working capital – stock, debtors, cash/overdrafts and short-term creditors. This is because the money is needed to finance the day to day operations of a business.

3.1 Managing stocks

Stocks may be held in different forms:

- **Raw materials**.
- **Work in progress**.
- **Finished goods**.

The level of stocks held will be determined by a number of factors connected to the business and its industry:

- The current and future availability of stocks.
- The forecast of future demands for stocks.
- The current purchase price, anticipated price changes, discounts and credit terms.
- The costs of holding stocks in terms of storage, insurance, theft, deterioration, and obsolescence.
- The rate of production and/or the time taken purchase finished goods.
- The pattern of sales over the year.
- The reliability of stock control records and systems.
- The availability of finance and the cost of borrowing to finance to the purchase of stock.

3.2 Managing debtors

Debtors represent what is owed to the business in the short term. **Trade debtors** reflect sales by the business to customers on credit. Other short-term amounts owing are called **other debtors**.

Although some businesses, such as retailers, operate largely on a cash basis and have few if any trade debtors, many businesses do not ask for immediate payment for goods and services and give customers a period of credit where cash payment is deferred for an agreed period.

The terms of credit granted to debtors are likely to depend on such factors as:

- The tradition in the industry.
- The need to increase credit so as to increase sales and profits.
- The customer's reputation based on past payment records.
- The costs associated with debts including administration, bad debts and the opportunity cost of allowing the debt.
- The effectiveness of a businesses credit control system in terms of granting, regulating and controlling debts.

raw materials
Goods purchased for incorporation into products for sale.

work in progress
The estimated cost of incomplete work that is not yet ready to be transferred to finished stock.

finished goods
Manufactured goods ready for sale or despatch.

trade debtors
Customers who have made purchases from the business on credit.

other debtors
Short-term amounts owing which are not trade debts.

3.3   Managing creditors

Credit granted by suppliers on the purchase of goods is one important source of short-term funds to most businesses. In effect, a business uses the money it owes to creditors to finance part or all of its current assets. Many businesses rely on creditors to keep down the level of investment required by the business in working capital. Using creditors is a relatively cheap way to finance current assets and the longer the period of time a business takes to pay its creditors the more of that money is available for other purposes.

In theory a business should pay its creditors at the last possible moment. However, the creditors are a business too, and delaying payment may cause them to refuse to supply further credit, take legal action or blacklist a business. The business needs to be aware too that in delaying payment to creditors they could lose out on prompt payment discounts. The credit controller has a difficult but vital role to play in managing working capital and cash. The credit controller needs to balance the cash books from both sides, without unnecessarily upsetting relationships between the business, its customers and its suppliers.

3.4   Managing cash

Cash and money in the bank are part of the working capital of a business because they are needed to pay the bills. Cash, like stocks and debtors, should be kept at a minimum level. The aim is to have sufficient cash to meet all debts as they fall due, but this may not involve holding cash for this purpose. For example a business may be able to borrow money quickly, say by a bank overdraft, so reducing the need to hold cash. A business should also consider the possibility that in holding large cash balances, they do not take advantage of more profitable opportunities that might occur.

Test *yourself*   9.2

(a)   List TWO reasons which explain why a business cannot keep delaying the payment of trade creditors.

(b)   List THREE ways in which the operating cycle of a business can be reduced.

Putting the case 9.1

The following information has been collected in respect of the working capital of the company. The information relates to the current financial year.

	Current Financial Year
Trade debtors collection period	44 days
Trade creditors payment period	64 days
Raw materials turnover period	128 days
Production period	44 days
Finished stock turnover period	63 days

Working capital

	£
Current assets	170,000
Less: Creditors	29,000
Working capital	**141,000**

The following questions will be discussed at a meeting with factory managers. To prepare for the meeting you are required to:

1 Calculate the operating cycle in days for *both* the previous financial year and the current financial year.

2 Compare and comment on the changes in the working capital of the company over the two financial years.

3 List FOUR suggestions the company could employ for managing the changed working capital position.

 1 The operating cycle in days for the two years is:

	Previous financial year – days	Current financial year – days	Increase/(Decrease) – days
Raw materials turnover period	90 days	128 days	38 days
Production period	29 days	44 days	15 days
Finished stock turnover period	68 days	63 days	(5) days
Trade debtors collection period	44 days	44 days	0
Totals	231 days	279 days	48 days
Trade creditors payment period	53 days	64 days	11 days
Operating cycle	178 days	215 days	37 days

Putting the case *(continued)*   9.1

2   The working capital of the business has increased over the two years as follows:

	Previous Financial Year £	Current Financial Year £
Current assets	122,000	170,000
Less Current liabilities	20,000	29,000
Working Capital	**102,000**	**141,000**

The working capital is expected to increase by £39,000. This represents a percentage increase of approximately 38%.

Following the increase in working capital, the operating cycle has lengthened by 37 days, from 178 days to 215 days. The length of the cycle will then have risen by about 21%. This increase can be analysed as follows:

	Increase/(Decrease) – days
Raw materials turnover period	38 days
Production period	15 days
Finished stock turnover period	(5) days
Trade debtors collection period	0
	48 days
Trade creditors payment period	11 days
Operating cycle	37 days

Each of the above figures points to the need for additional finance. Funds will have to be invested to cover the increase in working capital. Unless additional capital can be raised from outside the business or the length of the operating cycle can be reduced, the business may be heading for liquidity problems.

3   The operating cycle could be shortened by:

- Reducing the level of work-in-progress. This is the same thing as shortening the production period.
- Reducing stocks of raw materials and finished goods.
- Shortening the period of credit allowed to customers. This may not be easy as the debt collection period is expected to remain constant at 44 days.
- Taking longer to pay suppliers.

Before deciding on the course of action the firm should assess the wider implications. For example, reduction of raw material stock could lead to stock-outs and lost production, while increasing the time taken to pay creditors may result in cut-off of supplies.

Test *yourself*   9.3

> (a) 'All capital is good so working capital should be kept as high as possible.' Explain
>   why you agree or disagree with this statement.
>
> (b) List FIVE factors which will influence the level of stocks held by a business.
>
> (c) Identify the forms in which stocks may be held by a manufacturing company and a
>   retailer respectively.

4   Cash budgets and the management of cash

A **cash budget** is an essential tool of the financial manager: it converts all the activities
of the business into cash flows. This allows the business to identify cash shortfalls and
surpluses throughout the budget period. A cash budget working sheet is illustrated in
Sample 9.1.

Sample cash budget sheet   9.1

		January	February	March	Etc.
Cash balance at beginning of month					
Add	Cash receipts				
	e.g. Cash sales				
	Payments by debtors				
	Loans				
Less	Cash payments				
	e.g. Cash purchases				
	Payments to creditors				
	Wages				
	Salaries				
	Taxation				
Cash balance at end of month					

cash budget

A detailed budget
of the receipts into
an organisation
and payments from
an organisation,
incorporating both
revenue and capital
items. The budget
identifies the
resultant effect
upon bank
balances or
overdrafts.

Worked example

9.2

Cash Budget

Silvermark Limited is a manufacturing business. The following information relates to the activities of the next six months.

	Sales	Purchases
	£	£
January	150,000	50,000
February	180,000	70,000
March	120,000	80,000
April	140,000	90,000
May	160,000	100,000
June	170,000	120,000

The following additional information is provided:

1   All sales are on credit and 20% of customers are expected to pay in the month of sale and the remainder in the next month.

2   All purchases are on one month's credit from suppliers.

3   Additional equipment costing £50,000 will be purchased in March. A loan of £20,000 has been negotiated from the bank from the same date.

4   Wages are expected to be £30,000 per month and are paid during the month.

5   Rent of £48,000 per annum is paid quarterly in March, June, September and December.

6   Depreciation on fixed assets amounts to £24,000 per annum.

7   The accountant has aggregated the remaining expenses into fixed and variable overheads:

   ● Variable overheads amounting to 10% of sales are payable one month in arrears.

   ● Fixed overheads of £360,000 per annum are payable one month in arrears.

8   The balances on the accounts at 31 December were:

   ● Amounts owed by customers £96,000.

   ● Amounts owed to suppliers for purchases £50,000.

   ● For overheads: Fixed £30,000; Variable £10,000.

   ● Balance at bank £20,000.

Prepare a cash budget for the six months ended June.

4.1   Uses of the cash budget

Cash budgets:

- Act as a yardstick against which comparisons can be made throughout the year.
- Bring all the receipts and payments together and allows a forecast bank balance to be worked out.
- Allow managers to take corrective action to deal with bank balances on a daily basis. Surplus cash can be invested or cash shortfalls can be dealt with by negotiating borrowings and overdraft facilities.

Worked example (continued)   9.2

A

Silvermark Ltd
Cash Budget for 6 months to June

	January	February	March	April	May	June
	£	£	£	£	£	£
Receipts						
Debtors from previous month	96,000	120,000	144,000	96,000	112,000	128,000
Received in month	30,000	36,000	24,000	28,000	32,000	34,000
Loan			20,000			
Total receipts (A)	126,000	156,000	188,000	124,000	144,000	162,000
Payments						
Suppliers: Materials	50,000	50,000	70,000	80,000	90,000	100,000
Variable overhead	10,000	15,000	18,000	12,000	14,000	16,000
Fixed overhead	30,000	30,000	30,000	30,000	30,000	30,000
Wages	30,000	30,000	30,000	30,000	30,000	30,000
Rent			12,000			12,000
Purchase of equipment			50,000			
Total payments (B)	120,000	125,000	210,000	152,000	164,000	188,000
Net cash in/(out) flow (A – B)	6,000	31,000	(22,000)	(28,000)	(20,000)	(26,000)
Opening balance at bank	20,000	26,000	57,000	35,000	7,000	(13,000)
Closing balance at bank	26,000	57,000	35,000	7,000	(13,000)	(39,000)

A look at the closing balances suggests that Silvermark Ltd will be in overdraft by the end of May. The sales may be cyclical and the pattern of purchases is unclear but the trend is worrying. Added to that, the firm financed 60% of the new asset out of its own cash. This clearly shows the need for careful budgeting if the firm wants to avoid an overdraft. If an overdraft is required it would be sound financial management to negotiate this well in advance of the need arising.

- Allow managers to be aware of any potential cash crisis well in advance and so plan to overcome this.
- Allow the timing and impact of capital budgeting decisions to be reviewed throughout the year.
- Allow overdrafts to be calculated and consequently the interest costs of alternative borrowing strategies.

Test *yourself* 9.4

(a) Why does the depreciation of fixed assets not appear in a cash budget?

(b) Which of the following THREE options is correct? Cash budgets of a manufacturing company should be reviewed annually or monthly or daily.

Summary

- The working capital of a business is the difference between the short-term assets and the short-term debt. In simple terms it is current assets less current liabilities.
- The working capital cycle should be managed in such a way as to minimise the cost to the business whilst ensuring its profitability and liquidity. A business has to make profit in the long term, but this cannot be achieved unless the business continues to trade.
- There is no fixed level of working capital or a time period for the operating cycle. The level of working capital and the length of the cycle is dependent amongst other things on the nature of the business, its seasonality and the credit-worthiness of the business.
- Credit granted by suppliers on the purchase of goods is one important source of short-term funds to most businesses. Many businesses rely on creditors to keep down the level of investment required by the business in working capital. In effect a business uses the money it owes to creditors to finance part or whole of its current assets.
- Cash and money in the bank are needed to pay the bills of a business and thus form a part of the working capital of a business. Cash, like stock and debtors, should be kept at a minimum level. The aim is explained as having sufficient cash to meet all debts as they fall due but may not necessarily involve holding cash for this purpose. Cash budgets are recognised as an essential tool of the financial manager. It converts all the activities of the business into cash flows. This allows the business to identify cash shortfalls and surpluses throughout the budget period.

Cost accounting for reporting and decision-making

10

Introduction

Many decisions made by business managers are based on information about the cost of making a product or providing a service, so it makes sense for business managers to understand something of how these costs are arrived at. This chapter discusses what is meant by the cost of a product and examines how the cost of something is established. Accountants usually set up cost centres and cost units against which the cost of something can be established. The costs are grouped systematically according to common characteristics or properties. Key terms and concepts such as direct and indirect costs are explained.

The chapter then looks at fixed costs – those costs that in general remain constant even when the level of business activity fluctuates. These are contrasted with variable costs which tend to vary directly with the level of output. The relevance of this distinction for business managers is introduced.

The chapter concludes with an introduction to common costing methods. These are grouped under two headings: specific orders and continuous operations. The specific order methods are described in terms of job costing, contract costing and batch costing. Continuous operation/process costing is explained as the grouping of costing methods used where goods or services result from a sequence of continuous or repetitive operations or processes. These are illustrated by reference to process costing and service/function costing.

1 Cost accounting and the business manager

Business managers are not expected to have a detailed knowledge of how accountants prepare the annual financial statements of a business. However, the financial statements do reflect the total financial resources the organisation uses to deliver products or services to its customers. It is highly probable that managers will want to break down these total figures to a level of detail which will help them manage a particular area or activity. The manager might want answers to questions such as:

- What are the costs of the materials and labour used to produce a particular product?
- What are the overheads, such as rent, heating, lighting, cleaning costs, etc. of running a business?
- What costs should be included if a manager is trying to calculate the selling price of a product or service?

Accounting, as is stressed throughout the study text, is not an exact science. Thus many of the figures supplied for decision-making are based on subjective judgements and assumptions made by the accountant. This is certainly true in financial accounting but is even more prevalent in cost accounting. If the cost accounting information is used as a basis for decision-making, it is sensible for business managers to understand how the costs are calculated. Managers should be able to ask questions of the accountants about how the figures have been produced. For example, what costs are included and what costs have been excluded from a particular calculation? How has the accountant allowed for possible changes in selling prices or sales volumes in their figures? Understanding how accountants arrive at figures upon which business managers make decisions should allow the business manager to have more confidence in the decisions they are making.

Other reasons for needing to understand how the figures have been calculated include the following:

- Business managers will be given responsibility to achieve certain objectives and many of these objectives will be expressed in monetary terms. For example, the objectives may include the responsibility for managing the costs of a particular department, say an assembly shop or a function such as advertising. Alternatively, their objective may be to achieve a profit figure for a particular area of responsibility such as a new product. In this case the manager will need to know about both the costs and revenues involved. Appropriate cost information will help the manager to plan for and control the achievement of such objectives.
- Managers will always be confronted with choices between alternative courses of action. Their decisions will be better informed if they understand the financial implications. For example, should a business manufacture a product itself or should the product be bought in?
- Businesses need to establish the cost of their products or services so they can set an appropriate selling price. The business manager will probably be involved in establishing the cost and negotiating the selling price, so it is essential they

appreciate how the costs have been established. This process is not restricted to managers who are directly involved in sales in customers outside the business. Many managers have to 'sell' and 'price' their services to internal customers; for example an information technology department may 'sell' its services to other departments, in the organisation.

- An understanding of the cost information allows the internal customer to question the costs and efficiency of the provider department.

Test *yourself*   10.1

(a) Give THREE reasons why business managers need to understand how the costs of their business are established.

(b) What do you understand by 'internal customers'?

2   Understanding and classifying costs

When accountants refer to the cost of a product or service they are referring to the amount of expenditure, actual or notional, incurred on or attributable to the activity. The use of the terms 'notional' and 'attributable' in the definition reveals that there is some element of estimation or judgement involved. It will become apparent throughout this chapter that while some costs are easy to quantify and verify, others are based on reasonable estimates or approximations.

2.1   Cost centres and cost units

Before examining how the cost of something is established it is useful to consider how accountants decide what is to be costed. In simple terms this can be explained as follows:

- Accountants can establish **cost centres** which are locations, functions or items of equipment in respect of which costs may be gathered for control purposes. These could include a geographical area such as a department, a shop or a factory; a person, for example, a sales person; a piece of equipment, for example, a cutting machine in a factory or a photocopying machine in a print shop.

- Similarly accountants can establish **cost units**, which are the quantitative units of a product or service in relation to which costs may be gathered for control purposes. These could include a kilogram of material, a barrel of beer, a passenger mile on a train, a room occupied in a hotel, etc.

- There is clearly a link between the cost centre and the cost unit. For example, a factory may be the cost centre and it can produce the cost units in the form of a kilogram of material; similarly a hotel can be a cost centre providing cost units in the form of a room occupied. It is the level of detail in the costing which differentiates and links the two.

cost centre
Locations, functions or items of equipment in respect of which costs may be gathered for control purposes.

cost unit
A unit of product or service in relation to which costs are ascertained.

2.2   Method of classifying costs

A useful starting point for examining how the cost of something is established is to classify the costs; this means grouping them systematically according to common characteristics or properties. Management may be interested in reporting costs in different ways. For example it is possible to categorise cost in terms of the following:

Organisational function or department

In a manufacturing business, cost information may be collected on the basis of the following functions/departments:

- Production.
- Sales and distribution.
- Technical.
- Engineering.
- Commercial.
- Support roles such as Finance, Human Resources, Administration, IT, Purchasing.

In a service organisation cost information may be collected on the basis of the following functions/departments:

- Administration and Finance.
- Product Development.
- Marketing.
- Personnel.

Types of cost

Costs can by further subdivided within each functional or department area on the basis of the type of cost. In smaller organisations there may not, of course, be an initial cost categorisation based on function or department.

Costs are normally grouped under the following broad categories:

- *Materials costs* – the raw materials and commodities used by the business. For example, a computer manufacturer could include electronic components for assembly, or a car manufacturer could include the components used to manufacture the final product.
- *Labour costs* – the paid human labour involved in delivering the work of the business and would include wages, salaries, and national insurance and pension contributions paid by the company.
- *Other expenses* – all non-material and non-labour costs. Examples of this type of cost would be rent, rates, heating, lighting, depreciation, advertising, stationery and printing.

Test *yourself*   10.2

(a) Explain the difference between a cost centre and a cost unit.

(b) What do you understand by the term cost classification?

2.3   Direct costs and indirect costs

Direct costs are costs which occur solely because a product or service is being made or provided. In other words, they are incurred directly in the production of a product or the provision of a service. The costs would not be incurred if the thing being costed did not exist. This means there is no suggestion of sharing a cost between several items that are being costed. These include:

- *Direct materials costs* which relate to the raw materials and commodities used by the business in producing a product. For example, the flour used by a bread manufacturer to manufacture the final product, or the cost of the paper involved in producing this study text.
- *Direct labour costs* which relate to the paid human effort involved in producing the product or service. These include wages, salaries, and national insurance and pension contributions paid by the company. An example is the wage of the printer involved in printing this study text.
- *Direct expenses* are expenses other than materials and labour that have been incurred as direct consequence of making a product or providing a service. For example any copyright fees payable in relation to the production of this study text. The total of all the direct costs of a product or service is often referred to as the **prime cost**.

Indirect costs are costs that are difficult to allocate directly to a particular product or service. Indirect costs include such items as rent, rates, administrative wages and salaries, etc. They are often referred to as overheads. An overhead or indirect cost is one which does not depend solely on what is being costed and is a common or joint cost incurred by two or more things being costed. These overheads could be grouped on a departmental or functional basis for example:

- Production overheads:
  - indirect materials such as grease
  - indirect labour such as the wages of supervisors or cleaners
  - indirect expenses such as rent
- **Selling overheads**:
  - salaries/expenses of sales people.
  - advertising.
- **Distribution overheads**:
  - maintenance of delivery vehicles
  - warehouse costs

To calculate the total **production cost** of making a product or providing a service the direct and indirect costs are added together.

>   Direct labour
> \+ Direct materials
> \+ Direct expenses
> = Prime cost

direct costs
Costs incurred solely because the product or service is being made or provided.

prime cost
The total of all the direct costs of a product or service.

indirect costs
Expenditure on labour, materials or services which cannot be economically identified with a specific saleable cost unit. Also known as overheads.

selling overheads
Cost incurred in securing orders, usually including salaries, commissions and travelling expenses.

distribution overheads
The cost of warehousing saleable products and delivering them.

production cost
Prime cost plus absorbed production overhead.

+ Indirect (overhead) factory expenses

= **Production cost**

+ Office and administrative expenses

+ Selling and distribution expenses

+ Financial expenses

= **Total cost**

Worked example 10.1 illustrates how the total costs can be calculated in practice.

Worked example   10.1

Direct and indirect costs

Dough Ltd is a factory which makes bread. The costs for the first quarter of production (representing 1.5 million items) are as follows:

Analysis of Costs – Quarter 1

	£	£	Cost (£) per item
Direct materials			
Flour	150,000		
Vegetable fat	10,000		
Water	20,000		
Yeast	<u>15,000</u>	195,000	0.13
Direct labour			
Factory wages		300,000	0.20
Prime cost		495,000	0.33
Factory overheads			
Factory supervisors' salaries	60,000		
Depreciation – factory	20,000		
Repairs and maintenance	18,000		
Insurance	12,000		
Rent and rates	14,000	124,000	0.08
Total production cost		619,000	0.41

Worked example *(continued)* 10.1

	£	£	Cost (£) per item
Selling and distribution costs			
Warehouse wages	80,000		
Sales salaries	60,000		
Sales commission	30,000		
Depreciation – warehouse	8,000		
Insurance – warehouse	8,000		
Packing and delivery – warehouse	12,000		
Rent and rates – warehouse	12,000	210,000	0.14
Administration costs			
Salaries	40,000		
Depreciation	5,000		
Insurance	7,000		
Rent and rates	8,000		
Office expenses	15,000	75,000	0.05
Total Costs		904,000	£0.60

The information has been presented under headings which are useful for control purposes, particularly if compared with budgeted information.

This example uses a firm that makes a single product so it was able to distinguish easily between costs relating to the factory, warehouse, the office and sales and allocate them to the product. In practice, this situation is unlikely. The firm may produce more than one type of bread and pastry and will want to calculate the cost for each type. If this were the case, the costs of the factory supervisors would be classified as indirect as it would be impossible to say which bread production line they are supervising.

Similarly, the firm may incur costs which cannot be accurately allocated to a department or product. Charges such as telephone, stationery, electricity are difficult to allocate precisely without setting up measurement systems which are uneconomic to operate. This means that arbitrary apportionments of costs have to be made which will reduce the accuracy of the information.

2.4 Fixed and variable costs

Costs can be classified according to their behaviour. In other words, they can be classified by the way they alter in relation to output changes. At first sight business managers might suggest that all costs change with different levels of output or activity,

fixed costs

Costs incurred for a period, and which, within certain output and turnover limits, tend to be unaffected by fluctuations in the levels of activity (output or turnover).

variable costs

Costs which tend to vary according to the level of activity.

semi-variable costs

A cost containing both fixed and variable components and so is partly affected by fluctuations in the level of activity.

but by classifying costs according to how they behave might suggest differently. Thus **fixed costs** in general remain constant, at least in the short term, regardless of changes in sales output or production increase/decreases. These costs include items such as rent, rates, telephone costs, insurance payments and managerial salaries. Fixed costs may change in the long term, for example if a business significantly increases/decreases its production capacity. Thus in general terms it is fairly easy to predict the level of fixed costs for a short period of time into the future, or until a fundamental change in the way the business operates takes place. Managers can be confident that even if sales or production levels change within quite wide limits over the short term, fixed costs will generally remain the same.

Variable costs tend to alter directly with the level of output. For example, as production goes up a business can expect the total cost of raw materials to increase. This is because variable costs are those costs that change in a direct relationship to a change in output or activity. Thus a business manager can assume that these variable costs will always tend to be a fixed percentage of the value of an organisation's output if price levels remain constant.

Some costs contain both fixed and variable elements. These are known as **semi-variable costs**. These do not fit into one or other of these tightly defined categories. For example, the cost of telephones in a factory will be fixed at a certain level, i.e. the line rental, but will also tend to increase as the use of the telephone increases, i.e. a charge per unit used.

Test *yourself* 10.3

(a) Explain, with an example, what is understood by the term an indirect cost.

(b) What is the prime cost of a product?

(c) Explain, with an example, the term semi-variable cost.

Putting the case 10.1

 You are required to respond to the manager of one of Blackstock factories which manufactures bread pastry products. You are required to:

1   Identify which of these costs at the bakery are the Direct and Indirect costs of producing bread pastry products.

2   Identify in which department/functional budget would the cost be included.

3   Explain the difference between a direct and indirect cost by use of specific examples from the materials and labour costs incurred by the factory.

Putting the case *(continued)* 10.1

Description	Direct Cost	Indirect Cost	Function/ Department
Flour			
Salary of team leader in bakery			
Cleaning the factory			
Lighting in the factory			
Heating in the Human Resources Department			
Machine maintenance			
Lease payments on computing equipment			
Wrapping materials			
Bread logos			
Factory supervisor's salary			
Depreciation of warehouse			
Insurance costs			
Scrap dough			
Sales commission			
Costs of ICSA training courses			
Servicing of vans			

Putting the case *(continued)*   10.1

 1 and 2

Description	Direct Cost	Indirect Cost	Function/Department
Flour	Yes		Bakery
Salary of team leader in bakery	Yes		Bakery
Cleaning the factory		Yes – Production overhead	Hygiene
Lighting in the factory		Yes – Production overhead	Bakery
Heating in the Human Resources Dept		Yes – Support overhead	Human Resources
Machine maintenance		Yes – Production overhead	Engineering
Lease payments on computing equipment		Yes – Administration overhead	IT
Wrapping materials.	Yes		Bakery
Bread logos	Yes		Bakery
Factory supervisor's salary		Yes – Production overhead	Bakery
Depreciation of warehouse		Yes – Production overhead	Despatch
Insurance costs		Yes – Administration overhead	Administration
Scrap dough	Yes		Bakery
Sales commission		Yes – Selling and distribution overhead	Sales
Costs of ICSA training courses		Yes – Administration overhead	Human Resources
Servicing of vans		Yes – Selling and distribution overhead	Sales – vehicle maintenance

3   Both of the categories of cost i.e. materials and labour can be broken down into direct and indirect costs. For example, under the heading of material costs a manufacturing bread and pastry making company could have costs such as:
– Wholemeal flour
– Yeast
– Water
– Vegetable fat

Putting the case *(continued)*   10.1

– Machine lubricants
– Cleaning materials

Flour, yeast, water and vegetable fat are classified as direct costs because they are the raw materials from which the finished products are manufactured. However, machine lubricants and cleaning materials are not converted into a final product, and therefore are classed as indirect costs.

Similarly way labour costs can be classified as direct or indirect costs. Direct labour costs in a production-based company include wages and other payments to staff directly involved in the production process. Indirect labour costs include wages and salary payments to staff not directly involved in the production process – support roles such as supervisors, office staff, sales people, technical people, commercial, finance and administrators.

3 Costing methods

Different methods of costing are used to suit the particular requirements of a business. Think of the differences between a business manufacturing engineering parts according to the individual requirements of its customers and a business manufacturing processed food. In turn, an accounting business providing a service will employ different costing methods to either the engineering company or the food processor. The costing methods may be grouped under those for specific orders and those for continuous operations.

3.1 Specific order costing

This is the basic cost accounting method applied where the work consists of separate contracts, jobs or batches. These are usually authorised by a special order or contract and each of the contracts or jobs are different from each other. The main methods of specific order costing are as follows:

Job costing is ideally suited to organisations that tend to supply goods and services on a project-type basis where the customer's individual needs will largely determine both the cost and selling price. Examples include the supply and installation of specialised plant and equipment; the provision of a service, such as accountancy services by a firm of accountants; the repair and servicing of motor vehicles. With this method, the job itself is the cost unit to which costs are allocated. A job-costing sheet is used to estimate costs and provide a basis for pricing or quotation. As the job progresses, individual costs can be charged to the job and a comparison made between actual and estimated costs. This enables any estimated costs that were perhaps shown to be inaccurate, to be adjusted for assisting in making future estimates or quotations. Any price quoted to a potential customer would include all the direct costs and appropriate overheads plus a profit element.

job costing
Where costs are attributed to specific jobs, e.g. the supply and installation of plant and equipment.

An example of a job-costing sheet is illustrated in Sample 10.1.

Sample Job-costing sheet   10.1

					Job No. 12584	
Customer: J. Keegan Ltd, London EC1					Order No. Ab8532/April 200X	
Details: Construction of Copper Widget						
Materials					Actual £	Estimate £
Date	Requisition No.	Details	Qty	Price		
16/05	367	Timber	50mts	£12	600.00	550.00
20/05	421	Copper	90kls	£30	2,700.00	2,800.00
Labour						
Date	Cost Centre	Operative	Hours	Rate		
17/05–23/05	Factory Shop 1	Skilled	26	£16	416.00	384.00
		Semi-Skilled	33	£10	333.00	350.00
Factory overhead						
Cost Centre		Rate				
Factory A		£25 per direct labour hour × 59 hours (26 + 33)			1,475.00	1,475.00
Total factory cost					5,524.00	5,559.00
Selling and administration overhead 50%					2,762.00	2,780.00
Total cost					8,286.00	8,339.00
Profit (25 % on total cost price)					2,072.00	2,085.00
Selling price						
					10,358.00	10,424.00
Invoice: No. 6542 Date 30/05						

Each job is given a unique job number (in this case 12584) and a copy of the production order will be sent to the factory accountant who will raise a job cost sheet. The accountant will create one account for each order so that the costs relating to each individual job can be separately accumulated. The estimated costs are included on the job cost sheet and the actual costs are monitored as the job progresses. The details recorded are the direct materials, the direct wages and direct expenses. The information is extracted from stores/materials requisitions, invoices and timesheets. Production overhead is included by the application of overhead absorption rates and when the job is completed the non-production overheads (shown in the example as 50%) will added together with the profit element (shown here as 25% of cost price). The customer is then invoiced accordingly.

- **Contract costing** is similar to job costing in that it is work carried out to meet a customer's detailed requirements. However, contract costing is usually for construction work which can last several years, for example the construction of military aircraft or ships, or the construction of a large building, bridge or tunnel. The contracts usually have a high monetary value and are based on a detailed legal contract specifying such things as the materials to be used, the quality of the work expected, and the timescale involved. From a financial viewpoint there is a need to specify that the customer will make **staged payments** – progress payments at specific stages of the work or at agreed intervals. These payments are usually made after the contract architect has agreed and certified the value and the quality of the work completed to date.

- **Batch costing** Organisations involved in producing goods or providing services in batches, such as a bakery producing loaves in batches, often use a variation of job costing, sometimes known as batch costing. Again, batch costing is similar to job costing in that a batch is treated as the job during manufacture. The total costs involved in producing that batch are calculated and used as the basis for determining the cost of each individual job unit – in the example 'per loaf'. Batch costing is used in industries where the customer orders a quantity of identical items such as shoes, shirts, books, car and computer components, etc.

Test *yourself* 10.4

(a) List FIVE items which may be found on a job-costing sheet.

(b) Provide THREE features of contract costing.

3.2 Continuous operation/process costing

This is the grouping of costing methods used where goods or services result from a sequence of continuous or repetitive operations or processes. Costs are averaged over the units produced during the period. This method is sometimes called *unit costing* as it aims to identify the average cost per unit during a period for a number of identical cost units. The main methods of continuous operation/process costing are as follows:

- **Process costing** is most appropriate in continuous process operations such as float glass, steel and chemicals. It can also be used in some service activities. It is ideally suited to situations where it is very difficult to link elements of direct costs with specific units of output. In making petrol, for example, it is necessary to blend crude oil with a number of other chemicals and this is further complicated in that the process may yield valuable by-products. The production of coal gas also produces coke and coal tar. Process costing requires detailed records to be kept for each process of units and part-units completed and of the cost incurred. As there is no individual unit being produced, but a quantity of units, this method

---

contract costing
Similar to job costing in that costs are attributed to individual contracts but usually used for high value, long term projects such as construction.

staged payments
Progress payments made at specific stages of a contract or at agreed intervals.

batch costing
A form of specific order costing; the attribution of costs to batches, a quantity of identical items, e.g. shoes, computer components.

continuous operation/process costing
The costing method applicable where goods or services result from a sequence of continuous or repetitive operations or processes. Costs are averaged over the units produced during the period.

process costing
The costing method where goods or services result from a sequence of continuous or repetitive processes. Costs are averaged over the units produced during the period.

uses the average cost of each unit of output as its basis of calculation. The average cost of each process can be calculated by dividing the costs incurred by both the fully and partly completed units. To achieve this, the partly completed units are converted into equivalent units. Thus if there are 1000 partly completed, which are estimated to be 75% complete, this represents 750 equivalent units of work in progress. In the chemical industry, for example, direct costs could be expressed as an average cost per litre or tonne. Finally, the quantity/volume/weight output from a process will be less than the quantity/volume/weight input. This will be due to losses in the processing due to evaporation, breakages, etc. Process costing will allow for normal process losses, i.e. standard or expected levels but must also identify abnormal process losses i.e. unexpected or unplanned losses.

- **Service** /*function costing* is cost accounting for services or functions such as canteens, maintenance or personnel. These may be referred to as service centres, departments or functions. They involve services which are sold to customers including rail and air transport, restaurants, hotels, education, and cinemas. Their service is usually measured by a relevant cost unit including:

service costing

Cost accounting for services or functions, e.g. canteens, maintenance and personnel. These may be referred to as service centres, departments or functions.

Service	Cost unit
Rail and air transport	Passenger mile or miles travelled
Training	Student hour
Hotels	Room occupied
Hospitals	Patient day or operation or clinical test
Restaurants	Meal served or tables occupied
University	Full time equivalent student
Electricity/Gas	Kilowatt
Water	Cubic metre

The calculation of the cost per unit is:

$$\text{Cost per service unit} = \frac{\text{Total costs per period}}{\text{Number of service units supplied in the period}}$$

Worked example 10.2 shows the cost of a small maternity unit based on the number of patient days and the number of patient cases.

Worked example   10.2

Service costing

Expenditure	Annual cost	Cost per patient day	Cost per case
Medical staff salaries	86,000	17.20	86.00
Nursing staff salaries	200,000	40.00	200.00
Medical and surgical supplies	30,000	6.00	30.00
Pharmacy	25,000	5.00	25.00
Pathology	18,000	3.60	18.00
Radiography	16,000	3.20	16.00
Catering	50,000	10.00	50.00
Laundry	22,000	4.40	22.00
Etc.	53,000	10.60	53.00
Total	500,000	100.00	500.00

Number of patient days	5,000
Number of patient cases	1,000
Average stay per case	5 days

Stop and Think   10.1

What reasons support the argument that managers in not-for-profit organisations should be provided with a more detailed breakdown of its operating costs than is provided in their published accounts?

Test *yourself*   10.5

Explain the difference between costing methods for specific orders and those for continuous operations.

Summary

- Business managers need to understand how elements of cost are calculated in order to make decisions. Accountants usually use cost centres (locations, functions or items of equipment) and cost units (quantitative units of a product or service) to collect and collate costs for control purposes.
- Costs are normally grouped under the broad categories of materials costs, labour costs and other expenses.
- The chapter explains how an understanding of direct and indirect costs is relevant

for business managers. Direct costs are costs that occur solely because a product or service is being made or provided and include the direct materials costs, direct labour costs and direct expenses. The total of all the direct costs of a product or service is often referred to as the prime cost. Indirect costs, often referred to as overheads, are costs which are difficult to allocate directly to a particular product or service.

- The cost of production is calculated by adding indirect costs (overheads) to the prime cost. In order to establish the total costs other overheads, including office and administrative expenses, selling and distribution expenses, etc., have to be added.

- Finally, the chapter ends with a discussion of different costing methods. The costing methods may be grouped under those for specific orders and those for continuous operations.

Costing products and services

11

Introduction

This chapter explains how direct and indirect costs are charged to cost centres using expense codes and cost centre codes. This is important to the cost centre manager as they will need to ensure that the production overheads of their cost centre are charged to individual cost units.

This chapter also explains the distinction between cost allocation, cost apportionment and overhead absorption and the key ways of absorbing overheads will be described, demonstrated and criticised.

The chapter concludes by explaining that overhead costs are absorbed on the basis of the estimated activity level for the year which allows a predetermined overhead absorption rate to be calculated. This section will examine the uses and limitations of full cost information.

1   Charging costs to cost centres

We saw in chapter 10 how direct and indirect costs contribute to the total cost of product or service. Table 11.1 summarises how this is done.

Total labour cost	=	Direct labour	+	Indirect labour
+		+		+
Total material cost	=	Direct material	+	Indirect material
+		+		+
Total expenses	=	Direct expenses	+	Indirect expenses
=		=		=
Total cost	=	Prime cost	+	Overheads

Table 11.1 Total cost breakdown

expenditure code

A system of symbols designed to be applied to a set of items to give a brief accurate reference, facilitating entry, collation and analysis.

Direct and indirect costs are charged to cost centres using expense codes and cost centre codes. Cost codes are a series of numbers designed to be applied to a classified set of items to give a brief accurate reference which assists collation and analysis. For example:

EXPENDITURE CODE 233,694:

- The first three digits indicate the nature of the expenditure (for example labour, electricity, consumables). These groupings are **subjective classifications**.
- The last three digits indicate the cost centre or cost unit be charged (for example machine shop, canteen, electrical engineers, Product A, Product B, etc.). These groups are **objective classifications**.

subjective classification

The first few digits of a code might indicate the nature of the expenditure.

This is illustrated in Figure 11.1.

objective classification

The final few digits of a code might indicate the cost centre or cost unit to be charged.

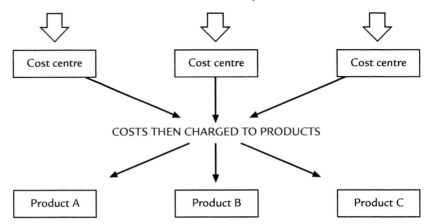

Figure 11.1

Test *yourself*   11.1

What is meant by objective and subjective classifications of expenditure?

absorption costing

The procedure which charges fixed as well as variable overheads to cost units.

2   Absorption costing

Business managers may be given responsibility for managing the costs of a particular cost centre. Although this might look like a complicated arithmetic procedure it is important for them to be able to interpret the cost accounting information they receive for the following reasons:

- To use the information as a basis for controlling the expanses of the cost centre.
- To question the bases which the accountant uses to prepare the information.

The cost centre manager needs to be able to charge the production overheads of their cost centre to individual cost units. There are two types of cost centre – a production cost centre – for example, a machine shop, where the products are manufactured; a **service cost centre** – for example, the personnel or salaries and wages departments. The service departments provide services for the production cost centres – for example, payment of wages or recruitment of staff.

2.1   Allocation, apportionment and absorption

Production overheads are charged to a cost centre by **absorption costing** which follows the following procedure:

- Allocate as many costs as possible directly to cost centres and cost units. **Cost allocation** involves charging discrete identifiable items of cost to cost centres or cost units. This involves allocating direct labour, direct materials and direct expenses directly to the product using the appropriate expense code and product code.
- Share out or apportion service cost centre costs such as cleaning, materials handling, transport etc. to the production cost centres. **Cost apportionment** is the division of costs across two or more cost centres in proportion to consumption or the benefit received. For example, the overall cost of floor space could be shared across a number of departments according to how much actual space each department occupies. Cost apportionment is necessary because there are certain costs that cannot be allocated directly to cost units. Examples of cost apportionment are shown in Table 11.2.

Service Cost Centre	Method of Apportionment to Manufacturing/Production Cost Centre
Canteen, Personnel Department, Payroll Section	Number of employees
Cleaning, ground and building maintenance	Floor area
Stores handling	Number of requisitions raised
Transport section	Number of vehicle miles

Table 11.2 Examples of cost apportionment

- Absorb the production overhead of the production cost centres into the specific cost units. **Overhead absorption** is where all the indirect costs in the firm are grouped together in such a way that they can be added to the product cost. Initially, all indirect costs are apportioned to various cost centres using rational apportionment methods. For instance, expenses such as rent and rates might be apportioned between administration, selling and production functions on the basis of floor area; catering facilities on the basis of employees; insurance on the insurable value.

service cost centre
Service departments provide services for the production cost centres. For example the personnel department could provide services including the payment of wages and/or the recruitment of staff.

absorption rate
A rate charged to a cost unit intended to account for the overhead at a predetermined level of activity.

cost allocation
The process of charging a specific cost to a cost centre or cost unit.

cost apportionment
That part of cost attribution which shares costs among two or more cost centres or cost units in proportion to the estimated benefit received.

overhead absorption
The charging of overhead to products or services by means of absorption rates.

All of these indirect costs must then be charged to the product. This is at the heart of any absorption or **full cost pricing** system. There are many ways of doing this but all solutions depend on identifying the factor that best reflects the productive activity of the firm and thereby the incurring of indirect costs. Remember that the solution is only a compromise and is not necessarily the correct answer or only solution.

Worked example 11.1

Methods of cost apportionment

The rent and rates of a factory are £300,000 per annum. The business wishes to apportion the rent and rates to the three production departments. The business can do this in one of two ways: 1) on floor area occupied, or 2) on the number of employees in the production departments. The relevant information is:

	Department 1	Department 2	Department 3	Total
Area in m²	12,600	9,600	7,700	29,900
No. employees	24	19	17	60

		Rent and rates apportioned on floor area
Department 1	£300,000 × $\frac{12,600}{29,900}$	£126,421
Department 2	£300,000 × $\frac{9,600}{29,900}$	£96,321
Department 3	£300,000 × $\frac{7,700}{29,900}$	£77,258

		Rent and rates apportioned on basis of number of employees
Department 1	£300,000 × $\frac{24}{60}$	£120,000
Department 2	£300,000 × $\frac{19}{60}$	£95,000
Department 3	£300,000 × $\frac{17}{60}$	£85,000

Either method can be used, but each leads to a different distribution of the overhead. For example, Department 3 would be charged £85,000 of overhead if it uses employee numbers as a method of apportionment compared with £77,258 on the basis of floor area.

It is not always easy to find an equitable method of apportionment and on occasions an arbitrary distribution will have to be made. This is often because the information necessary to apportion the costs fairly is not available, e.g. exact square metres occupied and the extra cost of obtaining the information exceeds the benefits. Cost allocation is usually preferred to cost apportionment, if accurate information is available.

Test *yourself*   11.2

(a) What is a production cost centre?

(b) What is the difference between cost allocation and cost apportionment?

2.2   Overhead absorption rates

If we take the overhead which we are trying to absorb and divide it by some factor of production this will give an overhead absorption or recovery rate.

The productive factor could be:

- Units produced.
- Direct labour hours worked.
- Direct machine hours worked.
- Direct labour costs.
- Direct material costs.
- Prime cost.

The overhead absorption rate is built around the following basic assumption:

$$\text{Cost centre overhead absorption rate} = \frac{\text{Total cost centre overhead}}{\text{Total cost centre activity}}$$

2.3   Overhead absorption methods

There is no one best method but six common methods are:

$$\textbf{Specific units method} = \frac{\text{Total cost centre overhead}}{\text{Number of units produced in the cost centre}}$$

$$\textbf{Machine hour rate} = \frac{\text{Total cost centre overhead}}{\text{Total cost centre machine hours}}$$

$$\textbf{Direct labour hour rate} = \frac{\text{Total cost centre overhead}}{\text{Total cost centre direct labour hours}}$$

$$\textbf{Direct labour cost rate} = \frac{\text{Total cost centre overhead}}{\text{Total cost centre direct labour cost}} \times 100\%$$

$$\textbf{Direct materials cost rate} = \frac{\text{Total cost centre overhead}}{\text{Total cost centre direct materials cost}} \times 100\%$$

$$\textbf{Prime cost rate} = \frac{\text{Total cost centre overhead}}{\text{Prime cost}} \times 100\%$$

full cost pricing
A pricing method where the cost of the unit of output is calculated taking into account all direct costs, and an apportionment of indirect production costs and other overheads. A fixed percentage is then added to this to cover profit.

specific units method
An overhead absorption rate based on cost units processed.

machine hour rate
An overhead absorption rate based on machine hours.

direct labour hour rate
An overhead absorption rate based on direct labour hours.

direct labour cost rate
An overhead absorption rate based on direct labour cost.

direct materials cost rate
An overhead absorption rate based on direct materials cost.

prime cost rate
An overhead absorption rate based on total prime cost.

Worked example 11.2

Using overhead absorption methods

Dough Ltd. has a budgeted factory overhead of £250,000.

Calculate the overhead recovery rate and apply it to job X using the following data.

Budgeted number of units	50,000
Budgeted labour hours	100,000
Budgeted machine hours	200,000
Budgeted direct labour costs	£800,000
Budgeted direct material costs	£250,000

Answer

Overhead absorption method	Overhead absorption or recovery rate
Specific units	Rate = $\frac{£250,000}{50,000}$ = £5.00 per unit
Machine hour rate	Rate = $\frac{£250,000}{200,000}$ = £1.25 per machine hour
Labour hour rate	Rate = $\frac{£250,000}{100,000}$ = £2.50 per direct labour hour
Direct labour cost rate	Rate = $\frac{£250,000}{£800,000}$ × 100% = 31.25% on direct labour cost
Direct material cost rate	Rate = $\frac{£250,000}{£250,000}$ × 100% = 100% on direct material cost
Prime cost rate	Rate = $\frac{£250,000}{(£800,000 + £250,000)}$ × 100% = 24% on prime cost

Depending on which absorption method was chosen, any jobs produced in the factory cost centre would have production overheads added as follows:

- Each unit produced in the factory would have £5 of overhead added to its costs.
- If a job in the factory uses 5 machine hours, overhead of 5 hours at £1.25 = £6.25 will be charged.
- If a job in the factory uses 10 hours of direct labour, overhead of 10 hours at £2.50 = £25 will be charged.
- If the direct labour cost of a job was £50 overhead of £50 x 31.25% = £15.63 will be charged.
- If the direct material cost of a job was £80 overhead of £80 x 100% = £80 will be charged.
- If the prime cost of a job was £130 overhead of £130 x 24% = £31.20 will be charged.

In effect the business is charging a part of the total cost centre overhead to the product using the overhead absorption rate. The selection of recovery method would be determined by the firm and applied consistently across all work.

Test *yourself*   11.3

(a) What is calculated by the following formula?

$$\frac{\text{Total cost centre overhead}}{\text{Total cost centre direct material cost}} \times 100\%$$

(b) What is the difference between the labour hour rate and direct labour cost absorption rates?

2.4 Selecting the overhead absorption or recovery rate

The treatment of overheads is one the most subjective areas in costing. The overhead recovery method chosen will produce six different costs for a product or job. None of the overhead absorption methods is the 'right one'. However, the key point to note is that whichever type of absorption rate is selected, the total amount of overheads charged to all products will be the same in each case, even though individual products will differ under different systems of absorption. As business managers recognise that there is no 'right answer'; the method chosen will be based on balancing the cost and convenience of collecting the information required to make the calculations.

Table 11.3 illustrates comments to be borne in mind when selecting the method:

Overhead Absorption Method	Comments
Specific units	This method is simple and practical to apply and is suitable when all the cost units are identical.
Machine hour rate	This is suitable when production is carried on machines. There is probably a strong relationship between modern machine intensive production methods and overheads incurred in a factory.
Labour hour rate	This is suitable where **production cost centres** are labour-intensive, i.e. mainly manual methods of production. The absorption method produces a standard rate and is unaffected by differences in wage rates or skills.
Direct labour cost rate	This method is widely used in practice as the information is readily available. It is most suitable where there is single rate of pay and one type of labour. If there are different rates of pay then higher paid workers will absorb more overhead.
Direct material cost rate	This method is practical and easy to apply. However, overheads tend to be generated on a time basis and have little relationship to the direct material cost.
Prime cost rate	This method has the weaknesses of the previous two methods as it is combination of them. There is unlikely to be a relationship between overhead and prime cost.

production cost centre

These are locations where the products are manufactured for example a machine shop.

Table 11.3 Selecting overhead absorption rates

It is important to select a method which ensures that cost units are charged with a fair share of the overhead. Business managers should remember when selecting the overhead absorption method that overhead generally accrues on a time basis, so the longer a cost unit spends in production the more overhead an individual cost unit will generate. This means that the time based methods namely the labour hour rate and the machine hour rate, are preferred for labour-intensive cost centres and machine-intensive cost centres respectively.

Stop and Think   11.1

What method would you suggest for apportioning the following overhead?

(a) Insurance of fixed assets.

(b) Heating of offices.

(c) Costs of a central IT department.

3   Pricing and costing using full cost information

Overhead costs for the year are usually calculated in advance of the actual figures being known. These estimated figures are included in the annual budget and are used to calculate the overhead absorption rates, which in turn allow a business to calculate the full cost of its products and determine selling prices. These estimated overhead figures are based on the estimated activity level for the year and include estimates of total labour hours, machine hours, total units, direct material costs and direct labour hours. However, the actual figures may differ from the estimated or budgeted figures for the following reasons:

- The actual overheads may change throughout the year, e.g. if the rent or insurance increases the overhead absorption rate will be too low. The opposite applies with fall in overheads.
- The actual production activity may change from the planned level. This would make the predetermined overhead rate invalid, e.g. if production activity decreases, and the overhead costs do not change, the overhead absorption rate will be too low. The opposite applies with a rise in production activity.

This is illustrated in Worked example 11.3.

Worked example

11.3

Effect of using predetermined absorption rates

Predetermined overhead absorption rate = $\dfrac{£250,000}{50,000 \text{ units}}$ = £5.00 per unit

Say the actual overheads were £280,000 and the activity remained unchanged at 50,000 units. This would result in an under-recovery of £30,000 of overheads. It is an adverse variance or difference.

Alternatively, suppose the actual number of units produced was 48,000 and overheads remained at £250,000. This would result in overheads of £240,000 (48,000 units × £5) being recovered, which would be an under-recovery of £10,000. This is an adverse variance or difference.

Such a situation does not undermine the case for setting predetermined overhead absorption rates. Business managers need to plan for overhead costs and activity levels but these plans need to be continually monitored. The predetermined rate allows business managers to receive cost statements at any time and so exercise cost control. The costing report will highlight variances between actual and expected performance which business managers can investigate.

3.1   Uses and benefits of full cost information

- Setting prices when the profit element is added to the full cost. This is known as cost plus pricing.
- To determine the cost of individual cost units as a means of planning and controlling the responsibility centres of the business.
- It is easily understood and widely practised.

3.2   Limitations of full cost information

- The total cost figures rely on accurate collection and recording of costing information.
- The overhead absorption methods are based on subjective judgements of managers and accountants. Thus the calculated total costs will vary with the judgements made.
- The emphasis on recovering overheads may mean managers are tempted to produce not for the market, but to absorb allocated overheads and so reduce unit costs.

3.3   Full cost pricing

Some businesses work on the basis of full cost pricing to determine their selling price. The cost of the unit of output is calculated taking into account all direct costs and an apportionment of indirect production costs and other overheads, using one of the absorption methods described above. A fixed percentage is then added to cover profit.

Full cost pricing as a technique of costing and then pricing products does have its uses – after all, firms need to cover their costs if they are to make a profit. However, it is not the type of pricing policy that should be adopted by a business that wishes to remain competitive by being flexible and able to react to changing market conditions.

**job cost card
or sheet**
A record of time
spent on a job. It
may include the
cost of labour and
materials and
attributed
overhead.

Pricing should be determined by conditions in the marketplace – what the customer is
prepared to pay – rather than by calculations made by accountants.

Test *yourself*   11.4

(a) List TWO reasons for setting predetermined overhead absorption rates.

(b) Fill in the gaps in the following statement: 'Overheads tend to be generated on a ——
     basis and have little relationship to the direct —— cost.

(c) List THREE uses of full cost information.

(d) What is cost plus pricing?

Putting the case   11.1

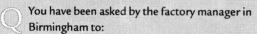

You have been asked by the factory manager in
Birmingham to:

1   Prepare a briefing note for the factory
     manger which identifies FIVE key features of
     job costing and of process costing.

2   Prepare the factory cost of Job No. Ed 5555
     using the data provided in the case study.

The FIVE key features of job costing are:

1   Costs of materials, labour and overheads are
     accumulated in a job cost sheet.

2   Costs of individual jobs are kept separate.

3   Overhead is allocated to jobs on a
     predetermined rate based on direct labour
     hours, machine hours, direct labour costs,
     etc.

4   The profit element of the job is added to the
     total cost.

5   Each job is given a unique number by which
     costs are charged as the job progresses
     through the business.

The FIVE key features of process costing are:

1   Costs of materials, labour and overheads are
     accumulated for each process in a process
     cost sheet.

2   Accurate records are kept of units produced
     and units in work-in-progress.

3   Production for the period is stated in
     equivalent units.

4   Cost per equivalent unit is calculated for
     materials, labour and overheads.

5   Normal losses and abnormal losses need to
     be recorded.

Putting the case *(continued)*   11.1

Job Cost Card					Job No. Ed 5555	
Customer:					Order No.	
Details						
Materials					Actual £	
Date	Requisition No.	Details	Qty	Price		
		Materials		£1,800.00	1,800.00	
Labour						
Date	Cost Centre	Operative	Hours	Rate		
	Machinery		30	£14	420.00	
			6	£28	168.00	
	Assembly		14	12	168.00	
	Finishing		8	£12.50	100.00	
					856.00	
Prime cost						
Factory overhead						
Cost Centre		Rate				
Machinery 36 hours		£40.91			1472.76	
Assembly 14 hours		£37.78			528.92	
Finishing 8 hours		£43.59			348.72	
Total factory cost					5006.40	

Workings – Overhead absorption rates – use BUDGET figures

Machining   Assembly

(use machine hour rate)   (use labour hour rate)

$\dfrac{£270,000}{6,600 \text{ machine hours}}$ = £40.91 $\dfrac{£170,000}{4,500 \text{ labour hours}}$ = £37.78

Finishing

(use labour hour rate)

$\dfrac{£85,000}{1,950 \text{ labour hours}}$ = £43.59

Summary

- Direct and indirect costs are charged to cost centres using expense codes and cost centre codes. Cost codes are a series of numbers designed to be applied to a classified set of items to give a brief, accurate reference to assist in collation and analysis.
- There are generally two types of cost centre: production cost centres – for example, a machine shop, where the products are manufactured; and service cost centres – for example, the personnel or salaries and wages departments. The service departments provide services for the production cost centres
- To arrive at the full cost of production, direct costs are allocated to production cost centres together with a share or apportionment of indirect, service centre costs. Overheads can be absorbed into production costs using agreed apportionment methods and rates.
- Overhead generally accrues on a time basis, so the longer a cost unit spends in production the more overhead an individual cost unit will generate. This means that the time-based methods – the labour hour rate and the machine hour rate – are preferred for labour-intensive cost centres and machine-intensive cost centres respectively.
- Full cost information helps managers in setting prices and for managing costs.

Cost behaviour and contribution analysis

12

Introduction

This chapter develops students' understanding of cost behaviour and its use in simple decision-making. Marginal costing attempts to identify the cost of producing one extra unit of output and the chapter introduces the important concept of contribution as being the difference between sales value and the variable cost of sales.

We also contrast absorption costing and marginal costing. A useful analysis of costs is in terms of variable and fixed costs but we still need to recognise that a firm must ensure that in the long term all costs are covered if it is to make a profit.

The chapter will be useful in encouraging cost centre managers to break down the total cost of a product or service into its individual components of fixed and variable costs. This will allow them to understand better how costs respond in relation to changing levels of business activity which should help improve forecasting and control costs. The chapter develops this by showing how the breakeven point can be calculated using both mathematical formulas and by the use of a chart and we review the assumptions and limitations of breakeven analysis.

1   Marginal costing and contribution

In chapter 11 the focus was on absorption costing as a method of costing widely used in business. An alternative costing method is marginal costing. **Marginal cost** is defined as the cost of one unit of product or service which would be avoided if that unit were not produced or provided. The marginal costs consist of the variable costs of production, namely the direct material cost, the direct labour cost, the variable production overhead and the variable costs of selling, distribution and administration. As we saw in chapter 10, variable costs are costs which tend to vary directly with the level of output. For example, as production increases, we can expect the total cost of raw materials to increase. In a similar way, if we are paying commission to sales agents, as sales output rises the commission paid will rise as well.

A **marginal costing** approach attempts to identify the cost of producing one extra unit of output and is defined as the accounting system in which variable costs are

marginal cost
The cost of one unit of product or service which would be avoided if that unit were not produced or provided.

marginal costing
The accounting system in which variable costs are charged to cost units and fixed costs of the period are written off in full against the aggregate contribution. Its special value is in decision-making.

contribution

Sales value less variable cost of sales. It may be expressed as total contribution, contribution per unit or as a percentage of sales.

charged to cost units and the fixed costs of the period are written off in full against the aggregate contribution (see Worked example 12.1). To achieve this a business needs to be able to distinguish between costs which vary with output and those that remain fixed. In marginal costing only variable costs are charged as part of cost of goods sold. The variable costs of goods sold are deducted from the value of sales to identify the contribution. The fixed costs are then deducted from the contribution to calculate the profit for the period. The contrast between marginal costing and absorption costing is illustrated in Worked example 12.1.

Worked example 12.1

Absorption costing

	£
Sales income	100,000
Less cost of goods sold	85,000
Profit	15,000

Suppose the cost of goods sold include £25,000 of fixed costs then the marginal costing method will present the figures as follows:

Marginal costing

	£
Sales income	100,000
Less marginal cost sales	60,000
Contribution	40,000
Less fixed costs	25,000
Profit	15,000

Contribution is the difference between sales value and the variable cost of sales. In effect, it is the contribution towards covering the fixed overheads and making a profit.

Absorption costing is based on the assumption that all the costs incurred by a business can be allocated or absorbed by each individual unit of production or output. The problem of course is that many of the costs incurred by a business are not directly related to the actual production. These costs, known as fixed costs (see chapter 10), are the costs that a business will incur regardless of the level of output. In an absorption costing system, as the units of output change, the cost per unit will change. If the units of output are less than budgeted, the cost per unit will increase, and vice versa. Similarly, the fixed costs applied to each unit of output will rise as the output falls. Equally, if the actual output achieved is more than expected, then the fixed costs per unit of output will fall. This variation in the cost of each individual unit of output can make it difficult to calculate accurately in advance the real costs of one unit of output and this can have serious implications when pricing decisions are being made. The technique of marginal costing tries to make sense of this dilemma.

1.1   Comparison between absorption and marginal costing

The marginal costing method is based on the assumption that the process of full allocation of costs as exemplified in overhead absorption is a waste of time. It is argued that the only analysis that is required is that for variable and fixed cost. This approach is likely to be easier and less subject to the inaccuracies of the allocation and apportionment process. Proponents of marginal costing argue that full costing is out of date in competitive markets where price is more likely to be determined by consumer demand than what the producer believes the product is worth. For example, in the electrical appliances sector it is possible to identify appliances such as televisions at approximately the same price from most manufacturers. Although the manufacturer will have worked out the total cost, the price is likely to be determined by what the competitors are charging for the equivalent model rather than on the basis of total cost plus profit. Marginal costing presents information in a simple way with analysis mainly restricted to variable costs, with fixed costs dealt with as an additional, unallocated sum.

These arguments in favour of marginal costing can be countered by suggesting that all firms must understand their cost structures. Overhead absorption does involve arbitrary allocation of costs to a product or service but firms need to ensure that in the long term all costs are covered if a firm is to make a profit.

Worked example   12.2

Comparison between absorption and marginal costing

A business manufactures three products. The accountant has produced a statement of the profitability of the three products based on absorption costing as follows:

	A	B	C	Total
	£	£	£	£
Sales	64,000	100,000	90,000	254,000
Total costs	72,000	78,000	66,000	216,000
Net profit/(loss)	(8,000)	22,000	24,000	38,000

The statement reveals that the three products make a total profit of £38,000 with product A making a loss of £8,000. This information might lead managers to decide that product A should be dropped. However, it ignores the fact that many of the costs incurred by the business are not directly related to the actual production. These fixed costs are costs that the business will tend to incur regardless of the level of output, and will therefore remain the same. On investigating the total costs of £216,000 the accountant finds that one third of the total costs are fixed and the remainder are variable. This means that the variable cost of the three products is £48,000, £52,000 and £ 44,000 respectively. The cost table can now be presented using the marginal cost method:

Worked example *(continued)*   12.2

	A	B	C	Total
	£	£	£	£
Sales	64,000	100,000	90,000	254,000
Less variable costs	48,000	52,000	44,000	144,000
Contribution	16,000	48,000	46,000	110,000
Less fixed costs				72,000
Profit				38,000

The second table shows that product A, although loss-making, does make a positive contribution towards the payment of the unavoidable fixed costs, hence there is case that it should be retained in the product range.

Test *yourself*   12.1

(a) Identify THREE marginal costs of production

(b) Define what is understood by the term marginal costing.

2   Marginal costing as an aid to decision-making

In deciding the course of action a business should follow it is useful to understand the cost and revenue implications involved. In predicting the consequences of proposed changes, an understanding of the behaviour of costs is essential. Costs can be classified in a number of different ways, depending on the purpose for which the information is required. It is useful in many decision-making situations to classify costs as either fixed or variable. As the names suggest, fixed costs are those costs which will not change, whereas variable costs are those that will alter as a result of some event. Clearly, in a business situation there is nothing which would fall strictly within this simplistic definition of fixed cost. Ultimately, all costs in a business can be altered, even if the change is brought about by something as dramatic as the termination of business. Thus whilst recognising that in the long run all costs are variable it is useful to make the distinction to assist decision-makers.

2.1   Classifying costs

Fixed costs were introduced and described in chapter 10. These are costs that in general remain constant even when the level of business activity fluctuates. They do not tend to change, at least in the short term, as sales output or production rises. These costs include items such as rent, rates, telephone costs, insurance payments and managerial salaries.

Fixed costs may change in the long term if the business increases or decreases its production capacity, for example. Changes in such costs as salaries, or rent and rates will also affect the level of fixed costs, but in general it is fairly easy to predict the level of fixed costs for at least 12 months in advance, or until a fundamental change in the way the business operates takes place.

A cost is fixed only relative to time or a specific event, and thus should be understood in relation to a specified time frame or event.

We saw in chapter 10 that variable costs are the costs which tend to vary directly with the level of output. For example, as production increases we can expect the total cost of raw materials to increase. Similarly, if we are paying commission to sales agents, as sales output rises the commission paid will rise as well.

Marginal costing emphasises the point that variable costs will always tend to be a fixed percentage of the value of an organisation's output if price levels remain constant.

We also saw that some costs, semi-variable costs, contain both fixed and variable elements. Examples would be the cost of electricity in a factory which is fixed to a certain level, tends to rise as production and levels increase.

2.2 Cost behaviour

Breaking down total costs into individual components of fixed and variable costs, and understanding how costs behave in relation to changing levels of business activity, we can begin the process of accurately defining and controlling current costs and forecasting future costs.

cost behaviour
The way in which costs of output are affected by fluctuations in the level of activity.

Stop and Think   12.1

Classify these costs under the various columns

	Fixed	Variable	Semi- variable
Printing and stationery			
Production wages			
Premises insurance			
Premises electricity			
Raw materials			
Managers' salaries			
Sales salaries (part commission)			
Vehicle running costs			

Stop and Think *(continued)*   12.1

Answer

	Fixed	Variable	Semi- variable
Printing and stationery	✓		
Production wages			✓
Premises insurance	✓		
Premises electricity			✓
Raw materials		✓	
Managers' salaries	✓		
Sales salaries (part commission)			✓
Vehicle running costs			✓

2.3 Contribution

The relevance of marginal costing in decision-making lies in the fact that in the short term the only costs that change are the variable costs or marginal costs. This means that in decision-making, the only relevant figures are the marginal or variable costs and the income of each alternative. The fixed costs can be ignored as they stay the same regardless of which alternative is selected. The use of marginal costing in decision-making is built around the concept of contribution (see section 1 above).

Marginal costing can be illustrated by the following:

Profit (Loss) = Total sales revenue – Total costs
Total costs = Fixed costs + Variable costs
Profit (Loss) = Total sales revenue – (Fixed costs + Variable costs)

As the fixed costs remain unaltered, the only relevant figures are the variable costs and the income of each alternative. This means identifying the contribution, which is the sales value less the variable cost of sales, expressed as follows:

Contribution = Sales – Variable costs = Contribution

The total contribution generated by a particular volume of sales has to be sufficient to cover the fixed costs for the period. Any excess contribution over the fixed costs represents the profit (loss) for the period.

3 Breakeven analysis

The above mathematics allows business managers to identify the **breakeven point**. This is the level of activity at which there is neither profit nor loss. The number of units that mangers need to sell in order to break even will be the total fixed costs divided by the contribution per unit. This is because the total contribution required to break even must be equal to the total fixed costs.

breakeven point
The level of activity at which there is neither profit nor loss.

Breakeven point (BEP) in units:

$$\text{Number of units to be sold to break even} = \frac{\text{Total fixed costs}}{\text{Contribution per unit}}$$

Worked example 12.3 gives a simple demonstration.

Worked example   12.3

Breakeven analysis

A business plans to sell 12,000 units of a product at £20 per unit. The variable cost per unit is £10 per unit and incurs £60,000 of fixed costs.

How many units does the business need to sell in order to break even?

Answer

Selling price per unit – Variable cost per unit = Contribution per unit

£20 – £10 = £10

$$\frac{\text{Total fixed costs}}{\text{Contribution per unit}} = \text{Number of units to be sold to break even}$$

$$\frac{£60,000}{£10} = 6,000 \text{ units}$$

3.1 Breakeven charts

The breakeven point can also be determined by the use of a chart. The **breakeven chart** is prepared by identifying the sales/output (in units or in value) on the horizontal axis and the values for sales revenue and costs on the vertical axis. The following lines can then be drawn on the chart:

breakeven chart
A chart which indicates approximate profit or loss at different levels of sales volume within a limited range.

- The *sales line* which starts at the origin, i.e. zero volume of sales = zero sales revenue and finishes at the point which reflects the forecast sales.
- The *fixed cost line* which is drawn parallel to the horizontal axis, starting at a point which represents the total fixed costs.
- The *total cost line* which represents the total fixed costs plus the total variable cost of the forecast sales in units. The line starts at the point where the fixed cost line meets the vertical axis (zero output) and finishes at the point which reflects the forecast sales.

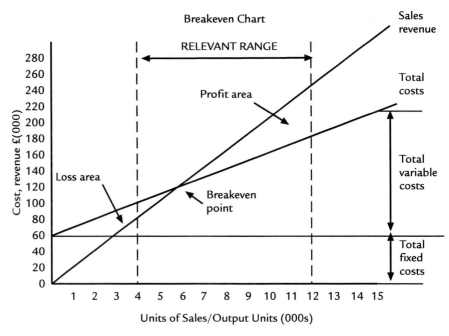

Figure 12.1 Breakeven chart

The breakeven point is located where the total cost line intersects the total sales line. The breakeven point in terms of the sales value and sales units can be read from the two axes at this point.

Worked example   12.4

Use figure 12.1 to determine:

1   The selling price per unit.
2   The fixed costs.
3   The variable cost per unit.
4   The breakeven point in units.
5   The breakeven point in sales revenue.

The items can be identified as follows:

1   The selling price per unit can be read off for example by identifying the sale of 12,000 units' produces total revenue of £240,000 or a selling price per unit of £20.
2   The fixed costs can be seen by reading £60,000 where the fixed cost line intersects the vertical cost line.
3   The variable cost per unit at 12,000 units is found by reading off the total cost of £180,000 less the total fixed costs of £60,000, i.e. £120,000 variable costs divided by 12,000 unit = £10 per unit.
4   The breakeven point in units can be read off the horizontal axis where the total cost line intersects the total revenue line, i.e. 6000 units.
5   The break-even point in sales revenue is 6000 units multiplied by the selling price per unit of £20, i.e. £120,000.

Note that the answers produce the same answers as those provided by Worked example 12.3.

3.2   Relevant range

In figure 12.1 there are two broken lines running vertically down the chart. The gap between these lines draws attention to the idea of the **relevant range of activity**, the activity levels within which the assumptions about cost behaviour in the breakeven chart remain valid. In this case the chart is pointing out that the costs and revenue relationships will only remain valid between say 4,000 and 12,000 units.

3.3   Margin of safety

The other point that can be identified by breakeven analysis is the **margin of safety**. This is the gap between the breakeven point and the planned or budgeted level of activity. In 12.1, the business planned to sell 12,000 units and the breakeven point is 6000 units giving a margin of safety of 6000 units. This means activity can fall by this amount, or 50%, before the business makes a loss. The greater the margin of safety, the smaller the risk. A low margin of safety would suggest that fixed costs are high and sufficient profits will not be made until there is a high level of activity. A small fall in productive capacity or in sales will lower profits considerably. A business with a high margin of safety can continue to make profits even if there is a serious drop in sales, provided the drop does not fall below break-even point.

3.4   Profit/volume (P/V) ratio

The contribution per unit measures the amount of contribution to fixed cost and profit from the sale of one unit of product. **The profit/volume (p/v) ratio** measures the contribution per £1 of sales.

$$\text{P/V Ratio:} \quad \frac{\text{(Unit) Contribution}}{\text{(Unit) Selling price/Sales revenue}}$$

A P/V ratio of 0.6 means that a product generates a contribution of 60 pence for every £1 of sales; whilst a contribution of 0.4 would mean that a product generated a contribution of only 40 pence for every £1 sales. The profit/volume (P/V) ratio measures the contribution per £1 of sales. The profit/volume ratio is also known as the contribution percentage.

3.5   Profit/volume chart

The breakeven chart presented in figure 12.1 has one major weakness in that it is not easy to identify the actual amount of profit or loss at different levels of activity. In the breakeven chart the profit had to be calculated by the value of the gap between the total revenue line and the total cost line. This profit/volume chart (Figure 12.2) shows the impact on profit of changes in turnover. The example below is based on the data used in the earlier breakeven graph.

relevant range of activity

The activity levels within which assumptions about cost behaviour in a break-even chart remain valid.

margin of safety

The amount by which the forecast turnover exceeds or falls short of breakeven.

profit/volume (p/v) ratio

The relationship between revenue and the contribution it generates (e.g. if an item sells for £60 and generates £15 contribution, its p/v ratio is 25%).

profit/volume chart

Chart showing the impact on profit of changes in turnover.

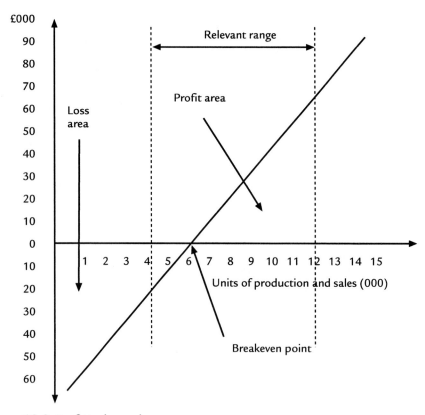

Figure 12.2 Profit/volume chart

The profit volume chart is prepared by:

1 The horizontal axis which represents the units of production, the sales value or the percentage of activity.
2 The vertical axis which represents losses or profits for various levels of activity.
3 The sales line which is drawn on the chart.

The profit volume chart reveals the following:

1 The breakeven point is located on the chart where the total cost line intersects the total sales line.
2 The breakeven point in terms of the sales units (6000) can be identified at this point.
3 There is a loss of £60,000, when there are no sales, which is equal to the fixed costs.
4 There is profit of £90,000 when sales of 15,000 units are achieved.

Test *yourself*   12.2

(a) What is meant by the term contribution?
(b) How would you construct a break-even chart?
(c) What is meant by the margin of safety?

4   Assumptions underlying breakeven analysis

The use of breakeven analysis depends on assumptions made about costs and revenues included in the analysis. These assumptions are as follows:

● Variable costs vary in direct proportion with changes in output. This assumption implies there is a linear relationship between variable costs and output. This linearity is represented by straight lines on a breakeven chart. This is illustrated as follows:

Figure 12.3 illustrates the assumption that variable costs remain constant per unit of activity.

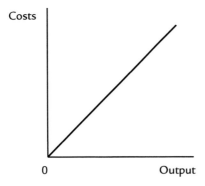

Figure 12.3 Variable costs remain constant per unit of activity

● The breakeven model assumes a single product is made and where there are several products it assumes a constant mix and the use of average variable costs for the mix of products is acceptable.
● The analysis is applied within a relevant range of activity only.

4.1   Limitations of breakeven analysis

The limitations include the following:

● In reality the assumption of linearity is unlikely to apply. For example, the relationship can be convex where the production of one extra unit of output produces less than a proportionate increase in cost. For example, variable cost per unit may decline as suppliers offer discounts for bulk purchases or the business benefits from economies of scale. This is illustrated in Figure 12.4.

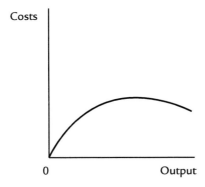

Figure 12.4 Reduction in variable costs with economies of scale

- The assumption that fixed costs will remain at a fixed level is unlikely to apply over a wide range of activity. Fixed costs tend to be 'stepped', i.e. they increase once a certain level of activity is reached. For example, a supervisor's salary may be seen as a fixed cost but once a certain number of employees are reached a supervisor may have to be employed. Thus fixed costs are likely to have steps at different points of activity. This is illustrated in Figure 12.5:

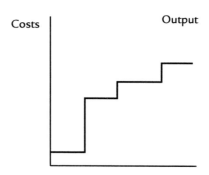

Figure 12.5 Stepped fixed costs

- It is not always possible to divide or classify costs into fixed or variable. Many such as labour costs cannot be classified as a variable cost as legislation makes it difficult to pay people solely according to activity and to make them redundant at short notice.
- The range of activity over which the assumptions apply is very difficult to determine with any accuracy.

Despite these shortcomings, breakeven analysis does have something to offer managers involved in short-term decision-making. For example, it may be better to allow activity to produce sales revenue to cover only variable costs, for example when a business has spare capacity, or to keep an experienced workforce together. This approach will generate some contribution towards fixed costs, which may be preferable to no contribution at all. The short-term approach may be to maximise contribution, but in the longer term all fixed costs must be covered.

Test *yourself*   2.3

(a) What is the one major weakness of a breakeven chart that is diminished by the use of a P/V chart?

(b) Breakeven analysis depends on the assumption of linear relationships. Explain what this means.

Putting the case
12.1

You have been asked by the factory manager in Newcastle to:

1 Prepare the two statements requested in the case study by the manager of the Newcastle factory.

2 Calculate the number of units that must be sold for the product to break even.

3 Identify both the margin of safety and the total profit that would be made if the factory production was reduced by 3,000 units.

1 The profit presented in traditional way:

	£	£
Sales (£15 × 15,000)		225,000
Variable costs (£10 × 15,000)	150,000	
Plus fixed costs	50,000	
Total costs		200,000
Profit		25,000

A profit expressed using contribution:

	Total £	Per Unit £
Sales (£15 × 15,000)	225,000	15
Less variable costs (£10 × 15,000)	150,000	10
Contribution	75,000	5
Less fixed cost	50,000	
Profit	25,000	

Under the second layout it can be seen that sales are covering the variable costs and then, if there is anything left, contributing towards fixed costs and finally any balance goes towards profit. Any surplus after covering variable cost *contributes* first to fixed costs and then to profit.

2 Breakeven point

If we take the contribution for one unit (selling price per unit minus variable cost per unit) and then divide that into the fixed costs we can see how many units we need to sell to cover all the fixed costs, i.e. to break even. In the above case the contribution per unit is therefore £15 – £10 = £5

$$\text{Breakeven: } \frac{\text{Fixed costs}}{\text{Contribution per unit}} = \frac{£50,000}{£5} = 10,000 \text{ units}$$

Putting the case *(continued)*   12.1

3 Sales drop by 3,000 units to 12,000 units

	£
Contribution per unit £5 × 12,000 units (revised sales figure) =	60,000
Less Total fixed costs	50,000
Total profit	10,000

Planned sales	12,000
Break-even sales	10,000
Margin of safety	2,000

Summary

- Marginal cost is defined as the cost of one unit of product or service which would be avoided if that unit were not produced or provided. If a marginal costing approach is taken, the aim is to identify the marginal costs a business incurs in producing and selling its product or service.
- The marginal costs consist of the variable costs of production.
- Marginal costing is the accounting system in which variable costs are charged to cost units and fixed costs of the period are written off in full against the aggregate contribution.
- Contribution is the difference between sales value and the variable cost of sales. In effect it is the contribution towards covering the fixed overheads and making a profit.
- Absorption costing is based on the assumption that all the costs incurred by a business can be allocated or absorbed by each individual unit of production or output. In contrast, marginal costing is based on the assumption that the process of full allocation of costs as in overhead absorption is pointless. It is argued that the only analysis that is required is that for variable and fixed cost.
- Break-even analysis – finding the level of activity at which there is neither profit nor loss – can be calculated using a simple mathematical formula and can also be calculated using a chart which will also show the relevant range of activity, margin of safety and the profit/volume (p/v) ratio.
- Breakeven analysis is based on the linear assumption that costs rise in direct proportion with output and that fixed costs remain fixed. In reality neither of these hold true over time, but despite these limitations, breakeven analysis is a useful tool for short-term decision-making.

Part Three Practice Questions

3.1 Identify SIX functions/departments on which a manufacturing company may base its costing information.

3.2 Define and illustrate with examples the following categories of costs:
- Materials.
- Labour.
- Other expenses.

3.3 Provide examples of cost units which could be used to ascertain costs in relation to the following services:

Service	Cost Unit
Hotel accommodation	
Accounting practice	
Human resource department	
Airline company	
Regional hospital	
Parcel delivery	
Restaurant	
University department	

3.4 The production manager of a business manufacturing garden sheds has provided the following estimates for the month of January 200X:

	Department X	Department Y
Material usage (metres per shed)	1.5	4.5
Material cost per metre	£6.70	£4.50
Labour hours per shed	0.5	2
Labour cost per hour	£8.20	£5.25
Machine hours per shed	1.75	Nil

The production manager has estimated the productive capacity for Department X for January 200X in terms of 6,678 machine hours and 3,625 labour hours. The equivalent figures for Department Y are 0 machine hours and 21,140 labour hours. The factory accountant has estimated that the overheads allocated to Departments X and Y are £66,780 and £105,700 respectively.

Calculate the full cost of producing one garden shed.

3.5

  a) Explain how the following indirect costs can be apportioned to cost centres:
    - Rent and rates.
    - Canteen facilities.
    - Insurance premiums
  b) Discuss the assertion that overhead absorption methods provide an accurate way of charging indirect costs to a cost centre.

3.6 Identify THREE reasons why a business needs to hold cash.

3.7 What are the costs and benefits of a business holding large levels of stock or inventory?

3.8 In terms of breakeven analysis, identify how the following can be calculated:
  (i)   Volume of sales in units to break even.
  (ii) Volume of sales in units to achieve a required profit.
  (iii) Profit-to-volume ratio.
  (iv) Margin of safety.

3.9 Explain what you understand by the term marginal cost and how it can help decision-makers.

3.10 Identify the respective advantages of a marginal costing system and an absorption costing system.

Using Budgets to Manage Business Resources

PART FOUR

Contents

Overview

This final part will help managers to use budgets to plan, monitor and control the use of their resources. Students will be introduced to definitions of budgeting and explanations of their objectives within the context of an organisation.

Having set the scene for budgets, we move on to consider the construction and operation of budgets. We consider different approaches to budget preparation and describe the process of preparing the various budgets within an organisation. These are illustrated by the preparation of simple budgets from relevant data.

Part 4 will also increase a manager's appreciation of the importance of supplying information for budgetary purposes. It is hoped that the experience of seeing how budgets fit together and of producing simple budgets will help managers at work.

Part 4 concludes by introducing managers to interpreting and acting on the information produced by budgetary control systems. This involves describing the use of budgets in exercising control over business resources. This part of the book should be relevant to managers' experience in the workplace. Managers will frequently receive budget reports which ask them to explain actual budget performance against the budgeted figures. The identification, explanation and correction of budget variances are likely to be part of many business managers' responsibilities. The practical application of this part of the syllabus should make the study of it both enjoyable and rewarding.

Learning objectives

▶ Understand that businesses have long-term objectives which are achieved through strategic plans and operational tactics.

▶ Define and explain the purpose of preparing budgets and the key procedures by which a budget is prepared.

- ▶ Demonstrate an understanding of the various types of budget and the methods of preparation.
- ▶ Explain the interrelationships between the various budgets in a business.
- ▶ Construct a simple budget.
- ▶ Begin to recognise the human aspects involved in the budgetary process.
- ▶ Explain the key elements of a budgetary control system and design a simple budgetary control statement.
- ▶ Analyse the results of a comparison of actual performance with the budget.

Budgeting

Joe Smith has a small business with several shops located across southeast London. You are employed as a business administrator based in the central accounting department. Your main role is to help in communicating information and advice between the accounting department and shop managers. The shops are all expected to make a profit and each manager has many tasks and responsibilities, particularly in relation to budgeting. Each shop manager produces revenue and capital budgets.

The managers are becoming increasingly frustrated at the amount of time taken up with budgets in particular, and planning in general. One of them describes the level of detail required in the budgeting process as excessive – for example, preparing capital budgets as well as revenue budgets seems a waste of time. Similarly the shop managers and their deputies are planning to spend a residential weekend together discussing the long-term strategic objectives of the business. They know when they get back to work on Monday morning they will be faced with a mountain of paperwork including a 20-page budget reference manual. The managers are all of the opinion that their time would be better spent managing the shops.

At a recent meeting between the chief accountant and the shop managers further concerns about the budgetary control system were raised. In particular the shop managers are concerned that the budgets they have to manage are imposed by the top management. They expressed a view that this top-down approach was not one to be followed in a twenty-first-century business. At the same meeting the shop managers also voiced their apprehension about the budgetary control reports they receive each month. These were frequently used as a stick to criticise them. The chief accountant has promised to investigate their concerns.

A list of issues to be discussed at the residential week end is presented below. You have been asked to prepare responses to the questions raised by the shop managers. It is important that where possible you provide relevant examples to support the advice you are giving. You are required to provide answers to the case questions as they appear throughout Part 4.

The nature and purpose of budgets 13

Introduction

This chapter discusses how organisations have long-term objectives which underpin their strategic plan. The organisation needs to develop the tactics or methods used in implementing the strategic plan. This chapter explains that these are likely to cover the short term, usually one year. The tactics will be developed to cover all operational activities of the organisation, including sales, production, personnel, land and buildings, marketing, finance, etc. It is at this stage that the annual budget or annual operating plan comes into play as it sets financial targets for the year.

The annual budget is a financial and quantitative statement of policy. It is more than a simple statement of income and expenditure expected during a period. It covers a wide range of functions such as planning, coordination, communicating, authorising, motivating and controlling events to enable managers to control the business and achieve the annual budget. The chapter concludes by discussing various types of budgets and the methods of preparing them.

1   Strategy and planning

All organisations, whether a one-person business, a multinational corporation or a charity, need to plan ahead. This process involves setting clear objectives, identifying the key issues facing the organisation, reducing uncertainty and providing a clear guide as to the way forward. In simple terms this involves going through at least the following three stages:

1   Identify the long-term objectives for the organisation. These are likely to be for a given period and be applied to different parts of the organisation and its activities. These objectives make it easier for the organisation to identify and change priorities and to be more able to react to changing demands and needs.

   These objectives might focus on, for example, 'a 50% improvement in profits over a three-year period', 'a 3% reduction in overhead costs', 'a market share to be established in two countries in the Far East'. These objectives are set by senior managers and should become the focus of the activities of all personnel within the organisation.

strategic plan

The formulation, evaluation and selection of strategies for the purpose of preparing a long term plan of action to attain objectives.

2 Produce a **strategic plan** which will help the organisation's long-term objectives to be achieved. This will be included in a long-term plan covering a period of, say, three to five years. The plan will help provide the resources and structure to achieve the objectives. The strategy will involve an assessment of the market targeted by the organisation; the range of products and services to be provided; the methods of producing products and/or delivering a service; the resource requirements in terms of personnel, buildings, equipment and finance; the levels of profits expected by the owners of the business, etc. For example, a business with an overall objective to grow or become more profitable will need to look at four strategies to achieve this:

(a) selling more of its existing goods and services to its existing customers (penetration);

(b) finding new customers to buy the existing products (product development);

(c) developing or acquiring new products to sell to its existing customers (market development);

(d) selling completely new products to completely new customers (diversification).

3 Develop the tactics or methods which are to be employed in implementing a strategic plan. This will involve choosing one course of action, for example leasing a factory, at the expense of another, for example purchasing the factory, to achieve a particular end. These tactics are likely to cover the short term – usually one year – and will cover all operational business activities, including sales, production, personnel, land and buildings, marketing and finance. For example, if a retailer selects as its strategic objective increasing sales it may have to adopt the tactic of selling products in its existing shops to existing customers as the cost of this is lower than trying to break into new markets which would involve opening new shops and attracting new customers. It is at this stage that the annual budget comes into play as it sets financial targets for the year.

Test *yourself*   13.1

What do you understand by the term long-term business objectives?

Putting the case
13.1

The following question will be discussed at the residential weekend with the shop managers:

What are long-term strategic objectives of a business and how are they set?

The long-term strategic objectives of a business are concerned with identifying its long-term purpose and/or direction. Unless the business knows what it is trying to achieve it is unlikely to be able to plan and control the direction of the business.

The achievement of the objectives could cover, say, a five-year period. The objectives will be set by assessing both the external influences on the

business and the internal resources available to it. External influences include government policy, competitors, exchange rates, cultural values, demographics, etc. Internal resources include human, financial and physical resources. This review will allow a business to develop strategic objectives and plan. For example, a business may have a strategy of working together to become the leading provide of its product in southeast London by setting standards for customer satisfaction, financial performance and quality in all they do. The business may try to achieve this by focusing on continually improving their retailing procedures to satisfy customer needs and wants.

2   What is a budget?

A **budget** can be defined in terms of one or all of the following:

- A plan of action for a future period expressed in monetary and/or quantitative terms.
- A financial and quantitative statement of policy to be pursued.
- A plan prepared and approved prior to a defined period of time in order to attain the organisations objectives.
- A plan or target in quantities and/or money value prepared for a future period of time.

The annual budget shows the planned income and expenditure for the next financial year. The annual budget is complemented by a **capital budget** which shows the investment in fixed assets over a longer period of, say, three years. In all of the above definitions the budget is seen as expressing the organisation's objectives in monetary terms for a period of time.

budget
A plan for the future, expressed in money, showing income, expenditure and the capital to be employed.

capital budget
Budget of the cost of acquiring, producing or enhancing fixed assets.

2.1   Reasons for producing budgets

A budget is more than a simple statement of income and expenditure expected during a period. Budgeting is a negotiating process during which estimates of what it will cost to meet the business's operational expenditure plans are matched with the expectations of income. The reasons for producing budgets include the following:

- *Plan the annual operations of the business*. This will ensure that managers consider how conditions in the next year might change and what steps they should take now to respond to these changing conditions. This might involve how to generate cash resources during the year ahead to cover for potential cash shortfalls as they arise. This might involve negotiating bank overdraft facilities or ensuring debts are collected as quickly as possible.

● *Coordinate the activities of the various parts of the business.* The preparation of the annual budget can be a means through which the actions of the different parts of an organisation can be brought together and integrated into a common plan. For example, the marketing department may be considering an advertising promotion to increase sales which the production department cannot handle. The budget preparation process aims to reconcile such inconsistencies and correct them *before* the final budget is agreed. This may mean repeated drafting of the budget.

● *Communicate the overall objectives and plans to all the employees of the organisation.* Everyone in the organisation has to be made aware not only of the long- and short-term objectives of the business but also their role in achieving them. Through the budget process, senior management communicates its expectations to lower-level management. The budget preparation process is particularly important because it should allow a two-way communication process where vital ideas and information is shared. Obviously the finished budget is important but business managers need to recognise the benefits of the actual preparation process in its own right.

● *Authorise future expenditure.* Once a budget is prepared and approved by senior management it acts as a formal authority for the expenditure in the future to individuals who are responsible for it. In effect the budget process delegates authority to incur the expenditure in the future without seeking further approval.

● *Motivate employees to achieve the organisational objectives.* A budget provides a target which employees may be motivated to achieve. The involvement in the budgeting process can motivate employees to take responsibility for achieving budgets which they have been involved in setting. This involvement and the subsequent acceptance of a budget by the employees can result in their taking responsibility for the activities and costs which they can control.

● *Control the actual events to conform to the annual budget.* Business managers need to establish a system which continuously compares the budget against actual results. Business managers can then focus their attention on significant deviations from the expected results. The deviations or **budget variances** can be reviewed and reasons for the budget variances identified and corrective action taken if necessary.

budget variance
The difference between budget and actual cost for each cost in a budget and revenue, where appropriate.

● *Evaluate and reward the performance of managers.* Organisations can measure individual success in achieving budgets through continual monitoring. Budgets which involve managers at all stages can promote flair and enthusiasm. Such skills can be rewarded in terms of promotion opportunities, staff development and/or performance related pay.

2.2 Linking strategy and the annual budget

Before moving on to cover the mechanics of the annual budgets, managers are asked to consider the following issues:

● The annual budget is not a technical exercise produced in isolation. It has to mirror the long-term objectives and strategies of the organisation. Frequently, the annual budget is part of a three- or five-year rolling plan where the budget is continually updated, adding, say, another year and deducting the earliest period.

● The production of the annual budget is not the concern of the accountant only. The accountant will be able to offer the technical advice to assist managers in deciding their tactics. While the accountant can offer financial advice it should be remembered that other managers, such as sales, production and marketing, will have an important role to play in preparing the annual budget. The above process is summarised in Figure 13.1.

The budget translates the long-range plans into an *annual operating plan* which is prepared within the constraints laid down by the objectives and strategies of the business.

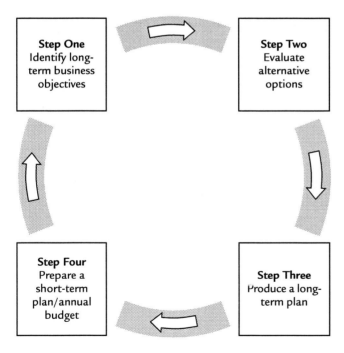

Figure 13.1 Strategy and the annual budget

Putting the case   13.2

 The following question will be discussed at the residential weekend with the shop managers:
How are the long-term strategies of the business linked to the annual budgeting process?

 The strategic plan sets out to achieve long-term objectives. The business will now prepare an annual plan/budget which will set out the annual detailed financial implications of achieving the long-term objectives. For example, the annual shop budgets may reflect the cost of changing selling processes and/or staffing levels to improve the quality of their service and so improve customer satisfaction. The individual shop budgets will be combined to produce a master budget.

The annual budget should not only reflect the strategic objectives of the business but also be the basis for monitoring and controlling their achievement. Thus any variances from the planned budget will be investigated and corrective action taken to get back on track to achieve both the annual budget and the long-term objectives and strategy.

Test *yourself*   13.2

(a) Why should the accountant not be solely responsible for preparing the annual budget?

(b) Provide an example of how the preparation of the annual budget can play in coordinating the activities of a business?

Stop and Think   13.1

Why might business managers be reluctant to become involved in preparing budgets?

revenue or operating budget
Budget of the expenditure and income for a financial year. The expenditure will be spent on the supply and manufacture of goods and the provision of services in the accounting period in which they are consumed.

3 Types of budget

The two most common types of budget are capital budgets and **revenue budgets** or **operating budgets.** Capital budgets include expenditure on purchasing fixed assets. Revenue or operating budgets are concerned with expenditure and income incurred or generated on a daily basis. Revenue expenditure includes goods purchased for resale, salaries and wages, electricity charges and other day-to-day running expenses. Revenue income includes income from the sale of goods or services to customers, rents and dividends.

Putting the case 13.3

 You are asked to write to all the shop managers providing answers to the following questions:

- Explain the key differences between the terms revenue and capital expenditure.

- Explain, giving reasons, which of the following would be classified as capital expenditure within a retailing business.

1 Purchase of an extra computer for controlling the accounts and stock records.

2 Cost of floppy disks, paper and printer cartridges.

3 Purchase of two cars for use by shop managers.

4 Delivery expenses and legal costs associated with the purchase and installation of computer network system.

5 Training staff in selling techniques.

6 Cost of redecorating the shops.

Capital expenditure is concerned with:

- Purchasing long-term permanent fixed assets for use in the business, e.g. ·purchase of buildings and equipment.

- The assets are bought to be used in the business and not to be sold.

- The assets are used to help the business sell its goods and services.

Revenue expenditure is concerned with:

- The day-to-day running of the business, including expenditure on such as salaries and wages, heating, loan interest, etc.

- Expenditure giving immediate benefit to the business i.e. in the year the expenditure is incurred.

The expenditure should be classified as follows:

1 Purchase of an extra computer for controlling the accounts, etc. – capital expenditure as it is the purchase of a long-term fixed asset.

2 Cost of floppy disks, paper and printer cartridges – computer consumables are revenue expenditure as they are used up in a few days/weeks.

3 Purchase of two cars for use by accountants – capital expenditure as they are fixed assets giving benefit over several accounting periods.

4 Delivery expenses and legal costs associated with the purchase and installation of computer network system – capital expenditure as these costs relate to acquiring or adding value to a fixed asset.

5 Training staff in selling techniques – revenue expenditure as training is an ongoing operating expense.

6 Cost of redecorating the shops – revenue expenditure as it is an ongoing operating expense.

4   Methods of budget preparation

An organisation can adopt various methods of budgeting:

- Incremental budgets.
- Zero-based budgets.
- Fixed budgets.
- Flexible budgets.

Before the annual budget is prepared, a base should be determined as a starting point.
Usually this is the current level of operating activity, which is then adjusted for

incremental budgeting
Projected expenditure and income is determined on the current level of operating activity, adjusted for anticipated activity changes and inflation.

anticipated changes due to growth and/or reductions in service levels inflation, etc. This method is called **incremental budgeting**. The disadvantage of this approach is that it continues previous inefficiencies. However, it is advocated by those who believe that the level of operating activity of most businesses will not change dramatically from year to year. It is also a relatively quick and inexpensive method as an incremental approach focuses on the changes and accepts the base.

An alternative approach to the incremental approach is **zero-based budgeting (ZBB)**. Here the budget starts from a zero base, with each year's budgets being compiled as though for the first time. Managers need to justify their budgets based on the following:

zero-based budgeting (ZBB)
A method of budgeting whereby all activities are re-evaluated each time a budget is set.

- Should the activity be performed at all?
- What level of activity should be performed?
- Are we delivering the activity in the most efficient way?
- What should it cost to deliver the activity?

Although it is time-consuming, the ZBB approach does attempt to share budget resources according to need and benefit rather than maintaining the status quo. The approach creates a questioning attitude and focuses on achieving value for money.

4.1   Fixed budget

fixed budgets
A budget which is designed to remain unchanged irrespective of the volume of output or turnover achieved.

This budget is designed to remain unchanged irrespective of the volume of output or turnover achieved. Consequently, if the actual activity is considerably above/below budget, then significant variances are likely to occur. Fixed budgets do not attempt to distinguish between fixed and variable costs.

4.2   Flexible budget

flexible budget
A budget which, by recognising different cost behaviour patterns, is designed to change as volume of output changes.

Managers are aware of the degree of variability of costs and the amount of costs of a fixed nature in a particular item of cost. As a consequence, it is possible to redraft budgets to reflect the cost for the level of activity attained. The flexible budget is designed to adjust the permitted cost levels to reflect the actual level of activity achieved. Where the principal factor on which the budget is based, for instance sales levels, is significantly different from budget, it may be appropriate to 'flex' the budget. After all if sales increase, it is likely that costs will increase. If the budget is fixed, this would result in unnecessary questions being asked about why costs have increased. For proper control to take place the budget holders should only be responsible for events that are within their influence. The flexible budget enables expenditure to be more closely controlled by relating actual expenditure to the budgeted expenditure for the actual level of activity achieved.

Test *yourself*   13.4

(a) Identify TWO differences between zero based budgeting and incremental budgeting.

(b) What is flexed in a flexible budget?

5   The planning process

Business managers need to appreciate that preparing the annual budget is more than a number-crunching exercise. This key point, which is referred to throughout this chapter, is reinforced in Figure 13.2.

Produce a statement which identifies the long-term objectives of the business. The objectives are set for a given period and applied all parts of the business.

⇩

Evaluate the external environment faced by the business and analyse the internal resources of the business.

⇩

Produce a strategic plan which will assist achievement of the long term objectives of the business. This will cover a 35-year period.

⇩

Develop the tactics or methods which are to be employed in executing a strategic plan. This will involve choosing courses of action to achieve particular ends. These tactics, covering all operational activities, are likely to cover the short term usually one year.

⇩

Prepare the annual budget which translates the long-range plans into an annual operating plan prepared within the constraints laid down by the objectives and strategies of the business.

Figure 13.2 The planning process

Summary

- A budget is the expression, in financial and quantitative terms, of a business plan for a defined period of time.
- The objectives of a business are the starting point in that they have to be converted into achievable plans. These plans need to be specified in measurable terms, have a time scale for their achievement and clear methods defined by which they are to be achieved.
- The strategies of the business will be decided upon after a review of the external influences on the business including government policy, competitors, the age, values and income of customers, etc. This external review will be put along side a review of the internal resources of the business namely finance, human resources and physical assets.
- The annual budget must conform to the business's longer-term objectives and take account of the external and internal constraints on the business. In effect the annual budget represents one stage in the achievement of the long-term objectives.

- The annual budget defines in financial terms the short-term plans of the business, allocates resources and identifies responsibilities. It is an instrument of reporting and control.
- Approaches to budgeting can be incremental, zero-based, flexible and fixed.

Preparing budgets

14

Introduction

This chapter describes the construction and operation of budgets, looking at different approaches to budget preparation and the process of preparing the various budgets within an organisation. These are illustrated by simple budgets from relevant data.

This chapter will increase students' appreciation of the importance of supplying information for budgetary purposes and put them in a better position to understand why and how budget information can be used in their organisation.

The budget process offers managers the opportunity to challenge existing practices. The chapter shows how budgets relate to each other, and how important it is for managers to work together in preparing and managing them. Finally, the chapter stresses the human issues in the budget process. Budgets can have positive effects on the behaviour of managers and can motivate staff. On the other hand, budgets prepared with little consultation and seemingly imposed from above can have a negative impact on the business.

1   Budget administration

1.1   The budget period

Most organisations follow a **budget period** of twelve months, which normally coincides with the organisation's financial year. Generally, the financial year is governed by the legal/taxation requirements of the organisation. The budget itself can be broken down into shorter periods, such as quarters or months, according to need, to assist financial control during the budget period. For example, because cash is so important to the survival of a business, the annual cash budget may be broken down to a daily basis for control purposes.

Some budgets, called **rolling budgets**, are prepared for a twelve-month period but are continuously updated by adding a further period, say a quarter, and deducting the earliest three months. This type of budget allows managers to react quickly to changes in say customer demand or costs.

budget period
The period for which a budget is prepared and used, which may then be subdivided into control periods.

rolling budget
A budget continuously updated by adding a further period, say a month or quarter and deducting the earliest period. Beneficial where future costs and/or activities cannot be forecast reliably.

budget committee

The group of managers/directors who are responsible for administering and coordinating the preparation of budgets in accordance with the organisation's objectives.

1.2   The budget committee

It is usual for the senior managers representing the major departments/activities of the organisation to form a budget committee. The committee's key task is to produce a coordinated and realistic budget. The Director of Finance has the role of ensuring that all the budgets presented by the heads of departments/activities are coordinated for the whole business. The Director of Finance usually prepares a budget reference manual, which describes the objectives and procedures involved in the budgeting process. The timetable for budget preparation will also be contained in the manual.

The budget committee will refer to the organisation's strategic plan which identifies the objectives for the next three to five years. The revenue budget needs to be set within the overall framework of the strategic business plan. Using the strategic plan the budget committee will identify, analyse and communicate the key events which are likely to impact on the business during the budget period. These could include details of:

- Units to be closed and/or opened.
- Products or services to be introduced and/or discontinued.
- Economic forecasts.
- Competitor activity.
- Pricing policy.
- International developments.
- Marketing strategy.
- Forecasts of the timing and level of pay and price increases.

This information will be sent to budget holders and will influence how they approach the preparation of their own budgets. The budget committee will also supply the following information:

- An organisation chart identifying the budget holders and the activity/department for which they are responsible.
- A list of the main budgets and the relationships between the budgets.
- A list of the budget holders' responsibilities.
- A timetable for the preparation of the budget which identifies the key events and the sequence in which the budgets are to be prepared.
- Copies of the relevant budget forms to be completed together with appropriate instructions.

limiting factor

Anything which limits the activity of an organisation, such as limits on space, or the operating capacity of a production line.

1.3   Limiting factors

Organisations are frequently faced with constraints which limit their ability to achieve greater financial success. There are certain key factors which can limit the activity of a business. These constraints are called limiting factors or key factors. Examples include:

- Limits on space, for example the square metres of shopping space in a supermarket.
- Limits on production, for example the operating capacity of the production line.

- Limits on personnel, for example a shortage of skilled computer software designers.
- Limits on the supply of raw materials, for example a shortage of flour grain due to weather conditions.
- Limits on output, for example production constraints imposed by patents, franchises and licences.
- Limits on demand at required price levels apply to all products and services.

The limiting factor is the starting point for budget preparation. The most common limiting factor is usually sales.

Test *yourself*   14.1

(a) List THREE key events which a budget committee might identify, analyse and communicate to budget holders as likely to impact on the business during the budget period.

(b) What is a rolling budget?

(c) What do you understand by the term limiting factor in relation to budget preparation?

2   Preparing budgets

Budget preparation should be a bottom-up process. The budget originates at the lowest levels and is subsequently refined and coordinated at higher levels. Managers at the lowest levels submit their budgets to their superior for approval. This process is repeated at each level as the manager incorporates their subordinates' budget. The budget holders negotiate and agree the final budget so that everyone participates fully. As negotiation proceeds, the Finance Director may identify inconsistencies and imbalances between budgets. This means notifying the managers concerned and may cause the budgets to be reworked from the bottom several times. When all inconsistencies have been identified and resolved, they are summarised in a **master budget**. When the master budget is agreed and approved, it is passed down through the business to the appropriate budget holders. Approval of the master budget is the authority for each manager to carry out the agreed activities and incur the budgeted expenditure.

The master budget is built up from the individual budgets, which are combined to produce the cash budget, the profit and loss budget and the balance sheet budget (see 2.5 below). There is no blueprint for how budgets should be prepared but the following indicates the relationship between the most common types of budgets.

master budget
The overall budgets of an organisation, built up from a range of individual budgets and comprising the cash budget, the forecast profit and loss account, and the forecast balance sheet.

2.1   The sales budget

The sales manager can produce forecasts of demand for products and services setting out the sales volume, mix and seasonal patterns, although sometimes preparing the sales budget will involve carrying out market research on the demand for products and services. Some organisations prepare three sales forecasts – most pessimistic, most optimistic and most likely.

2.2 The production budget

This is prepared after the sales budget. It involves preparing and costing a production plan to meet sales. This includes assessing the stock levels needed to meet demand. In a manufacturing business it will involve preparing a direct materials usage budget, a materials purchase budget, a budgeted direct labour hours and costs budget and a machine utilisation budget in terms of operating hours required.

Worked example   14.1

Preparation of part of the production budget

Assume a business manufactures one product and the following are the budgeted sales for the three months ending 31 March 200X are:

Budgeted sales	January 200X	75,000 units
	February 200X	90,000 units
	March 200X	80,000 units

Stocks of finished goods are estimated at 25,000 units at 1 January 200X and at 23,000 units at 31 March 200X. It is the policy of the business that stocks of finished goods at the end of each month will represent 20% of the following month's budgeted sales.

You are required to produce the production budget (finished units) for each month for the three months ending 31 March 200X.

Answer

Production budget in finished units for three months ending 31 March 200X

	January	February	March	Total for Quarter
Sales (Units)	75,000	90,000	80,000	245,000
Add: Stock at end of month (units)*	18,000	16,000	23,000	23,000
	93,000	106,000	103,000	268,000
Less: Stock at start of month (units)**	25,000	18,000	16,000	25,000
Required Production	68,000	88,000	87,000	243,000

Notes

*Stock of finished goods at the end of the month is to be kept at 20% of the following month's sales. Thus January 20% × 90,000 = 18,000; February 20% × 80,000 = 16,000; and March 23,000 as per question.

**Stock of finished goods at the start of the month is January 25,000 as per question; February and March are the closing stocks at the end of the previous month namely January and February.

2.3 Departmental/functional budgets

This is prepared by the managers responsible for budgets in their departments/functions including, marketing, distribution, information technology, human resources, accounting, etc.

departmental budget/functional budgets
A budget of income and/or expenditure applicable to a particular function.

2.4 The capital expenditure budget

The capital expenditure budget is a fixed asset purchase budget. This normally covers actual fixed purchases in the next twelve-month period but may also give a forecast for a longer period, say three years, because fixed assets often take longer to acquire. The capital budget also identifies the depreciation charges arising during the next twelve months as these have to be built into production and departmental budgets. The capital budget indicates the cash requirements arising during the year.

capital expenditure budget
Budgets for expenditure on purchasing fixed assets.

2.5 The master budget

This is a combination of the sales budget, production budget and other budgets. The master budget is made up of three parts:

- The ***cash budget*** converts all the activities of the business into cash flows. This allows the business to identify cash shortfalls and surpluses throughout the budget period.
- The *profit and loss budget* which identifies all the business's revenues, expenses and projected profit.
- The *budgeted balance sheet* is a forecast of what the balance sheet will look like at the end of the budget period.

cash budget
A detailed budget of the receipts into an organisation and payments from an organisation, incorporating both revenue and capital items. The budget identifies the resultant effect upon bank balances or overdrafts.

Test *yourself*   14.2

(a) How are the sales budget and the production budgets linked?

(b) What are the key issues to be considered when compiling an annual sales budget?

(c) What do you understand by the term master budget?

(d) A cash budget is made up of which of the following: i) Receipts and payments; or ii) Income and expenditure?

Worked example　　　　　　　　　　　　　　　　　14.2

Cash budget

An illustration of a cash budget for a year split into quarters is shown below.

The cash budget shows:

- The opening budgeted cash balance; in this case £50,000.
- The budgeted cash inflows or receipts in this case quarter by quarter.
- The budgeted cash outflows, again by quarters.
- The closing budgeted cash balances. In this case, the cash balance at the end of each quarter highlights cash surpluses of £98,500 and £153,700 at the end of the first two quarters. In contrast cash is overdrawn by −£286,700 and −£209,600 at the end of the third and fourth quarters.

	Qtr 1	Qtr 2	Qtr 3	Qtr 4	Total
London	168,500	146,500	169,400	165,200	649,600
Sheffield	65,400	70,500	50,800	70,600	257,300
Leeds	70,100	85,800	90,000	90,500	336,400
Manchester	89,500	93,800	94,200	94,600	372,100
Total Receipts	£393,500	£396,600	£404,400	£420,900	£1,615,400

	Qtr 1	Qtr 2	Qtr 3	Qtr 4	Total
Wages	187,500	187,600	194,500	185,600	755,200
Insurance	19,900	19,900	19,900	19,900	79,600
Light & heat	19,800	15,400	12,000	18,500	65,700
Other expenses	117,800	118,500	118,400	119,800	474,500
Purchase of new shop			500,000		500,000
Total Payments	£345,000	£341,400	£844,800	£343,800	£1,875,000
Excess of receipts over payments	£48,500	£55,200	−£440,400	£77,100	−£259,600
Cash at start of quarter	50,000	£98,500	153,700	−286,700	
Cash at end of quarter	£98,500	£153,700	−£286,700	−£209,600	

Putting the case　　　　　　　　　　　　　　　　14.1

 You are required to provide the following information to the shop managers:

FIVE potential benefits to a business of introducing a budgeting system.

SIX uses of a cash budget.

 Five potential benefits of budget systems.

They:

1　improve planning and control;

2　improve internal communications;

3　allow a detailed review or organisational functions and efficiency;

4　encourage the setting of realistic objectives and targets;

5　identify problem areas and encourages corrective action to get plans back on track;

6　improve staff morale and motivation.

3 An overview of the budget process

Preparing the annual budget can be a long and repetitive process. Figure 14.2 summarises the stages involved:

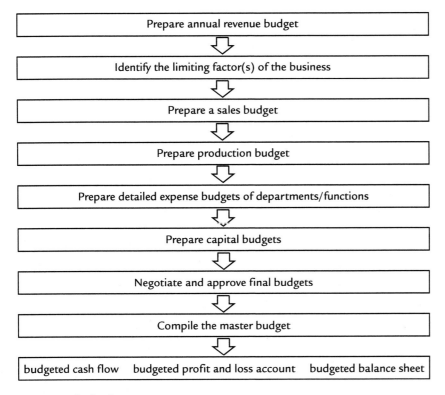

| Prepare annual revenue budget |
| Identify the limiting factor(s) of the business |
| Prepare a sales budget |
| Prepare production budget |
| Prepare detailed expense budgets of departments/functions |
| Prepare capital budgets |
| Negotiate and approve final budgets |
| Compile the master budget |
| budgeted cash flow   budgeted profit and loss account   budgeted balance sheet |

Figure 14.2 The budget process

4   Budgets and people

The budget is the device senior managers use to quantify objectives such as pounds or employees and communicate them through the organisation. Thus it is the budget which brings the human and social aspects of financial management face to face with the technical aspects. While there are undoubtedly benefits in preparing budgets, there can also be a practical difficulty in convincing people to accept and use a budget.

4.1   Negative responses to budgets

- The term 'budget' is not always viewed in a positive light by managers because budgets can be perceived as telling them what they can and cannot do. The budget can be seen as a constraint imposed by others on manager's decision-making powers.
- Managers are not always directly involved in budgeting process. Budget preparation can sometimes be a top-down exercise imposed by management. This approach can often inhibit initiative and morale.
- There can be a lack of authority over the items line managers are expected to control and have responsibility for.
- There is often a conflict between budget managers and personnel who are trying to deliver a quality service and/or product.

4.2   Participation in budgeting

One way of reducing these negative aspects of budgeting is to encourage participation in the budget process. The increased participation can lead to better interdepartmental co-operation and also to better planning as knowledge and ideas are shared.

Putting the case   14.2

 You are asked to chair a discussion with the shop managers at the residential school on the benefits and drawbacks of involving people in budget preparation. In order to prepare for the discussion you are asked identify and provide THREE examples of how the behaviour and human relations of managers can have a negative effect on budget preparation.

 THREE examples of aspects of people participation producing negative results:

1   In constructing budgets, managers have to compete for finite resources. This can result in them asking for more resources than they need in the belief that their bid may be reduced.

2   Managers may be overoptimistic about expected sales revenue to avoid a cut in the resources available to generate the sales. This building in of 'slack' not only distorts the budget process but also wastes valuable time and energy in constructing the budget.

3   Budgets are used to measure the performance of individuals and groups. This measurement may affect managers' behaviour. Thus if budgets are set at levels which are perceived to be either unachievable or too easy managers' motivation is likely to be affected. Improving motivation is promoted through budgets that are challenging but achievable.

Summary

- Most organisations follow a budget period of twelve months which mirrors their financial year. The budget is then broken down into shorter control periods of a month or even daily for monitoring and comparison. Rolling budgets can also be used for monitoring.
- The budgeting process is usually organised and coordinated by a budget committee, made up of senior representatives or heads from the main departments or functions in the organisation. It is the committee's responsibility to ensure that the budget follows the framework of the strategic plan and meets its objectives, and when the budget is finally agreed, to communicate it to the budget holders in the organisation. The budget will always be subject to limiting factors.
- Budgeting should be a bottom-up process, with individual sales and expenditure budgets contributing to the master budget.
- Participating in the budget process can be an important way of bringing departments and teams together, however, where consultation is minimal or non-existent, budgeting can have a negative effect on the organisation.

15 Budgets as a management tool

Introduction

The chapter introduces students to interpreting and acting on the information produced by budgetary control systems. Responsibility for a budget and its achievement lies with managers, who are responsible for a specific activity within the organisation. These areas are frequently called responsibility centres.

The key point of effective budgetary control is that responsibility is established and authority given to carry out specified functions. The chapter helps managers to consider the key issues when designing a budgetary control report which shows variances, the differences between actual figures and budgeted figures. The individual budget holders are responsible for interpreting the budgetary control report. This involves identifying the cause of any variances and taking corrective action.

It is important to build in an element of flexibility into the budgeting process with the aim of striking a balance between detailed controls and allowing some flexibility.

1   Budgeting and control

1.1   Planning and control

An important part of management control concerns budget preparation and budgetary control. Chapter 13 explains that annual budgets are short-term plans, which have been formalised and converted into monetary and/or quantitative terms. The control aspect of role of management involves:

- the communication of plans;
- the motivation of employees to achieve the plans;
- the reporting on the achievement or otherwise of the plans.

1.2 Budgetary control

Budgetary control is a system which uses budgets as a means of planning and controlling all aspects of a business's operations. The process of budgetary control involves the following steps:

- Preparation of budgets (see chapters 13 and 14).
- Communication of the budget details to a **responsibility centre**. This is a unit or function in a business headed by a manager (e.g. a factory manager, a hotel manager) having direct responsibility for its performance. (Students may recognise responsibility centres better under the more widely used terms of division, section, department and business unit.)
- Comparison of actual performance against budget.
- Identification and analysis of **variances** from the plan. A variance is the difference between budgeted and actual cost and for revenue where appropriate.
- Taking corrective action to correct or control the variances.

The **responsibility centre manager** (head of department or division) is given the authority to achieve the centre's objectives and is accountable for the centre's performance. This approach attempts to delegate responsibility for the business's activities to the employees closest to delivering the product or service.

From a budgeting viewpoint a responsibility centre manager will be accountable for their budget which will mirror the manager's authority. The budget reflects the plan or standard against which the manager will be judged. The budgetary control statements will reflect the financial performance of the responsibility centre.

Test *yourself* 15.1

(a) What do you understand by the term budgetary control?

(b) Providing TWO examples, explain what you understand by the term responsibility centre.

2 Budgetary control reports

The **budgetary control report** is the normal channel used in communicating feedback to managers. Report formats vary from business to business. The key points to consider when designing a report are the user's needs, the content and the timing of the report. Sample 15.1 shows what a simple report looks like.

---

budgetary control

A system which uses budgets as a means of planning and controlling all aspects of an organisation's operations, by comparing actual with budgeted results.

responsibility centre

A unit of an organisation such as a division or department headed by a manager who is directly responsible for its performance

variance

The difference between the budgeted cost and the actual cost; and similarly for revenue.

responsibility centre manager

A manager having direct responsibility for the performance of a responsibility centre.

budgetary control report

Report which shows the actual performance, the budget and the variances from budget.

Sample Simple budgetary control report   15.1

	Budget for Period	**Actual for Period**	**Variance**
Income	£ 1,500,000	£ 1,400,000	£ 100,000(Adverse)
Expenses	1,200,000	1,250,000	50,000 (Adverse)
Profit	300,000	150,000	150,000 (Adverse)

The report is useful in that it discloses:

⦿   The differences between actual figures and budgeted figures, which are called variances.

⦿   The variances that have a negative effect on budgeted profit are called **adverse**.

⦿   The variances that have a positive effect on budgeted profit are called **favourable**.

However, Sample 15.1 is very limited and does not provide the level of detail required by a budget holder to investigate the variance. The essential content which should feature in any budgetary control report includes:

⦿   Details of the budget centre, the budget holder, and period covered and date prepared.
⦿   The budgeted details for the period question.
⦿   The actual details for the period in question.
⦿   The cumulative budgeted details for the year to date.
⦿   The cumulative actual details for the year to date.
⦿   The variances (if any) arising.
⦿   The identification of the variances in terms of favourable and unfavourable.
⦿   Appropriate analysis of, and comment on, variances where appropriate.
⦿   Corrective action to be taken by budget holder.

Test *yourself*   15.2

(a) What is a variance?

(b) List FOUR items of information you would expect to be included in a monthly budgetary control report.

Sample 15.2 shows a more detailed budgetary control report which meets the above criteria in terms of content and layout.

Sample Detailed budgetary control report   15.2

		May 200X	May 200X	*May 200X*	200X Year to date	200X Year to date	200X Year to date
Item	Annual Budget	Budget this month	Actual this month	Variance this month	Budget for period	Actual for period	Variance to date
	£	£	£	£	£	£	£
Salaries	40,800	3,400	3,625	225U	17,000	17,560	560U
Offices	6,000	500	475	25F	2,500	2,450	50F
Advertising	24,000	2,000	2,240	240U	10,000	7,900	2,100F
Transport	12,000	1,000	1,100	100U	5,000	5,700	700U
Printing	20,000	1,600	1,550	50F	8,000	7,600	400F
Telephones	5,200	450	360	90F	2,250	2,300	50U
Overheads	36,000	3,000	2,950	50F	15,000	14,650	350F
Total Expenses	144,000	11,950	12,300	350U	59,750	58,160	1,590F

XYZ Department – Budgetary Control Report
Budget Holder: A. Smith
For 5 months to 31 May 200X

F = Favourable
U = Unfavourable

Comments on the budgetary control report

- This is a budget statement for a five-month period ending 31 May 200X.
- The budget this month is estimated as approximately one twelfth of the annual budget.
- The budget this period is estimated as approximately five-twelfths of the annual budget.
- All variances are calculated as the difference between the budget for month/period and the actual for month/period.
- The variances are identified as favourable when the actual expenditure is below the budgeted figures; unfavourable variances occur when the actual figures are greater than the budgeted figures.
- Some budget statements indicate unfavourable expenditure variances by including them in (parenthesis) as overspent expense items.

- The above statement is for a department that has a budget for expenditure only. Budget statements can, of course, include information on income if it is generated by the responsibility centre.
- The budget holder's performance will be assessed by comparing the planned expenditure against the actual expenditure.
- This statement has split the annual budget into monthly portions which assumes the expenditure will be fairly even over the year.
- Where the expenditure is more variable, say due to seasonal variations, then the annual budget can be profiled over the year based on past spending patterns etc.

Test *yourself*   15.3

(a) What does the £1,590 variance represent in the budget statement included above?

(b) Provide one benefit and one drawback of dividing budgeted expenditure into equal monthly portions.

Putting the case   15.1

You have been asked you to prepare some notes so that the chief accountant can respond to the shop managers' comments concerning a top-down approach to budgetary control. He asks you to provide a list of the possible benefits and drawbacks of a top-down approach as compared to a more participative approach. You are required to provide a list of THREE benefits and THREE drawbacks for both approaches to budgetary control.

Benefits of a top-down approach:

- It encourages senior managers to decide what the objectives of the business are. This means that there is less confusion about what is expected of lower-level managers.
- It avoids wasting the time and energy of employees by not requiring them to attend endless meetings to discuss what is going into the budget. Their time is better spent on selling goods and services.
- Increased involvement can lead to departments or functions becoming less self-centred and working together to achieve the business objectives.

Drawbacks of a top-down approach:

- Imposed budgets can lead to their rejection by lower-level managers and the subsequent failure to meet objectives.

- Lower-level managers may manipulate costs and income figures to meet the imposed targets.
- The view can develop among shop managers that budgets are primarily there to stop them doing things rather than being a helpful tool.

Advantages of a participative approach:

- Improved agreement between lower-level managers and senior managers on the objectives, strategies and tactics of the business. This agreement can be reflected in a better budget.
- The agreed budgetary system can motivate staff as they feel more ownership of the system.
- The participative approach can encourage more initiative and innovation on the part of managers.

Disadvantages of a participative approach:

- The actual process of consulting everyone costs time and money.
- Participation may not be real in that senior mangers may listen to managers' comments and then ignore them.
- The process of consultation and allowing everyone to participate means it is difficult to reach agreement given the wide variety of views.

3   Exercising financial control

We have seen that individual budget holders are responsible for interpreting the budgetary control report. This involves identifying the cause(s) of any variances and taking corrective action. The key point here is that control without action is of little use.

3.1   Causes of variances

In simple terms variances can and should be traced to their ultimate cause.

3.2   Variances in salaries and wages

- Poor estimate of the rate of pay.
- Having to use a higher grade of labour than budgeted for; this could be due to an inability to recruit staff at the budgeted rate.
- The need to pay for unplanned overtime due to special circumstances.
- There are vacancies in staff positions for a period during the year.
- Lower pay awards than anticipated.
- The business pays higher national insurance and pension contributions than planned for.

These reasons for variances tend to focus on the rate of pay paid to employees. However some of the reasons for the variances may be due to the efficiency of the employees been less/greater than planned ue to any of the following:

- Poorly trained employees providing poor quality goods and services.
- The poor supervision by managers.
- The low morale of employees.

3.3   Variances in raw materials and stocks of finished goods

- The price in the original budget was poorly estimated.
- The impact of nationally or internationally agreed price increases.
- The use of material which is of a better or worse quality than required in the budget.
- The business does not take discounts as expected.
- An ineffective buying policy is operated by the business.

These reasons for variances tend to focus on the price paid for the materials and finished goods. However, some of the reasons for the variances may be due to the usage of the materials and finished goods being less or greater than planned. This might be due to any of the following:

- Theft of materials and finished goods.
- Poor quality or deficiencies in materials leading to high levels of scrap.
- Poor production methods and/or faulty machinery leading to losses.

Test *yourself* 15.4

(a) What are two possible cause of an unfavourable variance in relation to staff salaries?

(b) What are two possible causes of a favourable variance in relation to raw material costs?

3.4 Investigating variances

How should managers investigate the variances? By identifying the variances and distinguishing between minor and significant variances. Significant variances are those that are likely to have an effect on the decisions and actions of management. Significant variances may be defined in terms of upper and lower limits of tolerance, for example all those 5% under/over the budget are significant. Significant adverse variances must be corrected as they will prove costly. Significant favourable variances should be investigated as they mean something is not going to plan. Business managers' time is valuable so do not waste it, or effort and money investigating minor variances; such variances should be monitored. Focusing on activities requiring attention and ignoring those that appear to running smoothly is often referred to as management by exception.

Budget holders' reactions to variances may involve:

* adjusting current actual performance; and/or
* adjusting future plans and strategies.

Budget holders should only investigate variances for items of expenditure or income for which they are responsible. Budget holders should not be blamed for costs or variances they cannot control. For example, it is pointless blaming a manager responsible for the labour budget for the consequences of actions taken by the purchaser trying to keep within the materials budget by buying poor quality materials.

3.5 Flexibility in budgetary control

Once a budget is approved it is almost inevitable that both income and expenditure will be subject to fluctuations. (Causes of variances have been discussed above.) It is therefore sensible to build in an element of flexibility into the budgeting process. However, in order to control any increases in expenditure or decreases in income it is advisable to adopt rules so that there can be no misunderstanding by managers of the authority for incurring expenditure which they have been granted. Such rules normally emphasise the fact that no expenditure should be incurred that involves the adoption of a new policy without prior approval of the budget committee. The aim should be to strike a balance between very detailed control and allowing flexibility appropriate budget holder.

3.6 Unspent budget balances

The normal practice is that any budget balance which remains unspent at the end of the financial year has to be forfeited and returned to the general funds of the business. This maintains tight financial control but can be demotivating for budget holders. Many businesses recognise that there may be good reasons for allowing unspent budgets to be carried forward to the following year. This could be to overcome the effects of delays in providing the goods or services which are outside the influence of the budget holder concerned. It is also employed to avoid any tendency for budget holders to spend the unspent budget provision without proper regard to achieving value for money.

Test *yourself* 15.5

(a) List TWO reasons for having some flexibility in the budgeting process.

(b) How would you identify a significant variance?

Putting the case 15.2

The chief accountant wishes to discuss the apprehensions the shop managers may have about the monthly budgetary control statements. In order to help him prepare for this meeting you are asked to:

List FIVE possible reasons for the shop managers' apprehension.

Suggest FIVE possible ways of alleviating the shop managers' apprehension.

FIVE possible reasons for the shop managers' apprehension concerning the monthly budget statements:

1 Lack of understanding of the financial terminology in the statements.

2 Lack of training and explanation on the content and use of the reports.

3 Untimely reporting systems to meet the shop managers needs.

4 Poor or inappropriate report formats.

5 Poor definition of the shop managers' areas of responsibility and authority.

FIVE possible ways of alleviating the apprehension includes:

1 Improved participation in the budgetary control process to increase motivation.

2 Recognition by senior management that there is a need for a flexible approach to budgetary control.

3 Training of shop managers in the aims and purposes of budgetary control in the context of the business.

4 Improved and regular communication between senior managers and the shop managers.

5 The setting appropriate and achievable budget targets. This does not mean the targets should not also be challenging.

Summary

- Planning and controlling financial operations using budgets is a major responsibility for responsibility centre managers.
- Responsibility centre managers will need to be able to interpret the budgetary control report which identifies favourable and averse variances against budget.
- This will involve identifying the cause of any variances and taking corrective action. Variances may be caused by poor estimating, unanticipated increases or decreases in costs, or external influences such as weather or government requirements.
- Managers should investigate significant variances, but do not need to spend time on minor differences. This approach, known as management by exception, will help mangers prioritise to make the best use their time.
- It is important to strike a balance between very detailed controls and allowing flexibility appropriate to the budget holder.

Part Four Practice Questions

4.1 Identify FIVE benefits of budgets and budgetary control.

4.2 What are the FOUR potential problems to a business from introducing a budgeting system?

4.3 List FIVE factors that have to be considered when setting a budget in a manufacturing business.

4.4 List FIVE expenditure headings that will make up a typical factory revenue budget.

Suggested Answers to Practice Questions

Part One

1.1 THREE economic decisions which shareholders may make based on accounting information include whether to buy more shares, sell their shares or hold on to their existing level of shares.

1.2 Accounting is a system for recording, analysing and summarising the financial impact of business transactions. This forms the basis of information about the financial activities of the business which is provided to the users of accounting information.

1.3 Financial accounting and management accounting.

1.4 THREE limitations of using accounting information to make decisions include the following:

- Financial statements are based on historical events and therefore have limited use in making decisions about the future.
- Accounting information tends to report on aspects of a decision that can be measured in monetary terms and often ignores the 'qualitative' aspects of decision-making.
- Accounting information is often based on judgements rather than precise numbers such as estimates of bad debts.

1.5 FIVE examples of type of information to support a credit reference to suppliers include: the length of time the company has been trading; names of owners; names of major customers; copy of the annual financial statements; and references from bank, credit agencies or other suppliers.

1.6 Going concern means the business will continue to operate in the foreseeable future. There is no intention to close the business, and no intention to make significant cutbacks to the nature of the business. In other words, the firm will continue in operational existence for the foreseeable future.

1.7 The accruals concept requires profit to be calculated by matching Income earned with expenditure incurred.

1.8 Revenue is recognised when the goods are delivered or the services provided and not when the sale proceeds are received. This will normally coincide with date on the invoice or the date of delivery if the issue of the invoice is delayed.

1.9 This means that periodically companies include more up-to-date valuations for some of a company's assets. This new valuation replaces historic cost. An example of modified historic cost could occur when land or buildings appreciate in value due to inflation and general price rises. This appreciation of property prices has been a common occurrence in major cities across the world.

1.10 Accepted accounting practice states that stock should be valued at the lower of historic cost and net realisable value. Thus if the stock of the company is likely to be sold at a price less than was originally paid for it, it follows that a loss is made. The accountant recognises this loss immediately by reducing the value of unsold stock to net realisable value. This will happen if the stock becomes obsolescent due to passing its sell by date or if the it is superseded due to technological developments or if consumers no longer wish to purchase the stock because it is no longer in fashion.

Part Two

2.1 These are liabilities of a business. They comprise the owner's capital which is the amount of the claim the owner has on the business normally made up the original capital investment plus any retained profits. They also comprise any external liabilities or obligations, usually legally enforceable, to people outside the business such as long term loans.

2.2 Cost of sales is calculated as follows:

	£
Opening stock	xxxx
Add purchases	xxxx
= Stock available for sale	xxxx
Less Closing stock	xxxx
Cost of sales	xxxx

2.3 The correct classification is shown below with the corrected items shown in bold text:

Assets	Liabilities
Cash in hand	Bank Loan
Buildings	**Creditors**
Office Furniture	**Loan from A. Jones**
Debtors	**Bank overdraft**
Stock of raw materials	

2.4 The completed table is as follows:

Assets	Liabilities	Capital
£	£	£
56,000	9,800	**46,200**
33,600	**8,600**	25,000
51,000	12,600	38,400

2.5 T. Judge on 31 January 2005

Cash at bank £6,300 + Stock £10,800 + Debtor A. Cowan £876 + Debtor A. Phillips £3,048 + Office Furniture £4,320 + Motor Vehicle £9,360 = Total Assets £34,704

Creditor S. Richards £648 + Creditor P. Fiddler £828 = Total Liabilities = £1,476

Total Assets £34,704 *minus* Total Liabilities £1,476 = **Capital £33,228**

2.6 Rent £ 6,640 + Rent owing £1,603 = £8,243

Insurance £2,160 – Insurance prepaid £524 = £1,636

Power £3,140 + Power owing £820 = £3,960

2.7 Current assets:

Prepayments (Insurance 2000 + Rent and Rates 2035) £4,035

Current Liabilities:

Accruals (Petrol 2,550 + Salaries 3,050) £5,600

2.8

Year	Annual Depreciation*	Balance Sheet Valuation
	£	£
1	22,500	102,500
2	22,500	80,000
3	22,500	57,500
4	22,500	35,000
5	22,500	12,500

Note: The annual depreciation charge is calculated as follows: (Capital Cost – Scrap Value)/expected life (£125,000 – £12,500)/5 years = £22,500

2.9

Year	Annual Depreciation*	Cumulative Depreciation	Balance sheet valuation
	£	£	£
1	18,000	18,000	107,000
2	48,000	66,000	59,000

* *Note:* (£125,000 – £5,000)/30,000 hours = £4 per hour.

Year 1: 4,500 hours × £4 = £18,000

Year 2: 12,000 hours × £4 = £48,000

Part Three

3.1 The following list is not exhaustive but does identify the most common SIX functions are illustrated below:

- Production.
- Marketing.
- Selling.
- Distribution.
- Personnel.
- Administration.

3.2 Materials costs relate to the raw materials and non-productive goods used by the business. For example, in the case of car manufacturing they include the metal, plastic, rubber, electric components, etc. used in assembling the vehicles. Non-productive goods include, e.g., the cost of cleaning materials, paper, pens, computer disKs used by a business. Non-productive materials are not used in the manufacture the final product.

Labour costs relate to the payments made to employees involved in supporting the product and/or service of the business This would include wages, salaries, and national insurance and pension contributions paid by the business.

Other costs are made up of all non-material and non-labour costs. These would include rent, rates, heating, lighting, depreciation, loan interest, stationery and printing, etc.

3.3 Examples of cost units which could be used to ascertain costs:

Service	Cost Unit
Hotel accommodation	Occupied room
Accounting practice	Chargeable hour
Human resource department	Employee
Airline company	Passenger mile
Regional hospital	Bed day or patient day
Freight delivery	Tonne/kg mile
Restaurant	Meal or cover
University department	Full-time student or full-time equivalent student

3.4

Direct Materials			
Department X	1.5 metres × £6.70	£10.05	
Department Y	4.5 metres × £4.50	£20.25	£30.30
Direct Labour			
Department X	0.5 hours × £8.20	£4.10	
Department Y	2 hours × £5.25	£10.50	£14.60
Overheads			
Department X	£10 × 1.75 machine hours	£17.50	
Department Y	£5 × 2 labour hours	£10	£27.50
Total cost of a garden shed			£72.40

Notes: Overhead absorption rates

Department X $\dfrac{£66,780}{6,678}$ = £10 per machine hour

Department Y $\dfrac{£105,700}{21,140}$ = £5 per labour hour

3.5

a)
  - Rent and rates could be apportioned on the basis of floor area.
  - Canteen facilities on the basis of employees.
  - Insurance premiums on the insurable value of fixed assets.

b) Indirect costs must be charged to products and services. There are many ways of charging these indirect costs and the aim of the chosen method depends should be to reflect the productive activity of the business and thereby the incurring of indirect costs. The productive factor could be:
  - Labour hours worked.
  - Machine hours worked.
  - Labour costs.
  - Material costs.

A key point is that any overhead absorption method is only a compromise and is does not necessarily the accurate correct answer or only solution.

3.6 THREE reasons why a business needs to hold cash:
  - To meet the need of business to make planned payments for example monthly salaries and purchase of fixed assets.

- To be able to take advantage of business opportunities as they arise for example the purchase of stock at a special discounted price offered by suppliers.
- To pay for unplanned or unexpected costs as they arise for example to make payments to creditors which are demanded earlier than expected.

3.7
- An advantage of holding large stocks is that there is less chance of stock-outs but there is risk of the stock deteriorating, becoming obsolete or being stolen.
- Whilst costs can be reduced in terms of the numbers of orders that have to be placed high stock levels generate costs in terms of increased storage costs such as rent and insurance.
- High stock levels can allow a business to negotiate favourable prices with suppliers but high stock levels have to be financed perhaps by an overdraft which will incur interest charges.

3.8

$$\frac{\text{Fixed costs}}{\text{Contribution per unit}} = \text{Breakeven volume of sales}$$

$$\frac{\text{Fixed costs} + \text{required profit}}{\text{Contribution per unit}} = \text{Sales volume to achieve a required profit}$$

$$\frac{\text{Contribution per unit}}{\text{Selling price per unit}} = \text{Profit to volume ratio}$$

Budgeted capacity – breakeven capacity = Margin of safety.

3.9 As a business produces an extra unit of a product or service it is likely to increase some but not all of its costs. Some costs will tend to be unaffected by fluctuations in the levels of activity; these costs such as rent and salaries are termed fixed costs. However, there are other costs which are termed variable costs as they tend to vary in total with activity; variable costs include such items as raw materials, electricity costs, etc.

This distinction of cost behaviour allows a business to calculate marginal cost which is the cost of producing one extra unit i.e. the extra variable cost of one extra unit. In effect the marginal cost of one unit of product or service is the cost which would be avoided if that unit were not produced or provided.

This approach has 'contribution' as its key feature namely selling price less variable cost 5 contribution. As fixed cost are assumed to remain unchanged as activity increases any increase in contribution will result in the same increase in profit. This allows decision makers to use break-even analysis and profit-volume ratios to inform their decisions.

3.10 Absorption costing systems do not require costs to be classified by their behaviour, i.e. fixed, variable and semi-fixed. Absorption costing is widely used and accepted in business this is in part due the fact that the method ensures that all costs will recovered in the long term. The method encourages prices to be set at full cost and so leads to stable prices.

By contrast marginal costing does not require the arbitrary apportionment of fixed costs between products. This in turn avoids an under/over absorption of overheads. The marginal costing approach is the basis of short-term decision-making techniques including contribution analysis, breakeven charts and cost volume profit analysis.

Part Four

4.1 Five benefits of budgets and budgetary control include:

- Management is forced to think ahead, to plan and to formalise these intentions.
- Standards are set, against which performance of managers can be controlled and measured.
- Business functions may be co-ordinated towards the achievement of agreed plans and targets.
- The agreed plans and subsequent performances are communicated to the relevant departments, functions and individuals.
- Delegation and participation can be encouraged.

4.2 Four potential problems include

- Overestimation of costs by managers seeking to keep within budget and to protect the level of budgets. This is called building in budget slack.
- De-motivation of employees for those not involved in the budget process.
- Unnecessary spending at year end to use up budget allocation.
- Changes outside the business, for example in the national economy, that make the budget plans unrealistic.

4.3 The following FIVE factors need to be considered:

- Competitors
- Suppliers
- Customers
- Operations
- Technology.

4.4 Five examples include:

- Direct materials cost
- Direct labour cost
- Factory management and supervision costs
- Factory consumables
- Depreciation of plant and equipment.

Sample Examination Paper and Suggested Answers

ACCOUNTING FOR BUSINESS

Important Notice

When reading these suggested answers, please note that the answers are intended as an indication of what is required rather than a definitive 'right' answer. In many cases there are several possible answers/approaches to a question. Be aware also that the length of the suggested answers given here may be somewhat exaggerated compared with what might be achieved in the reality of an unseen, time-constrained examination.

This Examination Paper consists of TWO sections. Section A is compulsory and carries 40 marks. Candidates are required to attempt TWO questions from Section B, all of which carry 30 marks each.

Total time allowed: 2 hours 15 minutes (inclusive of 15 minutes' reading time). Please note that candidates must not write anything during the 15-minute reading time.

SECTION A – COMPULSORY

You should allow yourself approximately 50 minutes in total to answer the questions in Section A.
Answer all parts of question 1 (2 marks for each part), and all parts of question 2 (4 marks for each part)

1.

    a)   **Identify FOUR different groups which use the published Annual Accounts of a business.** *(2 marks)*

        Suggested answer:

        The Inland Revenue, shareholders, creditors and employees.

    b)   **What are the TWO key elements that make up 'shareholders funds'?** *(2 marks)*

        Suggested answer:

        Share capital and retained profits or reserves.

    c)   **What is the term normally given to the overall budgeted profit and loss account, budgeted balance sheet and the budgeted cash flow statement?** *(2 marks)*

        Suggested answer:

        The Master Budget.

d) **What does the term 'adverse variance' mean?**   *(2marks)*

Suggested answer:

An 'adverse variance' occurs when a comparison of the budgeted expenditure or income for a period reveals an overspend or a shortfall of income.

e) **In what type of business will machinery, motor cars and computers not be treated as fixed assets?**   *(2 marks)*

Suggested answer:

These will not be fixed assets in a business, which manufactures and / or sells these types of assets. In this situation they will be current assets.

f) **What is the equivalent of the profit and loss account in a not-for-profit organisation?**   *(2 marks)*

Suggested answer:

An income and expenditure account (not a receipts and payment account).

g) **What is the accounting rule for the valuation of stock in a shop selling men's clothing?**   *(2 marks)*

Suggested answer:

Stock is valued at the lower of cost and net realisable value.

h) **What is the difference between the current ratio and the acid test ratio?**   *(2 marks)*

Suggested answer:

Current Ratio is current assets: current liabilities.
Acid Test Ratio is current assets minus stock: current liabilities.

i) **Give TWO disadvantages of incremental budgeting.**   *(2 marks)*

Suggested answer:

Allows errors and inefficiencies included in previous budgets to be continued.

It does not encourage managers to forget about the past and think afresh about their objectives and targets.

j) **A company paid £36,000 for a piece of equipment at the start of January 2004. The equipment was expected to have a useful life of 4 years and a scrap value of £4,000 at the end of 2007.**
What will be the net book value of the asset at the end of 2005, if the asset is depreciated on a straight-line basis?   *(2 marks)*

Suggested answer:

Cost   £36,000
Less scrap   4,000
                  32,000
£8,000 per annum
2 years = £16,000
                    £
Cost   36,000
Depreciation   16,000
Net Book Value   20,000   *(Total: 20 marks)*

2.

a) **Identify FOUR examples of financial information, which may be provided by a cost accountant in a manufacturing company.**   *(4 marks)*

Suggested answer:

Stock valuation records;
Analysis of labour costs over products or jobs;
Provision of information to set and evaluate selling price of products;
Preparation and control of budgets.

b) **The Capital International Travel Company has a financial year ending on 31 March. On 1 June 2004 the company purchased a company car. The annual insurance premium of £432 was paid on the same day.**

What is the correct amount that should be included for the cost of insurance in the profit and loss account for the year ended 31st March 2004? What accounting concept is being applied in calculating your answer?   *(4 marks)*

Suggested answer:

£432
12 months   = £36 per month _ 10 months

£360 charged to Profit and Loss Account.
This is an example of the accruals concept, with £72 being prepaid.

c) **Give THREE examples which illustrate the drawbacks of using manual accounting systems.**   *(4 marks)*

Suggested answer:

Speed of operation – manual writing up and recording of millions of data transactions in the banking sector.
Storage space – the paperwork generated by manual systems, e.g. in a multinational company processing invoices for debtors.

Human errors – greater involvement of human beings in manual systems increases the risk of errors in recording and manipulating figures.

d) **What does the term 'contribution per sales ratio' mean? Illustrate how it can be used in decision-making.** *(4 marks)*

Suggested answer:

The contribution per sales ratio or percentage measures the contribution per pound of sales. For example:

	£
Selling price per unit	200
Less Variable cost per unit	120
Contribution per unit	80

This means that the contribution per sales ratio or percentage is:

$$\frac{80}{200} - 100 = 40\%$$

Thus every pound of sale generates a contribution of £0.40. It is a way of describing the relative profitability of products, which is often required when capacity is limited and more of each product could be sold.

e) **Identify THREE disadvantages experienced by a business which has insufficient working capital.** *(4 marks)*

Suggested answer:

Companies are unable to take up an opportunity to buy stock, which is being offered at special prices.
Companies are unable to settle bills promptly with their suppliers, so as to take advantage of cash discounts offered by their suppliers.
Companies are unable to reduce or eliminate bank overdrafts as a response to rising short-term interest rates.

(Total: 20 marks)

SECTION B

Questions 3 to 7 are based on the pre-seen case study

Vertex Ltd

Vertex Ltd has several factories located throughout Europe, Africa and South East Asia. You are employed as a business administrator, located in the central accounting department. Your main role is to help in communicating information and advice between the accounting department and managers in the company factories. The factories are all expected to make a profit and each factory manager has many tasks and responsibilities delegated to them, particularly in relation to budgeting, financial record keeping and financial decision-making. You are frequently involved in sorting out queries relating to the inputting of financial transactions into the computer, as well as offering advice on the financial aspects of decisions.

You receive queries from the managers on a daily basis and currently have a series of outstanding tasks to complete, which revolve around the following pieces of information.

A factory manager in South East Asia provided you with the following information relating to the year-end adjustments to the expenses of the factory:

Accruals Information

Accruals Balance at	31 December 2003	31 December 2004
	£	£
Heating expenses	12,400	10,300
Cleaning materials	4,000	3,800
Rent	4,500	0

Cash payments made during 2004:

Heating expenses	£104,000
Cleaning materials	£45,600
Rent	£96,000

Debtors' information

	31 December 2003
	£
Debtors' balance	390,000
Provision for doubtful debts balance	17,400

During the year 2004, debtors totalling £39,000 were written off. At 31 December 2004, the factory had debtors amounting to £422,000. It is in the company policy to provide for doubtful debts by charging 5% of total debtors against profits.

There is a note from the factory manager attached to the above data asking for an explanation of what the figures are used for. The factory manager also comments that the information contains a number of estimates. It appears that accountants have a lot of flexibility in measuring and recording the financial transactions of the factory. The manager is confused as to how the accounts of the factory can be described as 'true and fair'. He is also concerned that many of the key assets of the business are not recorded on the balance sheet of the business.

Each of the factory managers produces revenue and capital budgets. The managers are getting increasingly frustrated at the amount of time taken up with budgets. One of the managers describes the level of detail required in the budgeting process as being 'over the top' and claims managers' time would be better spent on managing the factory production process.

Vertex Ltd has recently been expanding its factories. This has involved a significant investment in capital projects and fixed assets. All the factory managers view this growth in the capital base of the business as something to be proud of. It has resulted in many factories acquiring new plant and machinery, however at the same time they each received a memorandum from the accounting department. The memorandum insists that managers must invest more of their time in controlling and reducing the working capital of the business. It goes on to stress that the working capital has an important bearing on the liquidity of the business, which is as important as its profitability. The contents of the memorandum are not appreciated by all the factory managers, who fail to understand how, after a period of profitability and expansion, they are being criticised for having too much capital.

As part of the budgeting process, one factory manager in Europe has produced information to assist in the preparation of the budget for 2005. This factory produces one product which has a selling price of £60. The forecast sales over the four quarters of 2005 are as follows:

	Quarter 1	Quarter 2	Quarter 3	Quarter 4
Sales (units)	760	1040	920	680
Total costs (£)	20,160	24,640	22,720	18,880

The manager estimates that fixed costs of the factory (included in the above figures) will amount to £8,000 per quarter. He asks you to review the above figures and prepare for a meeting to discuss their implications in a couple of day's time.

The manager of a factory in Africa which makes annual profits of £50,000 is considering investing in a new piece of equipment at a cost of £165,000. The equipment will have an estimated life of five years or 30,000 machine hours. It is estimated the equipment will be sold for £15,000 at the end of its life. Vertex Ltd has estimated that the replacement cost of the asset in five years' time will be £200,000.

The factory managers have been informed that a new method of controlling petty cash payments is to be introduced in the next financial period. They have been asked to make better use of source documents in controlling petty cash disbursements. The factory managers have been circulated with the following format, which is to be used in petty cash books:

Receipts	Date	Details	Voucher Number	Payments Total	Premises	General Admin. Costs	Travel and Subsistence	Other Expenses

Section B – Questions

Answer TWO questions from the five in Section B. You should allow yourself approximately 35 minutes to answer each of the questions in this section. Each question is worth 30 marks.

3. **You are asked write to all the factory managers in the Vertex group, providing information on the following areas:**

   a. **Explain the key differences between the terms 'revenue' and 'capital expenditure'.** *(6 marks)*

   Suggested answer:

   Capital expenditure is concerned with purchasing long-term permanent fixed assets for use in the business. They are bought to be used and not sold. They are used to help the business make and sell its goods and services.

   Revenue expenditure is concerned with the day to day running of the business. The expenditure will include items such as salaries and wages, heating, loan interest etc. This expenditure gives immediate benefit to the business i.e. in the year the expenditure is incurred.

   b. **Provide THREE reasons why it is important for Vertex managers to appreciate the distinction between revenue and capital expenditure.** *(6 marks)*

   Suggested answer:

   The distinction is important because of their impact upon:
   - Cash flow – because of its financial size a capital transaction can have a significant impact on the cash flow of the business.
   - Annual impact – revenue expenditure gives benefit to one accounting period and is thus charged against one year's profits.
     Budgets – capital expenditure is approved and controlled via a capital budget, which is separate from the revenue budget.

   c. **Explain, with reasons, which of the following would be classified as capital items and which as revenue items in the accounting system of Vertex.**

      i. **Purchase of an extra computer for financial modelling.**
      ii. **Cost of floppy discs, paper and printer cartridges.**
      iii. **Purchase of two cars for use by accountants.**
      iv. **Delivery expenses and legal costs associated with the purchase and installation of computer network system.**
      v. **Training staff to use new hardware.**
      vi. **Cost of redecorating the computer room.**
      vii. **Servicing and repair of laser printers.** *(7 marks)*

As follows:

i. **Purchase of an extra computer for financial modelling** – capital expenditure as it is the purchase of a long-term fixed asset.

ii. **Cost of floppy discs, paper and printer cartridges** – computer consumables are revenue expenditure as they are used up in a few days / weeks.

iii. **Purchase of two cars for use by accountants** – capital expenditure as they are fixed assets giving benefit over several accounting periods.

iv. **Delivery expenses and legal costs associated with the purchase and installation of computer network system** – capital expenditure as it is cost of acquiring or adding value to a fixed asset.

v. **Training staff to use new hardware** – same as (iv) above.

vi. **Cost of redecorating the computer room** – revenue expenditure, as it is an ongoing everyday operating expense.

vii. **Servicing and repair of laser printers** – same as (vi) above.

d. **Give FIVE potential benefits to Vertex of introducing a budgeting system.**
(5 marks)

Suggested answer:

Budget systems:

i. **Improve planning and control;**
ii. **Improve internal communications;**
iii. **Allow a detailed review of organisational functions and efficiency;**
iv. **Encourage the setting of realistic objectives and targets;**
v. **Identify problem areas and encourage corrective action to get plans back on track;**
vi. **Improve staff morale and motivation.**

e. **Outline SIX uses of a cash budget to factory managers.** *(6 marks)*

Suggested answer:

Cash budgets:

i. **Act as a yardstick against which comparisons can be made throughout the year;**
ii. **Interlock with other budgets such as budgeted debtors and creditors as they move from month to month;**
iii. **Allow the timing and impact of capital budgeting decisions to be reviewed throughout the year;**
iv. **Bring all the receipts and payments together, so a forecast bank balance can be worked out;**
v. **Allow overdrafts to be calculated and consequently the interest costs of alternative borrowing strategies;**
vi. **Allow managers to take corrective action to deal with bank balances on a daily basis e.g. surplus cash can be invested and / or cash shortfalls can be dealt with via negotiating borrowings and overdraft facilities.**

(Total: 30 marks)

4.   **The factory manager in South East Asia has asked you to:**

a.   **Calculate the figures for heating, cleaning materials and rent to be included in the profit and loss account for the year ended 31 December 2004.**   *(6 marks)*

Suggested answer:

Accruals

	Heating Expenses £	Cleaning Materials £	Rent £
Opening Accruals	(12,400)	(4,000)	(4,500)
Cash Payments	104,000	45,600	96,000
Closing Accruals	10,300	3,800	0
	101,900	45,400	91,500

b.   **Provide the figures for both the bad debts and the provision for doubtful debts to be included in the profit and loss account for the year ended 31 December 2004.**   *(6 marks)*

Suggested answer:

Debtors
Debtors at 31 December 2004   £422,000

	£
Proposed provision for doubtful debt 5% _ £422,000	= 21,100
Provision for doubtful debts at beginning of year	17,400
Charge to P & L A/c for 2004	3,700

Bad debts w/o to P & L A/c for 2004   £39,000

c.   **Define the concepts of Prudence and Consistency. Explain, with an example, how *both* the concepts can be applied when presenting the financial position of the factory.**   *(12 marks)*

Suggested answer:

The prudence concept requires that accountants must always be cautious or prudent when preparing financial statements. If accountants have some doubts about whether income will be received, they should always plan for the worst. Thus the doubtful income should not be included in the financial statements. This is why the accountant not only provides for bad debts which have occurred, but also for doubtful debts which may occur in the future. The making of a provision for doubtful debts is therefore an example of the application of the prudence concept.

The consistency concept states that when accountants choose a method for presenting the financial position of a business, the method is not just used for one accounting year, but over several years. Thus if a business chooses the straight-line method of depreciation, this method must be consistently applied to its fixed assets. The business can change to a different method, e.g. the reducing balance method, but must disclose the reasons for the change and the effects of the change on annual profits. This is an example of applying the consistency concept.

d. **Provide FIVE examples of assets and / or liabilities, which are not generally included on the factory balance sheet. Which accounting concept underpins the omission of these items?** *(6 marks)*

Suggested answer:

Financial accounts are presented in money terms. The money measurement concept says that financial accounts can only include items, which can be measured objectively in money terms.

This means the following items are normally not included:
-   The expertise and skills of the workforce and its manager;
-   The fact that there are poor industrial relations which may result in a disruption of production;
-   The entry into the market place of a competitor who will take away long-standing customers;
-   The value of patent rights or copyright;
-   The value of internally generated goodwill i.e. the value in excess of the fair value of its assets.

The accounting concept is the money measurement concept.

(Total: 30 marks)

5. **The factory manager in Africa has asked you to:**

a. **Calculate both the annual depreciation charge and the net book value of the equipment at the end of its first year of use. The factory manager estimates that the equipment will be used for 11,000 machine hours during that year. Your figures should be based on:**

i. **The straight-line method;** *(3 marks)*
ii. **The machine hour method.** *(4 marks)*

Suggested answer:

Depreciation: Straight line method

$$\frac{\text{Cost} - \text{Scrap Value}}{\text{Estimated Life}} \qquad \frac{165{,}000 - 15000}{5 \text{ years}} = £30{,}000 \text{ per annum}$$

Net Book Value £165,000 – 30,000 = £135,000

Depreciation: Machine hour method

$$\frac{\text{Cost} - \text{Scrap Value}}{\text{Estimated Hours}} = \frac{165{,}000 - 15{,}000}{30{,}000 \text{ hours}} = \frac{150{,}000}{30{,}000} = £5 \text{ per machine per hour}$$

£5 per hour × 11,000 hours = £55,000
Net Book Value £165,000 − £55,000 = £110,000

b. Comment on the effect that each method will have on the factory's annual profit. *(5 marks)*

Suggested answer:

Impact on profit:

	£	£
Annual profit	50,000	50,000
Depreciation	30,000	55,000
	20,000 profit	5,000 loss

Plus the investment of £165,000 has negative impact on company cash flow.

In both cases the divisions reported profit declines, which may influence decision-makers about undertaking the investment. The adverse impact on divisional profits may mean that the manager is judged as not meeting objectives, should investment be undertaken.

c. State THREE reasons why depreciation should be charged annually to the profit and loss account. *(9 marks)*

Suggested answer:

. Three reasons for depreciation include:
   - To reduce book value of fixed assets to more realistic levels in the balance sheet;
   - To comply with the accruals or matching concept. The annual depreciation charge represents the annual cost of using the fixed asset to generate sales for the business;
   - To reflect the loss in value of the equipment due to wear and tear, usage and the passage of time.

d. Discuss the opinion that depreciation should be calculated on replacement cost instead of the original capital cost. *(9 marks)*

Suggested answer:

The basic principle is that fixed assets are valued at historic cost and depreciation charges are based on this figure. In times of rising prices, the value of a fixed asset may increase in value or more likely the cost of replacing the asset may have risen.

The argument is that either the new value or the replacement value is depreciated over the remaining years of the asset's life. By charging at the higher value, the amount set aside out of profits to replace the asset will protect the original capital of the business. However, estimating the replacement cost of an asset can be difficult. Technological change can make it difficult to find a comparable replacement for the asset.

It should be noted that depreciation charges, whether on an historic cost basis or a replacement cost basis, do not guarantee sufficient cash will be available to replace the assets. The decision to replace the asset and its method of finance will be a new investment decision and will be assessed at the end of the asset's useful life.

(Total: 30 marks)

6.   **The factory manager in Europe asks you to:**

a.   **Produce a table, which summarises both the quarterly and total results for 2005. Your table must show the sales revenue, variable costs, fixed costs, contribution and profit.**   *(12 marks)*

Suggested answer:

Workings as below:

	Quarter 1	Quarter 2	Quarter 3	Quarter 4	Total
Sales (units)	760	1040	920	680	3,400
Selling Price per unit	£60	£60	£60	£60	
Total costs (£)	20,160	24,640	22,720	18,880	86,400
Less Fixed costs (£)	8,000	8,000	8,000	8,000	32,000
Variable costs (£)	12,160	16,640	14,720	10,880	54,400
Variable Cost per Unit (£)	16	16	16	16	

	Quarter 1	Quarter 2	Quarter 3	Quarter 4	Total
Sales (units)	760	1040	920	680	3,400
Sales Revenue	45,600	62,400	55,200	40,800	204,000
Variable costs (£)	12,160	16,640	14,720	10,880	54,400
Contribution (£)	33,440	45,760	40,480	29,920	149,600
Less Fixed costs (£)	8,000	8,000	8,000	8,000	32,000
Total Profit (£)	25,440	37,760	32,480	21,920	117,600

b. **Calculate and explain the significance of:**

i. **The breakeven point;** *(3 marks)*
ii. **The margin of safety.** *(4 marks)*

Suggested answer:

Breakeven point
The breakeven point is the level of activity at which there is neither a profit nor loss. It can be ascertained by the following calculation:

Break even point = Fixed Costs
                   Contribution per unit (£60 − £16 = £44)

£32,000   = 728 units
  £44

Margin of safety
Indicates the level by which the forecast turnover exceeds or falls short of the breakeven point. In this case the forecast turnover of 3,400 units exceeds the breakeven of 728 units by 2,672 units or 79%. Thus sales can drop by this level before a loss-making situation is incurred.

c. **State TEN expenditure headings that will make up a typical Vertex factory revenue budget.** *(5 marks)*

Suggested answer:

Direct materials cost;
Direct labour cost;
Factory management and supervision costs;
Factory consumables;
Depreciation of plant and equipment;
Maintenance of equipment and buildings;
Heat and light;
Insurance of equipment;
Factory rent and rates;
Transport costs.

d. **State TWELVE key headings that should feature in a typical Vertex budgetary control report.** *(6 marks)*

Suggested answer:

Budget centre;
Budget holder;
Period ending;
Expenditure code;
Description of expenditure item;
Budget for current period;
Actual for current period;

Variance;
Cumulative budget to date;
Actual for period to date;
Variance;
Trend of variance;
Comments.   *(Total: 30 marks)*

7.   You are asked to write to all the factory managers in the Vertex group providing answers to the following questions:

a.   Define and explain the significance of working capital in the various businesses of the Vertex Group.   *(6 marks)*

Suggested answer:

Working capital is the investment which allows the business to trade on a day-to-day basis. In effect, it is the difference between current assets and current liabilities. The business needs working capital to allow it to trade e.g. it needs stocks of finished goods which it can sell for cash or on credit. Working capital is also required to finance the results of trading, as a firm which sells on credit will not receive the cash for some time. Working capital is needed to pay other running costs such as salaries and wages, until the cash is received from the debtor. Thus the significance of working capital is that it is necessary to be able to carry out day-to-day operations.

b.   What is the key point Vertex managers should bear in mind when fixing the level of working capital?   *(6 marks)*

Suggested answer:

The level of working capital varies between businesses, but it is generally set at a level which balances two competing needs. The first is the cost of tying money up in working capital. The money invested in stock for example, is not available for other purposes. Similarly, paying creditors more quickly than is necessary means that money is no longer available to the business. The second need influencing working capital levels is the need to have sufficient working capital items such as stock and cash to be able to carry out day-to-day activities. Thus running out of stock will disappoint potential customers and may result in a loss of business.

c.   What do you understand by the term source data in an accounting system? List FIVE examples of source documents managers can refer to.
                                                                     (7 marks)

Suggested answer:

Business transactions are nearly always recorded on source documents. These documents are a source of the information included in the accounts. They are the evidence which leads to and supports the making of an entry in the accounting system. Examples include:

- Purchase orders;
- Goods received notes;
- Credit notes used to correct errors;
- Cheques;
- Invoices to customers and from suppliers.

d. What is the likely use of a petty cash book in Vertex?   *(4 marks)*

Suggested answer:

A petty cash system is where a small amount of cash is kept on the premises for small value payments e.g. stamps, local travel costs, provisions etc. Petty cash books record the payments made supported by a petty cash voucher. The books also record cash received from the business bank account.

e. How would a petty cash imprest system operate within Vertex?
        (7 marks)

Suggested answer:

Petty cash is the responsibility of the petty cashier. An imprest system is where the petty cash is kept at an agreed sum or 'float' by topping up from the business bank account at regular intervals. Thus expense items are recorded in vouchers as they occur, so that at any time the following will apply:

	£
Petty cash vouchers	xxx
Plus cash still held in petty cash	xxx
Equals the agreed sum or float	xxx

The total of the petty cash vouchers is the amount reimbursed to the petty cashier at regular intervals.

(Total: 30 marks)

Glossary

The following terms are reproduced from Management Accounting Official Terminology (2000 edition). Copyright 2000 © Chartered Institute of Management Accountants and © Elsevier Ltd. with their permission.

absorption costing The procedure which charges are fixed as well as variable overheads to cost units.

absorption rate A rate charged to a cost unit intended to account for the overhead at a predetermined level of activity.

accounting Identifying, collecting, measuring, recording, summarising and communicating the financial aspects of an organisation's activities.

accounting concepts and conventions The broad, underlying assumptions that underpin accounting practice.

accounting software packages Collections of software or computer programs designed for computer hardware 'the physical equipment that makes up the computer' to undertake specific accounting tasks.

accounting standard An authoritative statement of how particular types of transactions and other events should be reflected in financial statements.

accounting standards Rules financial accountants and auditors must follow when preparing financial statements. In the UK the regulations are developed by the Accounting Standards Board.

Accounting Standards Board (ASB) The ASB is a subsidiary of the Financial Reporting Council. Its role is to produce, amend, issue and withdraw accounting standards on its own authority. Standards produced by the ASB are known as Financial Reporting Standards (FRSs).

accruals Costs which have not so far been taken into account at the end of a period because they have not yet been invoiced – for example, gas or electricity, invoiced in arrears.

accruals concept The principle that revenues and costs are matched with each other and dealt with in the profit and loss account of the period to which they relate, irrespective of the period of receipt or payment.

adverse variance Where the variance against budget produces an adverse impact on profit, e.g. where actual costs are higher, or actual sales are lower, than budgeted.

applications software Computer programs which undertake specific tasks such as payroll or word processing.

asset Any tangible or intangible possession which has value.

average cost The total cost of an item of material in stock divided by the total quantity in stock; used for pricing issues from store.

bad debt A debt which is, or is considered to be uncollectible and is, therefore, written off as a charge to the profit and loss account.

balance sheet A statement of the financial position of an entity at a given date, disclosing the assets, liabilities and accumulated funds.

batch costing A form of specific order costing; the attribution of costs to batches, a quantity of identical items, e.g. shoes, computer components.

books of prime entry A first record of transactions, such as sales or purchases, from which details or totals, as appropriate, are transferred to the ledgers.

breakeven chart A chart which indicates approximate profit or loss at different levels of sales volume within a limited range.

breakeven point The level of activity at which there is neither profit nor loss.

budget A plan for the future, expressed in money, showing income, expenditure and the capital to be employed.

budget committee The group of managers/directors who are responsible for administering and coordinating the preparation of budgets in accordance with the organisation's objectives.

budget period The period for which a budget is prepared and used, which may then be subdivided into control periods.

budget variance The difference between budget and actual cost for each cost in a budget and revenue, where appropriate.

budgetary control A system which uses budgets as a means of planning and controlling all aspects of an organisation's operations, by comparing actual with budgeted results.

budgetary control report Report which shows the actual performance, the budget and the variances from budget.

business entity concept The principle that financial accounting information relates only to the activities of the business entity and not to the activities of its owner(s).

capital The funds used by an entity for its operations.

capital budget Budget of the cost of acquiring, producing or enhancing fixed assets.

capital expenditure Expenditure that is likely to provide a benefit to the organisation for more than one accounting period/financial year.

capital expenditure budget Budgets for expenditure on purchasing fixed assets.

capital income The proceeds of selling fixed assets.

cash book A book which records the cash accounts of a business.

cash budget A detailed budget of the receipts into an organisation and payments from an organisation, incorporating both revenue and capital items. The budget identifies the resultant effect upon bank balances or overdrafts.

cash flow The difference between cash generated and cash spent in a period.

consistency concept The principle that there is uniformity of accounting treatment of like items within each accounting period and from one period to the next.

continuous operation/process costing The costing method applicable where goods or services result from a sequence of continuous or repetitive operations or processes. Costs are averaged over the units produced during the period.

contract costing Similar to job costing in that costs are attributed to individual contracts but usually used for high value, long term projects such as construction.

contribution Sales value less variable cost of sales. It may be expressed as total contribution, contribution per unit or as a percentage of sales.

cost allocation The process of charging a specific cost to a cost centre or cost unit.

cost apportionment That part of cost attribution which shares costs among two or more cost centres or cost units in proportion to the estimated benefit received.

cost behaviour The way in which costs of output are affected by fluctuations in the level of activity.

cost centre Locations, functions or items of equipment in respect of which costs may be gathered for control purposes.

cost of sales The sum of variable cost of sales plus factory overhead attributable to the turnover. It may also be referred to as production cost of sales or cost of goods sold.

cost unit A unit of product or service in relation to which costs are ascertained.

credit notes Prepared by a seller notifying the purchaser that the account is being reduced, e.g. because of return of goods or cancellation.

creditor A person or business entity to whom money is owed.

current assets Cash or other asset, e.g. stock, debtors and short-term investments, held for conversion into cash in the normal course of trading.

current liabilities Liabilities which fall due for payment within one year, including that part of the long-tem loans due for repayment within one year.

database Data records held in a structured way which can be searched according to specific criteria.

database management system (DBMS) The software that runs the database. The data is input, and the DBMS software organises it into the database.

debtors Money owed to the entity by customers (trade debtors) or others.

departmental budget/functional budgets A budget of income and/or expenditure applicable to a particular function.

depreciation The measure of wearing out, consumption or other reduction in the useful economic life of a fixed asset.

direct costs Costs incurred solely because the product or service is being made or provided.

direct labour cost rate An overhead absorption rate based on direct labour cost.

direct labour hour rate An overhead absorption rate based on direct labour hours.

direct materials cost rate An overhead absorption rate based on direct materials cost.

distribution overheads The cost of warehousing saleable products and delivering them.

double-entry bookkeeping A method of recording transactions in ledger accounts so that the monetary value of the debits and credits always balance each other.

doubtful debts An amount charged against profit and deducted from debtors which allows for the non-recovery of a proportion of the debts.

drawings Monies or goods taken out of the business by the owner for private use.

expenditure code A system of symbols designed to be applied to a set of items to give a brief accurate reference, facilitating entry, collation and analysis.

expenses The expenses of operating the business for the accounting period.

external audit An independent examination of the financial systems and controls of a business.

external auditor A suitably qualified person who certifies that the financial accounting statements for give a 'true and fair view' of the organisation's performance and financial position.

favourable variance Where the variance produces a favourable impact on profit, e.g. where the actual costs are lower or actual sales are higher than budgeted.

financial accounting Reporting the financial performance of an organisation for external users via the organisation's financial statements.

Financial Reporting Council (FRC) Independent body responsible for making, amending and withdrawing accounting standards.

Financial Reporting Exposure Draft (FRED) Draft of an FRS circulated for consultation and comment.

Financial Reporting Review Panel (FRRP) Part of the Financial Reporting Council responsible for ensuring that published company accounts comply with accounting requirements.

Financial Reporting Standards (FRSs) Accounting standards produced since 1990 by the Accounting Standards Board.

Financial Services Authority (FSA) The government authority that governs the regulatory framework of accounting in the UK.

finished goods Manufactured goods ready for sale or despatch.

first in first out A method of pricing the issue of material using the purchase price of the oldest unit in stock first.

fixed budgets A budget which is designed to remain unchanged irrespective of the volume of output or turnover achieved.

fixed costs Costs incurred for a period, and which, within certain output and turnover limits, tend to be unaffected by fluctuations in the levels of activity (output or turnover).

flexible budget A budget which, by recognising different cost behaviour patterns, is designed to change as volume of output changes.

full cost pricing A pricing method where the cost of the unit of output is calculated taking into account all direct costs, and an apportionment of indirect production costs and other overheads. A fixed percentage is then added to this to cover profit.

going concern concept The assumption that the entity will continue in operational existence for the foreseeable future.

goods received note A record of the receipt and inspection of stock, used to verify the supplier's invoice before it is passed for payment.

gross profit Sales less the cost of goods sold.

historic cost concept The principle that resources are normally stated in accounts at the amount which was paid to acquire them.

impersonal accounts A record of the revenues and expenditures, liabilities and assets classified by their nature, e.g. sales, rent, wages, electricity. Sometimes called nominal accounts.

imprest system A method of controlling cash or stock; when the cash or stock has been reduced by disbursements or issues it is restored to its original level.

incremental budgeting Projected expenditure and income is determined on the current level of operating activity, adjusted for anticipated activity changes and inflation.

indirect costs Expenditure on labour, materials or services which cannot be economically identified with a specific saleable cost unit. Also known as overheads.

integrated accounting software A set of accounting packages where each separate module is linked with others in the suite.

International Accounting Standards Board (IASB) The IASB is an independent, privately funded accounting standard-setter based in London. Standards issued by the International Accounting Standards Board are designated International Financial Reporting Standards (IFRSs).

invoice A document prepared by a supplier showing the description, quantities, prices and values of goods delivered or services rendered. To the supplier this is a sales invoice; to the purchaser the same document is a purchase invoice.

job cost card or sheet A record of time spent on a job. It may include the cost of labour and materials and attributed overhead.

job costing Where costs are attributed to specific jobs, e.g. the supply and installation of plant and equipment.

journal A record of financial transactions, such as transfers between accounts, not dealt with elsewhere.

last in first out A method of pricing the issue of material using, the purchase price of the latest unit in stock first.

liabilities The financial obligations of a business, e.g. creditors, bank and overdrafts.

limited liability company A legal entity which exists separately from its owners, directors and employees. The liability of the members is limited to the value of their shares.

limiting factor Anything which limits the activity of an organisation, such as limits on space, or the operating capacity of a production line.

liquidity The ability a business has to convert its assets into cash so as to meet its liabilities.

listed company A company whose shares are traded on a recognised investment exchange.

long-term liabilities Liabilities which fall due for payment after one year or more.

machine hour rate An overhead absorption rate based on machine hours.

management accounting Management accounts are prepared by management accountants for internal users within an organisation.

margin of safety The amount by which the forecast turnover exceeds or falls short of breakeven.

marginal cost The cost of one unit of product or service which would be avoided if that unit were not produced or provided.

marginal costing The accounting system in which variable costs are charged to cost units and fixed costs of the period are written off in full against the aggregate contribution. Its special value is in decision-making.

master budget The overall budgets of an organisation, built up from a range of individual budgets and comprising the cash budget, the forecast profit and loss account, and the forecast balance sheet.

materiality concept The principle that financial statements should separately disclose items which are significant enough to affect evaluation or decisions.

money measurement concept The principle that financial accounting information relates only to those activities which can be expressed in money terms.

net assets The excess of book value of assets over liabilities, including loan capital.

net book value The historic cost of an asset less any accumulated depreciation or other provision for the diminution in value e.g. reduction to net realisable value.

net profit Gross profit less expenses.

net realisable value (NRV) The price at which the stock could be currently sold less any costs which would be incurred to complete the sale.

nominal ledger A record of the revenues and expenditures, liabilities and assets classified by their nature, e.g. sales, rates, wages, electricity. Sometimes called impersonal accounts.

objective classification The final few digits of a code might indicate the cost centre or cost unit to be charged.

operating budget/plan Budget of the profit and loss account and its supporting schedules.

operating cycle or cash conversion cycle The length of time between the purchase of stocks and the receipt of cash from debtors for the sale of the stock; and between when the cash is paid out for stocks and the cash is received in from debtors.

other debts Short-term amounts owing which are not trade debts.

output data The outputs of a computerised ledger system.

overhead absorption The charging of overhead to products or services by means of absorption rates.

overhead absorption rate A means of attributing overhead to a product or service based, for example, on direct labour hours, direct labour cost or machine hours.

owners' funds The total of the original capital invested by the owner in the business, plus any retained profits or reserves from previous years, plus this year's profits less any drawings made by the owner during the year.

partnership A business where ownership is shared among two or more people.

personal accounts A record of amounts receivable from or payable to a person or an entity.

petty cash account A record of relatively small cash receipts and payments, the balance representing the cash in the control of an individual, usually dealt with under an imprest system.

petty cash book A book for recording receipts and payments made out of a petty cash account.

prepayments Expenditure on goods or services for future benefit, which is to be charged to future operations, e.g. rentals paid in advance.

prime cost The total of all the direct costs of a product or service.

prime cost rate An overhead absorption rate based on total prime cost.

process costing The costing method where goods or services result from a sequence of continuous or repetitive processes. Costs are averaged over the units produced during the period.

production cost Prime cost plus absorbed production overhead.

production cost centre These are locations where the products are manufactured for example a machine shop.

profit and loss account A statement which shows the income less the various expenses of an organisation to show the profit or loss for an accounting period.

profit/volume chart Chart showing the impact on profit of changes in turnover.

profit/volume (p/v) ratio The relationship between revenue and the contribution it generates (e.g. if an item sells for £60 and generates £15 contribution, its p/v ratio is 25%).

prudence concept The principle that income is included in the financial statements only when realised, while likely losses are included as soon as possible.

purchase order A written order for goods or services specifying quantities, price, delivery dates and contract terms.

purchases Raw materials purchased for incorporation into products or finished goods purchased for resale.

purchases or creditors' ledger A collection of the personal accounts payable to a person or an entity.

raw materials Goods purchased for incorporation into products for sale.

realisation concept The concept that profit is only accounted for when it is realised and not when it can be recognised.

relevant range of activity The activity levels within which assumptions about cost behaviour in a break-even chart remain valid.

residual value The actual or estimated value of a fixed asset, received on disposal.

responsibility centre A unit of an organisation such as a division or department headed by a manager who is directly responsible for its performance

responsibility centre manager A manager having direct responsibility for the performance of a responsibility centre.

retained profits Non-distributed profits retained as revenue reserve. In a not-for-profit entity these are described as accumulated funds.

revenue or operating budget Budget of the expenditure and income for a financial year. The expenditure will be spent on the supply and manufacture of goods and the provision of services in the accounting period in which they are consumed.

revenue expenditure Expenditure on the supply and manufacture of goods and provision of services charged in the accounting period in which they are consumed.

revenue income Amounts derived from the provision of goods and services falling within the company's ordinary activities, after deduction of returns, trade discounts and value added tax; also called turnover/sales.

rolling budget A budget continuously updated by adding a further period, say a month or quarter and deducting the earliest period. Beneficial where future costs and/or activities cannot be forecast reliably.

sales Amounts derived from the provision of goods or services, after deducting returns, trade discounts, and value added tax. It is also called revenue.

sales ledger A collection of the accounts or records receivable from each customer.

sales order An acknowledgement by a supplier of a purchase order. It may contain terms which override those of the purchaser.

selling overheads Cost incurred in securing orders, usually including salaries, commissions and travelling expenses.

semi-variable costs A cost containing both fixed and variable components and so is partly affected by fluctuations in the level of activity.

service costing Cost accounting for services or functions, e.g. canteens, maintenance and personnel. These may be referred to as service centres, departments or functions.

service cost centre Service departments provide services for the production cost centres. For example the personnel department could provide services including the payment of wages and/or the recruitment of staff.

share A fixed identifiable unit of capital, e.g. a share of £1.

sole trader A person carrying on business with sole legal responsibility for the business, not in partnership or as a company.

source documents Source documents contain the information that is put into an accounting system.

specific units method An overhead absorption rate based on cost units processed.

spreadsheet Software which allows data to be entered and stored in a 'grid' format. It provides a means of performing numerical and statistical calculations.

staged payments Progress payments made at specific stages of a contract or at agreed intervals.

standing data The master file of the records for individual accounts held on a ledger. The data tend to remain the same and change only occasionally

stocks Stocks are made up of goods purchased for resale. The intention is to resell the stock so it will normally be kept in the business for a relatively short time.

strategic plan The formulation, evaluation and selection of strategies for the purpose of preparing a long term plan of action to attain objectives.

subjective classification The first few digits of a code might indicate the nature of the expenditure.

trade debtors Customers who have made purchases from the business on credit.

trading account An account which shows the gross profit or loss generated by an entity for a period.

trial balance A list of account balances in a double-entry accounting system.

variable costs Costs which tend to vary according to the level of activity.

variance The difference between the budgeted cost and the actual cost; and similarly for revenue.

work in progress The estimated cost of incomplete work that is not yet ready to be transferred to finished stock.

working capital The capital available for conducting the day to day operations of an organisation; normally the excess of current assets over current liabilities.

zero-based budgeting (ZBB) A method of budgeting whereby all activities are re-evaluated each time a budget is set.

Directory

Further reading

Atrill, Peter and McLaney, Eddie, *Accounting and Finance for Non-Specialists,* fourth edition (Pearson 2003).

Dyson, J. R., *Accounting for Non-accounting Students*, fifth edition (Pearson 2003).

Hand, Len, Isaaks, Carolyn and Sanderson, Peter, *Introduction to Accounting for Non-specialists*, first edition (Thomson Learning 2005).

Web resources

www.accaglobal.com – choose an article, a paper, professional articles and technical articles.

www.accountancymag.co.uk – the website for *Accountancy* magazine. Contains articles on tax, audit and finance.

www.accountingweb.co.uk – resources on auditing and financial reporting.

www.bized.ac.uk – resources for business, economics and accounting. Includes glossaries, interactive worksheets and accounting theory.

www.economist.com. Website for *The Economist* magazine.

www.news.ft.com.uk. Website for *The Financial Times*.

Professional bodies

The Association of Chartered Certified Accountants – www.acca.co.uk.

The Chartered Institute of Public Finance and Accountancy – www.cipfa.org.uk (not-for-profit body)

The Institute of Chartered Accountants in England and Wales – www.icaew.co.uk.

The Chartered Institute of Management Accountants – www.cimaglobal.com. Good for online resources with articles from *Financial Management*, CIMA's professional magazine.

The Association of International Accountants – www.aia.org.uk.

Index